BEYOND THE CRYSTAL SEA
A Second Exodus

by

H. Nelson Freeman

Acknowledgments

A special thanks to all of the incredible men and women of
the Iowa Writers Corner for their full support,
encouragement, and assistance in writing.
To Birdie Hawks for her daily support and help.
To Maggie Rivers, whose expertise made this and my other
novels a reality.
To Dawn Hall, thank you for your invaluable help in
editing my work
To my Brothers and sister in Christ, Rev. Mickey Carvour
and Rev. Dick Johnson, two of God's servants, and Rev.
Michelle Leonard, who guide me to the ways of our Savior.

BEYOND THE CRYSTAL SEA

A SECOND EXODUS

"For God so loved the world, that He gave His only begotten Son, that whosoever believeth in Him should not perish, but have everlasting life."

John 3:16

The Holy Bible

Richard L. Johnson, Chaplain
chaprlj@yahoo.com

FORWARD

I've been both privileged and honored to know H. Nelson Freeman (Sgt. Freeman) for many years. I've enjoyed having him as a personal friend, a member of my parish, and a leader both in the church and the community. I've spent hours in his squad car while on patrol and accompanied him to crime scenes. In addition, we have enjoyed many hours of Bible study together and shared numerous hours of discussing our faith over cups of coffee.

Needless to say, he is a most creative person in many ways. His career is distinguished by the years he served in the U.S. Navy, Army Guard, and as a Police Officer, assisting multiple agencies with his training in every aspect of Law Enforcement.

But, in the past few years, God has given him the creative ability to write. His stories in historical fiction bring to life the reality of the times, and the fiction part of the books is developed from his given level of genius, faith, and creative juices.

In this story, ***Beyond the Crystal Sea***, there is a real active threat of terrorism, as we have seen carried out in our nation. But along with that is also the confrontation by those in high places of national leadership that is disparaging the faith of many, in particular, those who hold dearly to the history of our Judeo-Christian ethic.

This anti-Christian spirit continues to develop within our nation. The Sgt. builds a case for those of faith and the cost they have to pay because of their belief in a Holy God; Jesus Christ our Savior; the power of the Holy Spirit; and the authority of the Word of God.

But then, should that really surprise us? The Bible teaches very clearly that in the 'last days,' such emphasis will develop and create unbearable times for believers.

Our mutual friend, the Rev. Mickey Carvour (S/A FBI, Retired), reminds us of the words of truth found in the Book of Revelation, *"Woe to the earth and the sea, because the devil has come down to you, having great wrath knowing that he has only a short time.' (Rev. 12:12) Or as The Messenger reads, "For the Devil's come down on you with both feet; he's had a great fall; He's wild and raging with anger; he hasn't much time, and he knows it."* Satan is defeated, knows that, and is trying to cause as much destruction as he possibly can before God says, 'Enough.' And this evil one is terminated once and for all.

Freeman, however, never leaves us hanging in his story. Clearly, in this biblical sci-fy novel, with creative and 'expanded technology,' he builds in the need for a personal faith in Christ; the beauty of God's forgiveness of our sins; the hope of eternity and heaven, and the assurance of God's presence for any who place their trust in Christ. Added to this is the proven validity of God's Holy Word, the Bible, the Biblical mandate that the end of the world is coming and that men and women are called upon by God Himself 'to be ready.' In this story, the characters are confronted with the personal choice of how then to live.

For each of those reading this novel, remember that you will be confronted with the reality of having a loving, caring God and make ourselves ready for the final event of the 'end times.'

Maranatha! ("Our Lord cometh!")

Dick Johnson, Chaplain
chaprlj@yahoo.com

Introduction

Beyond the Crystal Sea is H. Nelson Freeman's latest book that tells an amazing and powerful story about Martin Philips, who, with the help of his wife Elinore, has been inspired to invent a clean energy machine sought by a corrupt government.

Because of their belief in God and the teachings of the Bible, they and others overcome troubling times, which is a blueprint for all who read this book.

"God is our refuge and strength, a <u>very present</u> help in trouble," Psalms 46:1 (KJV). <u>Very</u> means real; <u>present</u> means available. God is real and present in this story with some supernatural intervention. And ***<u>"in a moment, in the twinkling of an eye," I Corinthians 15:52 (KJV).</u>*** On to Chapter One.

Reverend Mickey Carvour
Special Agent, FBI (Retired)

BEYOND THE CRYSTAL SEA

CHAPTER ONE

Sirens blared from every direction as additional Homeland Security stormtroopers swept in. Their vehicles were the large ones that resembled tanks seen on television, painted flat black to be invisible at night when they emerged from their dens. Each vehicle had a half-inch thick special treated steel cupola on top, with a gunner standing up, his fingers on the trigger of a big fifty caliber machine gun. The five-and-a-half-inch long cartridge boasted a four-mile range. Anyone hit by a bullet from the weapon was highly unlikely to survive.

Every trooper wore uniforms as black as their vehicles, void of any patches or names to keep them anonymous. Their primary weapon of control rested in the fear they created. Not that they oozed peace and goodwill; to the contrary, these combat-trained killers practiced brutality daily against the citizens without the destroyed Constitution and Bill of Rights of the United States.

Their warning blared once from the loudspeakers; then, the commanding officer ordered the gunners to open fire. Everyone without hearing protection within a radius of two blocks could suffer hearing damage from the roar of the guns.

The big slugs hit the wooden structure at about twenty-nine-hundred feet per second, faster than anyone can think and move. Deadly shards of wood flew in every direction, along with anything else hit by the bullets. The rounds turned everything in the house into shrapnel, increasing the likelihood of injury or death.

Martin Philips heard a small voice whispering in his ear, "Martin, take Elinore and flee; you must leave *NOW*." The last word sounded like a scream, emphasizing urgency.

Martin bolted upright in bed, looking around wide-eyed, sweat soaking into his t-shirt. Then, finally, the frightened man looked out a window, his sense of alarm dissipating as he saw the quiet grounds in the early dawn of a sunny day.

Summer usually turns the mid-west into an oven, and Mother Nature again reminds everyone she controls the weather, despite the foolish attempts of man. Afternoon temperatures danced in the high nineties, and the real villain, the elevated humidity, made it almost suffocating when the breeze fell to near zero for those with no access to air conditioning. The source of the moisture didn't come from Lake Michigan but was brought northward on the breezes from the Gulf of Mexico.

Those people in the southern half of Illinois and states to the south suffered even more distress. The mingling air masses and widely spread temperatures clashed over the city, creating loud and sometimes vicious thunderstorms with dangerous lightning. One such storm came broiling out of the southwest, causing the more affluent people to flee to their homes and enjoy the air conditioning or fans. The rest, middle and lower classes, the homeless from incapacitation, and the lazy, disappeared into small tents and any cover or overpasses they could find.

Martin retreated to his abode, which sat on three acres of manicured land outside the suburban city limits and Chicago, Illinois. His air conditioner worked hard to spike his electric costs; the Socialist government had hiked the rates three times since January and promised additional increases during the peak usage days in the summer months. Those homes with basements were rushed into renovation for living quarters and in an effort to remain cool. The citizens living in apartments that couldn't afford the high cost of conditioned air or didn't have them in the first place relied on fans to create air movement and wiped their bodies with wet cloths.

Under the change from a representative republic government to a one-party socialist dictatorship, the former United States suffered a devastated economy. Most stores nationwide closed during the first years of the transition from individual and corporate businesses to government-owned stores. The people suffered the most. The scarce rights afforded to the people came from the socialists. With the end of the protection from a tyrannical government provided by the Constitution and Bill of Rights, the people found they had no redress.

Philips shook his head to clear out the cobwebs of politics and began checking the meager contents of the cupboards. He planned to put together an evening meal with his fiancée, Elinore Adelina Canfield. Miss Canfield worked at the nearby hospital as a trauma nurse. Her pre-med classes lay behind her as she prepared to begin medical school in the fall.

Elinore preferred being called Elie and loved the gentle Martin Philips, and the energetic nurse knew she would have one man, and that was Martin.

Martin promised to prepare a vegetable beef stew and had removed the last four pounds of beef from the deep freeze three days earlier.

While the scientist prepared the evening meal, his fiancée Elie returned from work; the nurse took a quick Navy-length shower and dressed for the evening.

"Elie, would you watch the pressure cooker? When the timer goes off, it should be ready. I'm going to clean up and be back in a few minutes." Martin said. Then, with a quick peck, they headed in two directions.

Elie began setting the table for two with an ear listening for the timer, as the house took on the delicious aroma of the beef.

The woman had a pure heart and strived to find the best in everyone, even those who always seemed angry. She and Martin attended the same church they'd grown up in and whose parents were the closest friends. Now the couple hoped to marry in the family church.

Elie and Martin cleaned the house together and enjoyed working the yards and plants as a team. The foundation they were forming would stand the test of time because of their faith in God. The home, a redesign of the nineteen-forties trend, had been a favorite type of house the couple liked.

Martin entered the living room and turned on his designed sound system. His choice of music for the evening consisted of a South Seas and natural forest piano mix from his collection.

Elie and Martin gave thanks for their meal and time together. After supper, the two cleaned up the kitchen and dishes. An hour later, they retired to the living room; to sit on the comfortable couch, engaging in small talk and relaxing to the music.

The engineer's mind did not relax; he began considering his tinkering with a different clean energy concept. His fertile mind turned to ideas of rotation and how to power it. But, as history has shown many times, the answer Martin sought may need to come to him unexpectedly.

Martin's research exhausted the previous use of magnets as a power supply for propulsion, which never panned out. It couldn't turn sufficient RPMs or maintain enough energy to produce work. Nevertheless, he wouldn't give up on a promising idea because that application failed. Martin's ideas challenged conventional wisdom regarding perpetual motion within the scientific community, resulting in his unofficial black-balling.

The intrepid scientist and engineer began to study magnetic properties and ways to enhance their power by inducing an external factor. Like his distant predecessor and hero, Thomas Edison, Martin started experimenting with ways to influence the magnet to become ultra-strong and find a substance that would intensely react to the magnetic field.

The key to success is constructing a device that produces as much or more energy as it requires. And that is what turned most scientists against him: the concept of perpetual motion was impossible.

Martin ran one thought through his head, *'No matter what success or lack thereof, he would not sacrifice his marriage to Elie by placing anything between them.'*

Martin looked at the resting form beside him. Elie wore a simple cotton sundress designed to afford maximum cooling effect, even from the slightest breezes. Her naturally blonde hair had been cut into a pixie, keeping her neck cool. Although in her mid-twenties, Elie retained her younger years touch of redness in her cheeks, making her look more youthful and innocent. Nature is the greatest architect of women's lips. Elie wore no lipstick or gloss; it would detract from her true beauty. Instead, her lips curved at the corners to reveal perfectly white teeth Hollywood stars pay thousands to create and maintain.

"How would you like some iced tea?" Martin asked.

Smiling, Elie replied, "I thought you would never ask?"

The woman's deep aqua-blue eyes paused Martin; then he had to look away, lest he'd lose himself in them.

As they sat sipping the cooling drink, they traded stories of the day's events. Finally, Elie inquired about his progress with his hobby, a name they called his magnetic project.

Not wanting to violate the law of confidentiality with the government, Martin gave her some information of interest, then switched the conversation's track to avoid his work dominating their discussion.

Elie smiled at his attempt to keep the discussion under control, but unknown to Martin, her interest in his work was genuine. The nurse found research and experimenting fascinating. Elie hadn't made her feeling about his work known until then, but the situation felt it was the right time. The delightful woman had a vested interest in Martin's work and wanted to become a partner rather than a cheering section.

Martin, like a vast number of men, is sometimes clueless about the mind of a woman. Then it surprises them when the facts set in.

"I've brought some work clothes; I'll be right back." Then Elie dashed up the stairs and returned a few minutes later wearing snug-fitting jeans and a plaid, lightweight shirt with the sleeves rolled past the elbow and a blue bandanna holding her blonde hair away from her face.

Martin's breath caught in his throat, *'She is the most dazzling and fascinating woman I have ever known'* blew through his mind. Elie's selection of clothes failed to hide her enticing attributes, and the impish glint in her eyes said her efforts met her intentions.

Martin opened the door leading to the extensive workshop, then Elie stopped halfway through, trapping Martin against the frame. She looked deep into his bright eyes and said, "Martin Philips, I love you," then wrapped herself around the surprised man, kissing him. Martin, who quickly recovered, held her equally tight. They came up for air, and Elie broke the hold and spell on her fiancée and led the way into the shop.

While building the workshop, Martin installed a motion detector-activated lighting system. As Elie stepped down a short flight of stairs into the spacious room, the detection sensor picked up her movement and switched on several led-based lights, illuminating the shop in sunlight-grade brilliance.

The scientist had built a shop most scientists can have in their dreams. One corner of the shop remained in a shaded area. The lighting control box required manual operation. Martin also installed electric-operated panels designed to seal the area from unauthorized eyes. As the new lady of the lab walked through it, she noticed the glint from what appeared to be a frame network in the ceiling in the shaded area.

"Martin dear, do you have a light problem in that corner?"

Philips chuckled, "No, that is an assembly area for larger projects, and the ceiling retracts on a frame and rail system and has a platform that rises to allow a vehicle to enter or leave."

"How clever," the radiant blonde replied.

"Come with me, if you will; I have something to show you,"

Elie followed Philips up the stairs, then to the south end of the house. A pair of French-styled windows at the end of the hallway provided a wide view of the manicured yard.

Elie took her time looking across the wide yard, then said, "That is a nice way to turn the yard from a ho-hum into an interesting place for kiddies to play. That circular arrangement of colorful flowers is an ingenious way to add color that brightens the atmosphere of happiness."

"Is that how you see it?"

"Oh, yes, it's delightful and unseen from the front of the house. I've never seen it before, maybe because I didn't look for it," Elie explained.

"Let me show you this," he turned and headed for the living room. Opening the door to the deck and setting a small drone on the floor, Martin turned on the large TV and adjusted the frequency to the drone's camera. Elie watched the show, wondering where it was going.

Martin launched the flying machine, taking it up to five-hundred feet. A large part of the block was visible on the screen until Martin lowered the altitude to two hundred feet, circling the house.

"I've never had one of these devices; I'm afraid I'd crash it the first time I tried to fly it," she said.

"It's like everything else, sweetheart; practice makes it easy. I crashed a couple of times before learning to fly. Now, what are you seeing?"

"The yard we looked at is the south side of the house."

"Yes, do you notice anything out of the ordinary, or might not be what it appears?"

After a few minutes of studying the picture on the screen, Elie mentioned, "It looks like a beautiful reward for a lot of work, but nothing nefarious."

"That's perfect." He responded.

"Martin, what are you showing me that I don't see?"

"Let's take a stroll through the yard."

Arm in arm, the two lovebirds walked from the deck around the south lawn, and Martin led Elie to the circle of a colorful assortment of flowers.

"These flowers are so bright and fresh; how do you keep them that way?"

"I don't have the green thumb, you think. So I hired a landscaper to maintain the lawn, bushes, and flowers. She does an excellent job, and her rates are more than reasonable. I let her use this to showcase her work, and she regularly escorts potential clients through the yards and timber section."

"And to think all this time, I was oblivious to it," Elie complained.

"Not really; this part is about a month old. Before, it was all yard grass before that," Martin explained.

"You still haven't mentioned the unknown issue behind it all."

"Certainly, let's go back inside."

Once in the basement, Martin flipped a switch, causing a low-volume hum to resound through the shop.

"I should have known you are too sharp to fool," Martin began. "First, I want to see if you could pick out anything abnormal in the yard, and you didn't. The flowers distracted you. That's what I had Jennifer, my landscape artist, create. The circle of flower planters sits slightly over the edge of the moveable roof in the shop to cover the mated, waterproof tongue and groove seal. The entire shop sits beneath the ground."

"That's pretty cloak and dagger stuff, Martin."

"Yes, it is, my dear. I must confide in you, and you must swear to secrecy the existence of this shop and the nature of our work."

"Martin, you're frightening me, and you know that isn't easy."

"We are safe, and there is a higher power at play; nobody has the slightest idea of all the works going on beneath the government's nose daily."

"Are you doing the Lord's bidding?" Elie asked.

"Yes, and you will also be."

"How do you know I will agree or maybe let the authorities know what you're doing."

Martin smiled, "I have it on good authority that you serve the Lord as much as I do. And until now, you haven't been commissioned."

"Commissioned?"

"Yes, by the Highest of authority."

Elie's hands flew to her mouth, and tears welled up in her eyes. "God wants me to work for Him?"

"Yes, we are working together for the Almighty's plans. But, this, too, must remain secret from everyone. First, neither our families nor parents know about this; later, they will."

"What are your plans for the research you've been conducting, and how can I help?" Elie asked.

"I've tried all the materials on the Periodic Table of Elements, and ferrous metals alone respond to magnetism," He said.

"That's the current table, using current technology and thinking. But, if you're going to find the elusive key to unlimited energy, we will have to think and plan outside the box," Elie lectured.

"We must go before the Master and ask for guidance on this. I have been working for the government, but our current government is the antithesis of God and his plan of salvation."

"I agree, time is running out; we need the Lord more than ever," Elie declared.

Elie and Martin knelt across from one another and held hands until the room became exceedingly quiet. Then, Martin began; he hailed the Lord, God, and humbled the two before their Creator, praising the love He had given the people of the earth and thanking Him for His Son, Jesus, who suffered on the cross for all the people to be called by His name.

Elie joined the praising; "Thank you, Lord God, for Jesus' continued work of knocking at the door of man's hearts to offer them eternal life with you in paradise."

Martin spoke again, "Father, you know our situation; how Satan has schemed to use lies, deceptions, dishonor, threats, and much more to undermine the nation you gave Christians to build, how the dragon has used the system against itself and beguiled its leaders into corruption. Elie and I fear our work on behalf of the government is contrary to your plans, and we ask for guidance for our paths. We also ask that you use us as you will. We lay all we have and all we are before you.

In Jesus' name, we petition you. Amen."

"What do you think we should do now?" Elie wondered.

"We continue with our work, and the Lord will guide us, but it will be in His time, and we wait upon Him."

Martin changed the conversation. "Let's grab a cup of coffee; I want to talk to you."

While Elie put together a snack, Martin made the coffee. By the time the cookies finished, the coffee had stopped percolating, and the scientist poured two cups. They shared their coffee preference of drinking it hot and black.

Elie took a sip of the black, steaming liquid, and Martin asked, "Elie, may I ask you a personal question?"

"Sure, I hold nothing from you; you know that."

"I've noticed you come in more tired than usual about three days a week. Are you all right, or is the hospital taking advantage of your dedication?"

Smiling, the petite blonde shook her head, "Haven't you heard about the string of assaults happening near the hospital?"

"I guess I haven't been paying attention to the news; it's mostly negative these days."

"I've taken a more positive stance in my ability to protect myself from attacks by attending self-protection classes. These include strenuous workouts and defensive movements.

Like most people, I thought kicking and punching an attacker was the preferred method. But it's so much more; it's a way of life to let go of ego and control anger. The best part is that there is no interference with my relationship with God. If anything, it helps me to concentrate on Him because I've learned to set everything else aside."

"Wow, that's pretty deep, but it makes sense."

"Yes, it does; now, tell me, what is our next move?" she asked.

"As I said earlier, I've tested the metallic substances and tried to enhance the responsive abilities of the ferrous materials without much success. After thinking about it for a bit, I thought of increasing the field strength by using a step-up transformer and inducing other means to create greater energy, thus enhancing the repelling effect. Our goal remains; if we produce more energy than we use, we are on the right track; otherwise, the experiment will fail," Martin said.

"Okay, as I see it, if we write down where this has been and where we propose to go, maybe fresh ideas will develop."

"I already have my notes and writings to this point; let me get them."

Martin directed Elie to the enclosed office area in one corner of the shop. Martin pulled the latest file containing experiments and results. Elie helped him set them out chronologically, and the two began reviewing the material.

An hour later, brand-new experiments came to light, and the steps for testing developed. Finally, Martin converted the processes into figures when applied to existing materials, but it failed to meet their goals.

The couple dived into the programming and made modifications to the circuit boards. The work continued until midnight when they finally shut the shop down and retired to the house. The exhausted pair parted company and disappeared into their separate bedrooms. Their fatigue immediately overwhelmed them, and they slipped into a well-needed sleep.

A MESSAGE

CHAPTER TWO

The grandfather clock's deep booming chimes sounded seven-thirty, waking the occupants of the two bedrooms.

Elie maintained a spare bedroom and spare clothing for rare stayovers like the previous night. She and Martin had separate bedrooms, keeping within the family rules and religious beliefs.

Saturday morning started with clear skies and temperatures that promised to continue the hot streak the weather had taken. Elie and Martin planned this weekend in hopes of relaxing and allowing their bodies and minds to rejuvenate. They had worked the previous two weeks almost non-stop, Martin in the shop and Elie at the hospital, pitching in to help Martin as she could.

Elinore prepared a breakfast of eggs, a slice of ham, toast, and a glass of cold vegetable juice. Martin watched his soon wife-to-be expertly make her way around the kitchen while putting the meal together. Finally, Martin set the table, and they held hands, thanking their Creator for the day and their bounty, then slowly ate as they discussed their plans for the day.

Martin's dream of the previous night kept haunting him. Happily, he dreamt of it once, but it left a lasting impression on him. His concern came from their Christian beliefs, in which dreams play important parts.

"Elie, you dream, don't you?"

"Sure, everyone dreams. For the most part, they run from neutral to good and sometimes happy dreams. But, now and then, a bad or unsettling dream sneaks in, usually after an upsetting scene at work, with people seriously injured, such as in a traffic accident. Why do you ask?"

"I had a bad one last night," Then he sat wondering how much to reveal to her.

"Well, tell me about your dream; it's better to talk about it than keep it bottled up." She said.

Martin stared at the wall, saying nothing.

"Wow, it must have been a doozy," Elie teased.

"Not at all," Martin said. A voice told me, "A package, not a big one, but heavy, would be delivered today or tomorrow, and it has instructions with the contents. Follow them carefully, and I will be in contact with you. Then a second one began. It began with sirens," he started. Then he opened up and told her the whole story, including the segment about the shooting. Then Martin looked at his woman and said, "I heard a voice tell me "You will know when to run, take Elie and flee to safety."

"That's some dream; you say you had it once?" She asked.

"Yeah, it was weird but too realistic to forget or ignore."

"Martin, we must be connected. I also had a dream that I hadn't been able to shake. It wasn't violent, such as yours, but astonishingly vivid. There was a stranger in my dream; he told me to help you, then when you said run, I was to take what I could carry and follow you. When was your dream?"

"Last night, how about you?"

Looking deeply into Martin's eyes, she said, "Last night." Then, finally, she took a deep breath and said, "This is beginning to frighten me. I've never had a dream like that before."

"Neither have I," he whispered.

The two sat quietly, each thinking about their dreams, and their urgent safety concerns weren't coincidental.

Martin said, "You know, there are many instances in the Bible where God has sent His angels to give people a message, and dreams are one of those methods. With both of us getting the same message, it could be a directive from the Holy One. Here is a pocket notebook and attached pen. Elie, you and I need to keep a record of these dreams with dates. I'm not taking anything for granted; I am going to pack a bag for a fast flight if needed."

'I'll put one together, and we can place them next to the car; that way, we can grab them on the run," Elie said.

"Good idea; let's do it before we forget about it."

Unexpectantly the door chimes rang, and Martin reached the front door in time to see a brown delivery truck drive away.

Looking on the front porch, he saw a box about twelve inches long, six inches wide, and four inches tall.

'Could this be the delivery I dreamed about?' He wondered.

Martin stooped over to pick up the seemingly lightweight box. Instead, he found the box far heavier than he believed. Taking both hands to lift the item and cradle it in his arms, Martin reached a counter in the kitchen and slid it off his arm.

"What's that?" Elie asked.

"I think it's the package I dreamt about."

Elie wiped her hands on a napkin as she walked toward Martin. "Is it as heavy as it sounded when it hit the counter?"

"Yes, would you hand me that small box cutter on the bottom shelf of the end cabinet?"

Elie handed over the mini cutter, and Martin carefully opened the top. When he folded back the cardboard tops, a folded piece of paper lay on top of a semi-clear plastic or vinyl container holding a grey-colored powder.

Martin opened the folded paper and began reading. 'This box contains a powder from a distant source and is irreplaceable. Follow the printed instructions meticulously.'

Martin read the instructions, finding them simple and complete. However, he had concerns about the claims of hardness and high-temperature resistance the writer said would result. And he had other problems with the statement regarding losing weight when heated to a boiling point.

Martin handed the instructions to Elie. "These are strange instructions and results," she said.

"Yes, they are; however, considering the supplier, I'm not about to second guess them," Martin promised.

"Good idea," Elie agreed.

An hour later, the two decided to change their plans for the day and sat in the shop office looking at plans for a prototype power device.

Taking an immediate interest in Martin's work, Elie reviewed the plans; she finished and said, "This has potential."

Chuckling, Martin mentioned, "I think you may have missed your calling by going into nursing."

"I doubt that; I can like two endeavors, you know, I enjoy working and studying mechanics; I've learned so much from you, I feel like I was born to this."

"If the power device works, we must create a drive system, cooling and heating systems, and an electrical grid for the vehicle."

"I have an idea; I can put together these subsystems while you work on creating the power source," Elie offered.

"Good idea; we should save time by working on two areas simultaneously." Martin gave several drawings of potential subsystem designs to Elie. "There is a drafting table with all the tools you'll need on the other side of that door," he nodded toward the door. Elie rolled them together, pulled a chair up to a drawing table, and went to work with a cup of hot coffee for support.

The nurse-turned-mechanic spent the next three hours laying out her thoughts, then modifying them when issues popped up. Thoroughly drawn into the world of creating mechanical devices, Elie didn't hear Martin slip into the small room, carrying a tray for her with a bowl of hot vegetable beef soup, a sandwich, and hot coffee.

"Where did you get time to make this food?" she asked.

"I heated the soup in the microwave.

"You should have been a chef."

"Not me; I watched those guys years ago, they could never be satisfied, and worse yet, the customers were worse. Besides, not everyone likes what I cook or how I cook it, so I think I'll keep cooking for us."

Following lunch and cleaning the kitchen area, Martin returned to the lab and Elie to the drafting room. Elie sat reviewing the drawings and notes on Martin's work when she failed to see any references to his work on the drive. Then she recalled him saying he hadn't developed a viable drive system that would work as the primary power supply.

"Yeow!" Elie heard Martin yelp and instantly the thumping of something hitting the floor, followed by the sound of breaking glass and another thump as something hit a wall.

Rushing to the lab, Elie called out, "Martin. Martin, are you all right?" The woman heard a groan from the far side of a table, and when she came around the end of the table, she found Martin lying on his back, groaning and holding his left shoulder. A glance at the scattering of paper and tools told the nurse Martin must have been in an accident.

Elie took two steps to reach Martin, and she completed a survey of dangers and injuries, noting Martin had a small tear in his shirt and was lightly bleeding from his shoulder. Then she saw a rivulet of blood on the floor from beneath Martin. She cradled his chest and head and rolled him upward enough to see a tear on the back of his shirt. Whatever hit him had penetrated his shoulder.

During her initial observation, Martin began showing signs of shock. Elie grabbed two thick paper binders from the table, laid them under his feet, and covered him with her lab coat to help alleviate the shock.

Elie rushed to the large first aid station nearby and pulled out a couple of compresses, four 4X4 gauze pads, and alcohol rubs, then began to treat and bandage the wounds. The nurse didn't see heavy bleeding, rich red or frothy blood, and Martin's color had started to return, all of which appeared to indicate he may not have suffered a serious wound.

The scientist opened his eyes, and when he started to get up, Elie was on him instantly, holding him down. "Martin lay still; you'll need medical treatment beyond what I can do. Whatever hit you went through your shoulder. I'm going to call for an ambulance, and I don't want you to move. Do you hear me?"

"Yes, Elie, I hear you; I won't move; it hurts too much."

A phone was two steps away, and she watched her betroth while calling in the accident. As a nurse, she could describe Martin's injury and condition in the unique medical language. Her unknown answer was how Martin received his injury.

Martin said, "I'm feeling better, but it hurts laying on my back." Elie helped him into a sitting position, with the uninjured area of his back against a steady table panel. "That's much better," he said.

Elie checked his pulse, finding it strong and steady. "You'll be fine but sore for a few days. What happened?"

"I followed the instructions with that powder, and when heated with the torch, it melted and coated a square piece of steel.

I had put together an untried circuit board with a unique design of current, frequency, and applications when there was what I can justly describe as an explosion. The next thing I knew, you bent over me saying something, but I had difficulty hearing you, probably because of the blast. Ouch, this does hurt; you say it went through me?"

"Yes, and we should recover whatever hit you. But, we have a lot of work ahead of us to figure out what happened and if it's the answer to our questions," Elie said.

The sounds of sirens began reaching through the sound-fortified lab, and Martin said, "Help me get to the anteroom; we don't want unknown visitors nosing around the lab, not now."

Elie took Martin by his good arm and steadied him into a standing position, and the two walked to the door. Martin locked it behind them, and they made it near the front door, where Martin sat in a comfortable upright chair. Elie rushed to the front doors, which she propped open for the First Responders.

A police officer and two medics trotted to the door, where Elie met them. She gave the medics the medical version of his injury, then turned to see the officer talking to Martin.

"Mr. Phillips. How are you feeling?"

"Much better than a few minutes ago, and certainly better than when I'm moving."

"I can believe that. Can you tell me who shot you?"

"Shot me?" Martin blurted back, "I wasn't shot; an object from a minor release of energy struck me. I'm a scientist, and accidents of this nature sometimes happen, but I assure you nobody shot me. We don't even have weapons in the house."

"Can you tell me what happened?"

"I was standing at the workbench, and my elbow brushed something, and there was a loud pop, and I went to the floor. I intend to investigate the incident scientifically for the answers when we finish here."

"What do you work with?"

" I work with metal and magnetism. So the logical thing I can come up with now is I suspect a piece of ferrous metal reacted to a magnetic force in a way I didn't expect."

"Officer," one of the medics who overheard the questioning intervened, "Whatever struck Mr. Phillips wasn't a bullet, at least in the conventional sense. The wound is thin and less than a half-inch long. It could have been round, like a penny, a spinning rectangle, or a square, but not a bullet."

"That's good, my report can reflect an accidental injury, and I'll close the case."

The medic said, "Where would you like us to take him for a check-up and treatment?"

"The Memorial Hospital it's just a couple of blocks away; that's where I work."

"We'll get your husband there in five minutes, and the medical folks there will probably treat and release him, but he will need a driver if you want to take your vehicle."

The officer and ambulance drove toward the street, and Elie rushed to gather fresh clothes for Martin, then headed for the hospital.

Elie made the short trip to the hospital in a few minutes, seeing the ambulance crew packing to leave. The nurse parked in an employee stall, then quickly, but in a nurse's professional manner, walked to the Emergency Room.

At the reception desk, Elie was relieved to see Charlene Buffington, a long-time friend on duty. "How's Martin doing, Charlene?"

"Hi Elie, are you all right? Martin is in the care of Doctor Weinberg, and from what I heard, he will make a full recovery. What happened?"

Elie explained the situation in general terms to protect the project. However, most staff members knew of Elie and Martins' engagement and that Martin was a scientist.

"Fortunately, whatever hit him, did so high enough to miss the major arteries and veins and his lung. Other than some pain, Martin will heal quickly."

Doctor Wienberg came from an entrance to the examination rooms. "Elie, here. I thought you had the day off, and you're still working."

Doctor Charles Weinberg, an up-and-coming excellent trauma physician, was engaged to a fine nurse at another hospital.

"Martin was lucky; he will have to exercise more caution in experiments. I gave him a mild sedative, and here is a prescription for the pain he will need when the injection wears off. One tab as needed for pain, but work him off it as soon as he can withstand the minor discomfort. This medication is addictive, and I wouldn't say I like providing it, except in controlled conditions or severe pain. Have him check in with his family Doctor, but Martin shouldn't remember he was ever injured in about four to five weeks."

"Thank you, Doctor Weinberg; I'll make sure he relaxes for a few days if I have to sit on him. By the way, next Sunday, we will be married if you and Marge would like to attend."

"I'll tell Marge, and if we aren't on the schedules, we'll try to be there. Martin is ready to leave as soon as the paperwork is complete. I'm glad you brought some clothes; his had to be cut or are bloody; I'm sure he will appreciate them."

Thanks again; I'm taking a few days off for the wedding and caring for Martin."

"Those sutures can come out in a week or ten days. You can take care of that at home."

Elie waved her acknowledgment as she walked to the ER treatment rooms. Elie found her fiancée semi-reclined in a bed, bare-chested, with bandages over the wound in his left shoulder. The pain injection had taken effect almost immediately, and Martin wasn't feeling any pain unless he moved suddenly.

Trying to appear subtle, the highly attractive nurse kissed Martin lightly on his cheek. "That's all you get for now."

"But, I'm wounded and need my lady." Martin joked.

"Sorry, my dear, any more attention will raise your blood pressure and bring on additional pain. I brought you a change of clothing; your other clothes were bloody and cut off."

Twenty minutes later, the two returned to the house, where Elie escorted Martin to his bedroom and helped him change into his pajamas.

Noting the time, the nurse asked, "How are you feeling?"

"Now that I'm relaxing, I don't notice any pain."

"The meds are still working. We'll give you a pain tablet before you sleep; it will help your body go a long way toward healing."

After ensuring the vehicles and home were ready for the night, Elie retired to her room, showered, and put on a set of PJs. She stepped across the hall, pushed open the ajar door, and then looked toward the bed. Martin appeared asleep, and the woman turned the lights off and quietly exited the room.

Back in her room, Elie sat on the edge of her bed, allowing the tension of the evening to drain away. Then she entered the presence of God, giving praises and thanks for the safe ending to the day. Elinore praised her Triune God and thanked Him for the understanding officer and helpful medics. Half an hour later, Elie lay down, physically exhausted. But the mystery of what happened in the lab haunted the woman. She mentally laid out her plan for the next day's hunt for the object that hurt Martin and may hold the answers to many questions she and Martin had pinned up within them and the storm of questions that were sure to arise.

Then, a disturbing concern popped into her head, *'What if their government supervisors learned of the incident and determined the key to a powerful energy source had surfaced, and in what way might they respond?'* Elie reopened her prayers and lay the issues at His feet, as she had learned. Then turned over and immediately fell asleep.

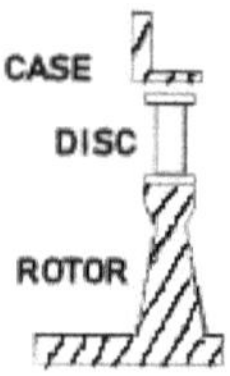

CHAPTER THREE

Sunday morning shined with a bright sun beaming through the eastern windows. Following their Sunday ritual, Elie and Martin dressed and headed for their church, half a mile away. Questions and hopeful solutions dominated the drive to church. They centered on the dreams they wanted to share with the Pastor. A sense of urgency hung over the young couple, like the feeling of high water pressuring a dam.

Elie looked at Martin, "Hun, I dislike this feeling of rushing to get things done. But I sense a voice telling me we must do it; then all will be safer. I can handle the trauma I see at the hospital, but this is spiritual, and the unknown threat frightens me."

"I have the same fears, Elie. Yet, the voice I heard wasn't threatening. Instead, I felt the voice was here to help. The only help in this situation is to talk with the Pastor at our earliest opportunity."

Elie and Martin met their parents at the church and joined the attendees entering the brick church. Pastor Mickey, and his delightful wife, Wife, greeted the folks coming in.

As Pastor Mickey greeted the family, Martin said, "Pastor, can we visit with you on an urgent issue? Then, could you and your wife join us for lunch?"

The Pastor looked at his wife, and she nodded; they had a free day following the service. An hour later, Pastor Mickey and wife said their 'good days' to the congregation as they left. Then, after locking the church, the eight people headed for a small but cozy restaurant.

"Pastor, Elie, and I have a potential problem to discuss with you, and we want our parents to know what is happening, and it involves an incident you may help us resolve."

The Philips and Canfields looked at one another and became seriously interested.

"Three nights ago," Martin began, "We both had a similar dream. In mine, it began with sirens, and he related the violence of the dream, then a voice said, "Take Elinore and run," and nothing more."

Elie took over, "I started with a normal drifting off into sleep that night, then without warning, an almost frantic voice said, "Take what you can carry, and run," Then the next day, Martin had his accident. Elie and Martin explained the accident as a simple loss of control of a metal piece and injury. Elie would investigate the accident as soon as possible.

Elie expounded, "Everyone dreams, but what is the chance of two people in a close relationship, apart, and receiving the same dream?"

Pastor Mickey thought for a moment, then said, "Extremely rare. When it happens, its source is usually traced to an outside entity. Putting the known facts together and the current political world, we know of their fixations and paranoia; I would have to consider the dreams as warnings and prepare to obey them. Those types of messages are Spiritual in origin. You must follow any directives from God and follow them to the letter."

Following lunch, conversations, and shared prayers, the group went their separate ways. Before Elie and Martin left their parents, Martin told the six of them, "I am becoming concerned about your safety and welfare. It would be best if you began to think in terms of police and military."

"What does that mean," Loraine Canfield asked.

"This will take practice, but you must always be aware of and familiar with people, your surroundings, and changes in conditions of vehicles, such as strange objects attached to the car not noted earlier, a house door unlocked or ajar when you know you locked it. Question anything in your homes that have been moved, and check air and heating vents for objects, especially those with wires attached.

The government has the ability to place listening and monitor devices in and around everything, clothing, shoes, anywhere in the house; they are devious devils. Watch for strange vehicles tailing you, then find them parked in the neighborhood with the same occupants. Look at clocks and framed photos for small glass circles in the picture or face of the clock in the area of any printing. These will probably be cameras. We will have to talk more about this as soon as we can, probably at the wedding."

Darlene Philips asked, "Why would they want to watch and listen in on the life of old folks like us?"

"Elie answered, "You aren't the subject of their investigation; Martin and I are. If we follow the Lord's directives, they will look for us, but they will also interrogate you and, before you know it, install audio and visual devices and surveillance to find us."

Clarence Philips' face betrayed his rising anger, "You must not tell us when you're leaving or where you're going. You can contact us when you're safe. We'll fend for ourselves."

Martin said, "We'll talk more about these contingencies after the wedding."

The group broke up, with Elie and Martin heading back to the house.

Martin, now fired up at the prospect of the government coming after Elie and him, said, "Let's find that piece of metal and see if we can't recreate the response it showed the other day."

"All right, but I'm not allowing you to push yourself, and I'll be at your side from now on," Elie said; the lack of a smile and the look in her azure eyes told Martin that he had no recourse.

Under the constant care of Elie, Martin finally gave in and allowed his body to heal. Then, although he wasn't a hundred percent healed, Martin got Elie to capitulate and agree to let him return to work under her supervision. The scientist didn't complain when Elie insisted on helping him pull his shirts over his red-scarred shoulder.

The two headed for the lab for the first time together since the accident. Unfortunately, Elie's investigation failed to account for the metal, and the incident was closed as accidental.

Elie had cleaned up the broken glass and debris from the accident, allowing another investigation to begin with Martin's presence. With a great deal of thought, Martin recreated the experimental setup with Elie's assistance. Then, aligning the angles as best he could remember, Martin estimated the possible trajectory of the square steel he coated with the powder.

"Elie, will you check that drawer by the door for a laser pointer? Attach it to the lab jig and activate the light if it's there." Martin sprayed a water mist in the beam's path to follow it to the wall. "Nothing," Martin said, " Let's expand the search. Elie, you take that side toward the north wall, and I'll go south." That wasn't an unexpected result at that point. The two began a search from the laser's pinpoint; Martin then spotted the small slit the projectile made as it penetrated the wall at the bottom of the wainscoting's top molding. Fortunately, Martin didn't miss the small horizontal penetration.

"Here it is, Elie."

Elie quickly walked to her betroth's side, holding several pop cycle sticks. "Here," she said, holding one out.

"Would you push the stick through the slit and out the opposite wallboard? I'll see what the height is."

Elie marked the hole by pushing the stick through the wall until it protruded on both sides. Martin noted the height of the penetration; it corresponded with the distance of the laser tip to the floor. The trajectory disclosed that the speed had to be sufficient to maintain level flight.

Erecting the laser at the location the stick exited the wall took a few minutes. Next, they located the point where the metal cut into the next wall, maintaining the level characteristic of flight and increasing the velocity value. The molten powder-coated square shot through the structure into the open air, where it disappeared. Again, it only took a few minutes to close and seal the missile's exit point.

With the information and facts discovered, Elie and Martin scratched their heads at the suggested velocity of the square sample. Their first requirement was to determine the metallurgy of the test material. An hour later, they found the base square was common steel, but the identity of the coating remained unidentified. Furthermore, there was no comparison in the Table of Elements for the melted-powdered layer.

Holding the disc in a pair of pliers, he waved it over every inch of the apparatus on the bench. He then noted in his book the procedure and its negative responses. Finally, reviewing his notes and the apparatus wiring, he noticed a magnet missing from its holder. After replacing the electromagnet, Martin waved the blank disc over the apparatus, and as it neared the electromagnet, the disc exhibited agitation, gaining intensity as the distance closed. More notes to his ledger. He noted the disc did not attempt to repel away but, as before, acted agitated.

Martin returned to reviewing his notes and comparing those to the diagrams of wiring and then the apparatus. Then, finally, it occurred to him that he had neglected to energize the circuit to the device.

"Elie, would you energize the battery circuit?"

With the blank disc still held in the grip of the pliers, Martin moved it closer to the front of the magnet. Then, at approximately ten inches to a foot from the magnet holder, the disc disappeared, and the pliers ripped from Martin's grasp. The disc disappeared through the wall as the first had.

Elie came up with the idea of taping white butcher paper to the wall in the test area, thus making it easier to track this missile. The two scientists followed the trajectory, repaired the damage, and then sat down to plan the next experiment.

Elie and Martin spent the next hour-and-a-half writing ideas in their notebooks, then applying them to the device. Finally, they came upon the idea of a brass shield in front of the magnet that extended to four by three feet, with a hole the size of the electromagnet in the center.

Under Martin's sharp eyes, Elie wired a single pole, spring-loaded switch in the positive wire from the battery. A single push would allow the contacts to close; the spring would immediately snap the button open. In addition, a ballistic chronograph stood by to capture the speed of the disc as it left its mount.

Elie watched as Martin reattached the 12-volt power supply to the motherboard grid, which included a six-sided coil tube aligned with the disc's trajectory, and they prepared for another test.

"Push the button, my dear."

"I believe the saying is, 'Fire in the Hole.'"

The disc disappeared, and the holding device flew across the floor as a sharp report assaulted their ears.

Martin glanced at the chronograph display, "It shows zeros across the screen. That means the reading is off the scale."

"Whatever it was, that bang hurt my ears; I can hardly hear you."

"That was the disc breaking the sound barrier in this enclosure.

The white paper showed where the disc went through the cover paper and the wall.

Martin became excited, "Elie," he shouted, "We did it."

As their hearing returned, Elie said, "Now we have to find a way to control the speed to apply the power to accomplish work."

Martin grunted, "Back to the drawing board. But now it shouldn't be too hard since we know and understand the mechanism to produce the flow of energy: converting the lateral movement into, say, revolution per minute and controlling the amount of that energy transfer."

"Martin, something bothers me."

"What's that?"

"We must wrap this into a watertight seal of secrecy; you know the government crazies will want to turn this into a cheap, deadly weapon."

The next morning, with the fog of exhaustion gone, Elie and Martin sat at the drawing table, brainstorming their next move. As they talked, Martin drew a rough drawing of a shaft with a serpentine belt pully on one end, which powered a vehicle alternator.

"That's pretty simple, isn't it?"

"And that's the beauty of it. See that crate in the corner with the red tarp?"

"What is it?" Elie asked.

"A steam turbine for an old water pump. There are several different sizes of couplings on the pallet, all of which fit the driven end of the shaft." After uncovering and opening the crate, Martin said, "It looks as if we're going to make on-the-job modifications to our plans."

"Martin, let's talk; it's time for coffee."

At the office table, they sipped coffee, then Elie spoke. "If I'm going to help you, I need to understand where all this is going. We started on one project, then switched to another with no apparent connections. So let me help you, but first, lay it out for me."

"You're right,"

"Slow down a little, and let me catch up to you," Elie pleaded.

"Right," Martin began, "As you know, the standard automobile engine derives its power from burning a fuel-air mixture, which expands as it's converted into a gaseous state. The reciprocating pistons move up and down, and the piston connecting rods are attached to the offset crankshaft and become rotary power. The rotary motion is connected to the transmission and, thus, to the drive wheels. The water pump is rotary and usually internally mounted, leaving the alternator and sometimes power steering and air conditioning connected by the serpentine belt.

In this case, we are replacing the fossil or electric engine with our design, the turbine wheel with molten powder-alloy discs attached to the turbine blade positions. And the weight of the turbine acts as the weighted flywheel to maintain smooth inertia."

Elie added, "The camera iris acts as the throttle by controlling the magnetic force on the discs."

"Exactly."

"Great, now the confusion becomes perfect sense."

The two labored for an hour, getting the heavy turbine and shaft secure in a custom-built frame on the bed of an engine stand. Next, the turbine easily rolled on castors to a modified lathe, where the overhead crane lifted the turbine and supported it until the heart of the untried engine was secured to the lathe by Elie and Martin.

Then the scientist machined and custom-prepared the tail of the turbine shaft to accept a serpentine pulley slid over the fore-shaft. Next, Martin followed the drawings and machined two locations for fitted journals to accept pillow block bearings to support and stabilize the power shaft.

"Martin, will those bearings handle the thrust?" Elie asked.

"There will be no axial thrust, as would normally be found in such a machine and pump. Instead, the thrust is when the magnetic stream strikes the discs, instantly dissipating as the shaft rotates," Martin explained.

Elie immediately grasped the mental picture of the turbine in operation. The pulley and serpentine belt provide the power for the accessories, and at the tail end, the transmission drives the wheels, a complete engine. But no fuel is required; therefore, there is no exhaust and no engine noise.

At the end of the turbine rotor, the turbine blades are dove-tailed onto the rotor. Such a method prevents the machined blades from dislodging from the rotor and damaging or destroying the rotor, other blades, and casting.

Five hours after the beginning, Martin removed the last blades from the rotor. Reverse engineering of the blade assembly allowed Martin to machine replacements with discs integrated into the ends.

Another day ended, leaving the scientists exhausted. A light dinner and prayer service relaxed the couple, and showers left them ready for sleep. The following morning, Elie finished setting aside her get-away bag. The contents gave her three days of clean underwear and socks, hygiene products, a change of outerwear, and cash for emergencies. Martin told her to refrain from taking any credit or bank cards; their move would be dark, and neither Elie nor Martin would take telephones.

In the drawing office, Elie said, "Martin, dear, I have to ask."

"Go ahead, Elie, no secrets between us."

"Aren't we trying to create perpetual motion by creating more energy than we use?"

"The theorists and other scientists say that is true. Here we are attempting to create a different kind of energy. Many attempts to use magnetism to generate energy or motion over the years have usually failed because magnets don't develop sufficient power." Martin thought for a few seconds, then continued, "I supposed we are trying to go against conventional wisdom, but the results we have seen tend to support our efforts."

"The excitement it's generating is sufficient for me to continue," the woman said with bright enthusiasm.

Martin gave Elie a set of plans for converting a 55-millimeter lens to a brass-leafed aperture with the glass lens removed and mounted on a non-metallic device. "Want to give this a try?"

A broad smile adorned Elie's face, and she scampered off to begin her work. Martin chuckled as he returned to assembling the turbine.

Work progressed, with Martin finishing the construction of the molten powder-alloy discs firmly integrated into the rotor. Finally, the scientist lowered the turbine into the engine cradle, where he installed the pillow block bearings.

With Martin's help, Elie completed the lens-holding device's manufacture and installed it on the frame of the novel engine assembly.

Elie painted a narrow stripe horizontally along the turbine shaft. Then, an RPM detector was mounted onto the frame, with its lens a quarter inch from the instrument. An internal light illuminated the silver stripe as the rotor turned to activate the counter, which Elie wired to an RPM repeater on the dashboard.

Next, the alternator, battery, and electric power steering device took their place in the growing electric system. Finally, Martin attached an electronic speed regulator and wired it into the system.

Elie and Martin created a checklist and reviewed it three times before applying it to the strange-looking machine before them. Next, the two scientists walked the checklist through the engine three times, triple-checking all wire connections.

"What do you think, Elie? Should we try it out?"

"After you were shot and all the work we put into this monster, you can bet your booties we're gonna give it a try," Elie said, not to be denied.

Martin handed her the computer keyboard-size control panel, "You have the honor, my dear. But let's take the precaution of the protective shield."

Once behind the shield, Martin added, "Start it by flipping the safety switch, which moves a ceramic barrier from the magnetic stream, do not touch the throttle; the governor should keep the RPMs to fifteen hundred. I've added an over-speed sensor as a cut-out at six thousand RPMs."

Elie took the board, then, looking at her husband-to-be, said, "I love you." Then, while gazing into his eyes, she flipped the barrier switch; a minute opening in the center of the iris allowed the tiniest magnetic stream to pass through. She immediately heard the engine begin spinning.

HUMVEE MILITARY VEHICLE

CHAPTER FOUR

The rotor turned smoothly on its axis as Martin reached for the knob, which controlled the iris between the energized electromagnet and aperture in the shield.

"One click might put this beast through the roof," Elie stated.

"That's why I installed the governor; it'll shut the iris and try to hold it to fifteen hundred RPM, but be ready for an emergency shutdown." Martin opened the iris with one click, hardly enough to see a light through the minuscule opening.

Immediately the turbine jumped to over two thousand RPMs, and the iris closed. A soft sound from the turbine as a slight whisper of air moving in the casing.

Elie looked at Martin and let out the breath she was holding.

Martin's hand hovered over the emergency shutdown while he watched the RPM indicator. The air in the casing acted as a form of break from its friction, and the RPM display began to show the slightest reduction in speed.

When the rotor reached fifteen hundred, the iris returned to the first opening, then began moving back and forth, attempting to maintain the set speed. Finally, Martin turned the knob off, interrupting the effect of magnetism on the rotor.

Elie yelped and threw her arms around her fiancé, "You did it, Martin; I'm so proud of you," as she held him for balance while she hopped up and down. Martin wrapped his arms around her, and they kissed, then he corrected her. "We did it. Now we have to put it together with all the parts and run a test with a load on the machine; that will be the proof in the pudding."

An assembly of a complicated, untried machine normally requires months, if not years, to perfect. However, in Philips and Canfield's case, time was short.

"Elie, will you begin attaching the electrical circuits? There are some which will need a different configuration or rebuilding. The diagrams are on the cart, and call me if you have any issues," Martin asked. "I'll start assembling the mechanical attachments so we can make the static tests."

"You bet; now I'm glad I took those home and auto electrical repair courses," Elie said.

Long hours passed quickly, and after a short break for lunch, Elie and Martin returned to their work, noting that their work began showing results.

Elie completed wiring the control panel to accept the feeds from the custom-made test bed holding the drive train, the peripheral, and the electrical components. At the same time, Martin finished installing the heating and cooling unit and attached the last light to the bed.

"Now, we begin an in-detail inspection of all nuts, bolts, and electrical connections. After that, we can attach the battery and begin the electrical tests."

"Sounds like a logical plan, Mr. Philips," Elie played with Martin.

The three clocks in the workshop all showed ten-thirty. Looking toward the skylight, Elie said, "Martin, it's after ten PM, time to shut it down and get some rest before we try any tests."

"You're kidding," Martin exclaimed. "Where did the time go?"

"You know time flies by when you're having fun," Elie smiled.

"I am tired; I guess I didn't stop long enough to feel it; let's shut it down; tomorrow promises to tell us what kind of mechanics we are."

Half an hour later, all was quiet.

****

Elie smacked Martin's door as she walked by his room.

A fresh pot of coffee finished perking as Martin stepped into the kitchen. Elie stood beside a counter, brushing hot butter on fresh cinnamon rolls.

"Pour us a cup of coffee, Martin, and I'll have the rolls on the table by the time you're ready."

"You will make a lucky man a fine wife," he teased.

"I'm trying to practice an unfamiliar lifestyle."

"It's pretty hard to improve on excellence."

"Now, you're brushing butter," Elie giggled.

Six hours after beginning work, the test bed waited silently, strapped to the shop floor.

Elie and Martin stood silently, praying for success.

Martin looked at the lady he planned on spending his life with; then, he opened the iris with one click as before. The turbine hit fifteen hundred RPM in a second, where it settled down at the regulated speed. Again, watching the gauges, electrical draws, and production, he made notes on every reading. Martin also prepared a log similar to navy engineering logs but customized to the project and filled in the values accordingly.

To ensure the engine and peripherals ran properly, Martin allotted a minimum of fifteen minutes of operation time before adding to the load on the system. First, he turned on the running lights, which included headlights, markers, and taillights, then switched to the high-beam headlights. With each additional load addition, Martin listened to the engine work. To his surprise, he heard no noticeable change in the whisper of the turbine. The meters registered the expected increase in the electrical draw, but the battery and engine remained unaffected. Elie took over recording the readings and adding them to the log.

Martin closed the air conditioning switch and started the compressor. At first, there was a slight movement in the amperage usage, but it immediately returned to the previous reading with the engine still idling. A minor change occurred in an increase of two RPMs; the draw at the battery showed far less than the supply availability.

"Elie, remember we talked about photographing the results of the project?"

"I'll get the camera and film. I have a plan in mind to take the photos in a logical manner to tell a story rather than a folder full of photographs."

"Do your thing while I monitor the board," Martin said. Then he checked the radios they installed. They had the AM/FM radio for local information and a Citizen's band radio to monitor back-and-forth communication; it was always busy. In addition, an enlarged military radio covered the military bands, including aircraft, with encryption and decryption modes. The AM/FM babbled their usual gab and music.

Martin thought about the radio noise, *'We can use the earphone connections, and with the quiet turbine running, they could remain unobserved and unheard.'*

Elie finished the photographic documentation, then took several pictures of the control panel, including closeup photos of the electrical gauges.

"Well, my dear," Elie said, "What's next on the agenda?"

"A test drive. First, we'll run the Humvee through the gears of the automatic transmission in the shop, then we take it for a trial drive, and the distance will depend on the readings as we go along. I know we're pushing the limits well beyond protocol, but we have no choice."

Elie acted as a ground guide for Martin as he put the Humvee through its limited paces. Testing identified four minor flaws that took a few minutes to correct. But, overall, testing more than fulfilled the scientist's wishes by working within the parameters of each system and part.

"Martin, it's almost eerie, this big vehicle operating as quietly as a kitten; sealing the engine compartment from the elements must have much to do with that."

"I agree; I keep looking for a failure in one component or another, yet everything works together in perfect unison. And the power ratio has remained almost unchanged. It makes you wonder how much power is available. With an unconventional concept and untried main drive, I would expect something would go wrong," Martin thought out loud.

"I would say there is divine guidance at work here," Elie said.

"We did ask for His help, and He found us wanting," Martin replied.

"We should give the Humvee a nickname. And I nominate 'Beast.' After all, there isn't anything pretty about it," Elie noted.

"I like it, Beast, it is."

Martin pulled the Beast into position to drive up the ramp to the driveway. First, Elie retracted the overhead, which also raised the ramp. Then, ensuring she had the remote control, the excited woman hopped into the modified front compartment and strapped herself into the comfortable bucket seat.

Martin had converted the throttle mechanism to operate like an unmodified vehicle. He shifted the Beast into drive and slightly depressed the foot throttle, opening the shutter assembly one notch. The Beast launched up the ramp, pushing the two occupants into their seats.

Besides a high response to the throttle, the heavy vehicle drove as the original manufacturers designed it. Martin looked at the electrical cluster, the gauges supported the lab findings, and the engine performed as it did during testing. Yet, with all the lights, radios, and heaters running, the draw showed a minuscule usage ratio to available energy. Elie had installed temperature sensors at all heat-developing locations, and they all registered in the normal range.

The city traffic flow had dissipated in favor of the usual nighttime drivers. But the high fuel costs and restrictions of the socialist government caused the late traffic to dwindle to a fraction of its former levels. This pleased Elie and Martin, which meant fewer people saw the military-painted vehicle. Those that had were used to seeing Humvees on the streets at night as they patrolled the streets for dissidents.

Elie said, "Martin, we've driven in and out of town, and today is Sunday. It's time to get rest for the church service in the morning; what do you say about heading for the house and bedding down the Beast? It worked so well; I'd give it a treat if it were alive."

Laughing, Martin answered, "I bet you would. The house is a few blocks away, and we're heading that way."

At the house, the Beast disappeared as Martin drove down the ramp, then Elie retracted the ramp and closed the overhead. Before shutting down the near-silent engine, Martin downloaded the operational data onto a flash drive. Elie had already retreated to her room, and Martin did the same, where he showered, crawled into bed, and slipped into a deep sleep.

****

Elie and Martin had been attending the same church most of their lives. So when Martin turned up with his arm in a sling, his friends crowded around him with sympathy and well wishes.

During the service, Pastor Mickey announced, "Next Sunday, we will have a special event, the wedding of Miss Elinore Canfield and Mr. Martin Philips, shortly after the main service. So, on behalf of Elie and Martin, please, no gifts or money. Your attendance will be the perfect gift."

After the parishioners left the church, the couple made their final arrangements for the wedding. Many couples stood outside the church in the sun, chatting and laughing with the Canfields and Philips when the betrothed emerged. Behind the two, Pastor Mickey and his wife locked the church and joined the families. As expected, the slightly blushing bride-to-be became the center of attention.

Pastor Carvour asked the Canfields and Philips to have lunch with them, and four vehicles followed the Minister to a popular eatery, where they parked in the lot. At the Pastor's request, the greeter seated them in an alcove where a good measure of privacy was available.

After ordering a light lunch, Pastor Mickey offered the blessing, including a special prayer for Elie and Martin.

The Minister looked around for possible eavesdroppers, then addressed the couple, "Any more messages?"

"No," the two chorused.

"Do you have somewhere to go, a place where you can be safe?" Mickey asked.

"Yes, but we're keeping that under wraps, even from our folks," Elie said. "If those who seek us ask our parents, they wouldn't have to lie, and if forced to take a polygraph, they could pass it with ease.

Mickey continued, " This is going to be a difficult time for all of you. Your lives are going to change radically, and you must prepare for a sudden departure from a planned action, and if the government is after you, they will tap any phones in your name, all your parents' phones, and your homes. So I suggest you pick up some burner phones, sign for them in a different name, and only use them in an emergency. What do you have for transportation?"

"Elie and I each have a vehicle, and…." The man went silent, not wanting to reveal the Beast.

Mickey continued, "Sell one vehicle now, then the other when you flee. I suspect you have a third vehicle you're reluctant to discuss. That's all right, keep it secret. Is it registered to you?"

"No, it's an unregistered salvaged ex-military vehicle."

"Good, keep it that way. Then, when you make your break, switch to the military unit after you sell your vehicle. And wear military camouflage uniforms to look the part. If you have weapons, do not have them on your person, that's the fastest way to get shot.

Answer the following questions Yes, or no.

Do you have access to communications outside burner phones?"

"Yes."

"Do you have any past arrest or investigative records with the law?"

Elie and Martin looked at one another, then said, "No."

"Have either of you ever had fingerprints or DNA collected by any government level?"

"Yes," they said.

"End of questions, the FBI, Homeland Security, and Intelligence agencies have access to all they need to identify you. If the government seeks you, then your safety is in deep cover," the former FBI agent said. "I must ask, how do you stand before the Lord?"

Both Elie and Martin stood before their Minister and parents and held hands. Elie began, "I am a sinner and have given my life to my Savior for whatever He wishes. I accepted Him as my Savior and God; He has taken my sins and sent them as far as the East is from the West. We go before Him daily, and He cleanses us of what sins we may have committed, and Jesus assures us of forgiveness. Therefore, as I stand here, I can assure my parents that we have honored your wishes."

Then, Martin declared, "I am a sinner, and I have been born again and cleansed by the blood of Christ. As a human, I still slide outside the wishes and laws of my God, but He gives me the opportunity to go before Him and ask for forgiveness, which He said he would grant.

Elie and I have enjoyed one another's company since childhood and have not dated another person. We committed to one another eight years ago and have exercised faithfulness with one another ever since."

Mickey and his wife glanced at the parents and saw the women filled with tears of joy, and the fathers, standing tall and proud. Then, turning to the young couple, the Pastor said, "There is nothing more for me to say, but God bless you, and Amen. We will conduct your ceremony as planned a week from today.

In the meantime, I recommend downloading all your files, scanning your drawings and photos, and loading them onto a portable hard drive. I would guess a terabyte should suffice; if not, they make two or more terabyte drives, but I'm not sure where to get them.

Then, and this is important, delete the information from all your computers. Since you work for the government, do you have the approved eradication disc?"

"Yes, it's in the safe."

"Once you're sure all the documents regarding your project, and those a month before your success have been copied, run the eradication program; it will leave no trace of your work. All paper documents must be shredded and burned."

"Why are you telling us to do this?"

"I received a message directing me to do so. And, God does not want man to have this technology; He has other plans."

Lorraine gasped, her hand flying to her mouth, "The rapture is near."

Mickey calmly corrected her, "The rapture will occur when it's God's decision, now or later. But, in the meantime, we must, without fear, walk the paths He has chosen for us; Maranatha."

The luncheon ended, sending each family on their way.

Martin and Elie had driven separate vehicles to church and lunch. Before leaving the eatery, Elie handed her keys to her mother, "Mom, the car is still registered to you, and I need you to take it back now."

Lorraine's face clouded, "Are you leaving us so soon?"

"No, Mother, but things are changing daily, and we feel compelled to prepare for whatever is coming, and I don't need your car now. Martin has his vehicle, and we will make do with it. You know this must happen?"

"Yes, I understand," then the older woman's stalwartness of old returned, transforming her into the warrior she once was. Her husband, Norman, saw the change and recognized the woman he fell in love with, and the former Special Forces Officer straightened and stood taller. Martin, Darlene, and Clarence witnessed what happened, filling their minds with questions, but respectfully remained silent and watched. Then the families said their goodbyes until Sunday.

As they approached home, Martin noticed a black vehicle occupied by two men. Additional radio antennas had been installed on the roof and the center of the trunk lid. The only missing mark was a decal screaming COP. No sooner than when Elie passed the car, it whipped out and followed her and Martin into their driveway. Martin exited their vehicle and stepped toward the black Ford bearing official government plates.

A beefy, tall passenger exited the front passenger seat and unfolded into a six-foot tall man with a football player's build. The driver remained in the government car, possibly as a backup, and it gave him access to his radio if he needed help. The tall man identified himself, "I'm Special Agent Miles Vickers with the Department of Homeland Security," he said.

"Of course you are; how can I help you?" Martin asked.

Vickers displayed his bi-folded credentials, then slipped them into his interior jacket pocket.

"Who might you be?" Vickers asked; in a glance, his eyes took in every tree, bush, and potential hiding place he could see.

"I'm Martin Philips; the lady in our car is Elie Canfield, my fiancée. I would be the person to whom you want to speak."

"As you know, we must maintain an update on your progress and if we may help in any way or if you need any material assistance. Unfortunately, we heard you suffered a minor accident and were injured. However, you are supporting your arm, so I assume it is more than a scratch. I trust your arm is healing well."

"You're right up to speed on the information net; that's impressive. Unfortunately, I did injure my shoulder in a moment of relaxing my observations, and I paid the price for inattention. I accidentally knocked over a container of sodium which came into contact with water from a broken drinking glass. I don't know your level of chemical knowledge, but…."

"It makes for a surprise when that combination all but explodes," the smiling agent said.

"It does that. Anyway, the explosion propelled a piece of metal, and my shoulder got in its way. I was treated at our local hospital and released. Tomorrow, we plan to isolate volatile substances to avoid any further problems. As you know, experimenting with energy is like handling a loaded weapon; you don't want to lose control of it."

"I understand; do you have any projection of when you can resume your work?" Vickers asked.

"Doctor Weinberg said to give it five weeks for a full recovery, but I usually heal quickly and may be able to shorten that time. So I'm anxious to get on with my work."

"I understand your caution; if I were in the scientific field, I would be cautious working with energy; you never know when you will hit a pothole and crash."

"I can attest to that, now," Martin agreed. "I suspect OSHA will pay me a visit."

"No doubt, I won't keep you, I know you're busy, and Sunday is a time of rest, and if anyone needs it, it's you; if we can help, give us a ring."

"Do you have a card?"

"Yes, here it is," he said, handing him a business card. "We have to head back; the paperwork never slackens. Take care." The black car backed into the street and left at a normal pace.

Elie and Martin watched the car disappear around the next corner, then Martin muttered, "Those guys were snooping; I wonder why Homeland Security has their hounds out?"

"They most likely received a call from the hospital." Elie said, "They are under a mandate to report anything that would fall into the category of a bullet or stab wound."

"I don't think we're going to see much rest today; those guys look pretty sneaky; I have no doubt they know what we're doing, but I don't think they know it's operational." Then he headed toward the house.

"You sound suspicious; what are you going to do?"

"I want to check the lab and house in detail."

"What are you looking for?" she asked.

"Not sure, possibly a bug or two, maybe even some cameras."

CHAPTER FIVE

"Do you think they bugged our house?" the upset woman growled.

"The lab or the house, and most likely both, if we find listening devices or cameras, we'll take our cars in for a check-over. Their appearance was too fast, and it wasn't by the 'next-in-line' concept; they knew I was injured before they arrived. From that, I, at least, suspect they bugged everything."

"Martin, how are we to locate these devices?"

"Anything they installed would be low power and transmit to a relay station and from there to their headquarters."

"A relay station. How big is that, and where would they hide it?" Elie persisted.

"Depending on their technology and budget, the DHS is high on the government's priority list. So even though it's several years old, they could have the COB technology."

"COB?"

"Components On Board; highly reduced in size electronic capacitors, resistors, and other parts reduced to a sixteenth of an inch in length, or less. That's what makes a wristwatch capable of having a radio in it. A relay station the size of a pack of gum isn't out of the question. Just tack it to a tree or any light or power pole, and they are in business. We can find the bugs with an RF detector if they are here. It indicates the strength of radio frequency output. Bugs and small cameras will do that if they are transmitting."

Elie and Martin stopped by their bedrooms and changed into work clothes and lab coats. Their planned day of rest was long gone. Elie prepared a pot of coffee and two cups. Martin headed straight to the lab.

Martin stopped for a minute, then said, "Elie, if we destroy one of their devices, it will alert them, and I fear they will come to detain us. So we aren't ready to leave yet."

"I'd like to start right away."

"So would I, but if we do, they will know and bring that blonde guy back here. They may have bugged us just to see our response. I think running at this minute would be playing into their hands. Besides, I need to plan our moves, and we won't have time once we start."

"After thinking about it, you're right. I'll fix a high-protein, low-calorie dinner," Elie said.

After cleaning the table and kitchen from dinner, Elie and Martin walked to the lab and shop. One modification to the Humvee included a front bench seat with belts for three people if needed. Elie sat next to Martin, her arm interlaced with his, as they discussed their next moves.

"You haven't mentioned where we will go. You know the government will have our photos and name posted on the most wanted list," she said.

"Probably, so we will have to follow Pastor Mickey's idea and go off the grid, or more accurately, disappear. Before that, we are going to marry. The first thing in the morning, I'll call the Pastor with a burner and tell him our plans. Before leaving, we must destroy our old cell phones, including the sim cards. Then, we can withdraw our funds from the banks and destroy all debit cards. I don't have a credit card, do you?"

"One, but there is no balance on it."

"Good, close it; we will have to go all cash now. Our next move is to sever all identification and locations we have had. After that, you will have to mail a resignation to the hospital. Simply stating, 'I hereby resign my position with the hospital,' and signing it.

I know it seems harsh and sudden, but this is needed for our survival until the Lord takes a hand."

"I agree, Martin, but I don't have to like it."

"You're right; the government has given us no other choice."

"We have never lived under a closed society, and I truly hate the dictatorship structure of the socialists, and the restrictive two-class structure they created, the people, their slaves, and the elites, the masters. However, I have one Master and will never bow before another. Now, as such, I am an outsider but in the best of company."

"Yes, we are," Martin agreed. "Here are the keys to my car; the title is in the glove box." Checking his watch, Martin continued, "It's almost two AM; time to get some sleep."

"I'm not going back into that house," Elie stated.

"You won't have to; we'll get a pair of motel rooms for the night. Then, we'll take the car for one last ride."

"I don't want to leave you, Martin," the unsettled woman said.

Elie and Martin knew they were being tailed, but that wasn't a problem. Couples will spend a night away from the house for a number of reasons, even to have a different evening.

Both rooms of the hotel were located on the top floor, across from one another. It provided an ideal opportunity to get a fair night's rest.

****

The phones in each room woke the occupants at six AM with sharp rings. The hot and cold showers worked wonders in preparing for the day. Elie watched from her open door for Martin to join him for breakfast.

"Despite the uncomfortable night in a strange bed, I would say it will suffice," Elie complained.

Martin smiled and turned toward the elevator, "Let's have some breakfast, then we can enjoy the coffee while we go over our plans."

"Good idea, I'm hungry."

After playing the role of a mundane couple, Elie and Martin returned to the house and the darkened area of the shop.

Sitting in the rear seat of the beast, Martin said, "Our first job is to bring into use the burner phones. Their use must be short, clipped, cryptic, and to specific people. Then, for the rest of the day, we can use our regular cell phones, but we must use phrases known to the caller and recipient. Other than that, any calls from us must be made from the burners. Finally, I must remember to call Pastor Mickey and set up a meeting as soon as possible for our marriage."

"We'll need to call our parents and ensure they can be there," Elie said. "Mom would never forgive me if I didn't."

"But first, we will need to change our last names; otherwise, all this will fall like a house of cards," Martin warned.

"Have you selected a name?"

"Yes, an easy one for the folks to remember, 'Cadin,' Elinore, and Mac Cadin."

"Explain, please?"

"Elinore, or Ali for short, is an exceptionally old English spelling of Eleanor, and Mac is a nickname my father picked up when he was in the army. Khadin means 'servant' in Arabic. Since we are servants of God, why not Servants? But to confound the government snoops, I altered it to Western standards, and hence, Cadin."

"Impressive; it should hold off the trackers for a couple of weeks."

"I thought it would be better than Smith or Jones," Martin said.

"That could be up for grabs, but I like the change," Elie added.

"Next, I need to contact our attorney and see what we can do about a legal name change; then, we can get an official driver's license and our marriage license."

"Then our old names are gone?" she asked.

"I'm afraid so; this government is extremely unforgiving toward anyone who withholds the potential for weapons and powerful drive machines, as we are doing. But, I'm not afraid, and neither should you fear them; we are servants of God, and we do the Lord's bidding."

Ali looked at the man she stood by and said, "Amen."

"Once we get the papers and license, we'll be married and on our way."

"I'm still bothered by how I am to explain it to my parents?"

"I have no doubt we will get the help when we need it. But first, it's time to clean the house.

Never before needing an RF detector, Martin thought about the circuitry for a minute, then laid out his tools and parts. It didn't take more than two hours to make the device, installing frequency bands of 3-30MHz, 30-300MHz, 300-3000MHz, and 3-30GHz, along with a meter for strength identification and an alert light with a reset. Then he calibrated it and checked it.

"Let's begin in the house; that will take the most time." Then, Martin suggested, "The lab and shop are larger; however, they have fewer dividers."

"I'm gonna be highly ticked off if someone is intruding into our life." Elie's growl screamed, 'Danger.'

Martin raised his eyebrows at the implied threat; he never envisioned his mate-to-be as a fighter, but lately, he had noticed a change from her medical persona. So, as an afterthought, he decided to make his future moves toward Elie with a bit more finesse and understanding.

"Now," Martin said, "You're beginning to see the picture. I've read stories of such behavior in the past. For example, the government ran deep surveillance programs on everyone involved in the 'Manhattan Project,' which produced the atomic bomb during World War II."

"We aren't at war," Elie growled again.

"No, we aren't, but since World War II, the government has been at war with someone, Elie. Even in the late twentieth and this century, there was serious government spying on citizens and other nations and their people, mostly political considerations or under national security. But, unfortunately, the government, especially the rabid socialist zealots, has taken the perceived need to spy on all or any of its citizens as necessary for self-preservation. It's contrary to the principles of the Founding Fathers. Under them, America spied only on individuals as an essential tool to preserve the safety of the people and the country. Enough history: we have work to do."

Elie said, "Take a break and then get your tools ready. I'll map out a search plan for the house. It will keep us from doubling back during the search."

"Why's that?"

"You don't want to start our married life with a woman who found out we had bugs and didn't catch them on the first sweep, now do you?" Elie giggled.

The two betrothed-turned-sleuths began in the kitchen. The alert light illuminated when Martin stepped through the doorway. He stopped, took a step, and the meter swung to the right. Elie's eyes popped wide open. Martin turned the device from right to left, with the strongest reading on the left. He moved toward the left counter, and the meter moved toward a hundred percent. Martin moved a paper towel used to catch any drain from a plant, and behind it was a pair of two-way communicators they used when working in the yard. The scientist grimaced and pulled the plug on the charging unit, canceling its output and resetting the light. He felt Elie's head plop against his back.

Martin took another step, with his female shadow on his six. Immediately the alert glowed, and the meter rose a third of the way across the meter. The needle moved further to the right when he stepped that way. An old Cathedral radio sat on the end of the right counter: Martin and Elie like the antique for its looks, and it still played well. Martin leaned over and pulled the radio's plug, and the meter remained pegged against a hundred percent. The man felt Elie's hand wrap around his belt and close into a fist.

Martin moved the swing latch aside at each corner, allowing the back to fall into his hand. Using a small led flashlight, he immediately spotted the foreign object facing the cloth front. Martin slowly removed the device using long tweezers, keeping its antenna intact. He showed it to Elie.

Martin had never seen Elie transform into a hardened woman. He didn't like what he saw. Her face reflected every word describing betrayal, hate, and disgust, twisting her lovely face into a fighting mask. He could hardly hear her voice, "Let's find the rest."

Martin set the listening device on a square of paper towels, then rammed a dozen sheets into a large coat pocket. *This isn't good; we're going to have to make our move tonight,'* he thought.

Turning away, Martin reset the light, expressed satisfaction that there were no other devices in the kitchen, and headed for the dining room. However, his approach was different upon entering the dining room; he hid the RF detector beneath his coat and casually looked around.

The scientist carefully looked at every nook and cranny; then it dawned on him how cavalier he took the living room in the past. The air vents sat low on the floor; heat and cooling utilizing the same duct flowed across the room to a return vent on the opposite side. The design warmed the feet in cold months, and the warm air rose upward to heat the rest of the body. Ceiling fans returned it to the return vents.

Elie went to the opposite side of the room and began checking the bottom of chairs and tables, finding two audio bugs.

Martin found another under the coffee table. Each was marked but remained unmolested.

Remembering Pastor Mickey's words, Martin looked at the grandfather clock and spotted the black quarter-inch circle of a camera lens. He opened the door enough for the lens to point at the bookshelf. Then, Martin retrieved the RF detector and worked around the known bugs and a second camera. Finally, he felt they identified the devices in two rooms.

Elie moved like a leopard, soundlessly stalking, listening, and viewing devices in her bedroom. Leopards are skillful and successful hunters. Elie displayed a sardonic grin as she held up two mini microphones and a camera by their antennas, as a hunter held its prey by their tails.

She whispered to Martin, "Those bastards have been watching me undress; I'm beginning to feel a need for a bath and retribution."

Concerned for Elie's beliefs, Martin reminded her, "Vengeance is mine, saith the Lord." Elie dear, what is done, is done and cannot be changed. God will take care of them. You can take comfort in knowing they viewed one of God's most beautiful gifts to your parents and your husband, and they will never taste the fruits of perfection."

Elie wrapped her arms around Martin and looked into his eyes, "I love you, Martin Philips; thank you for keeping me straight. Now let's see what you find."

Martin's bedroom gave up the same combination as found in Elie's. The angry woman asked, "When do we leave?"

"Tonight, the G-boys already know we found their toys."

"I have an idea, so they will have no doubt that we found them; let's put them in a large can and pour kerosene on top of them. Then run another sweep for any we missed, and if we did, add them to the can. Then, on our way out the door, light the kerosene," Elie proposed.

"I like it, and we still have the lab and workshop to check." In the Lab, Martin pulled a large portable light from a closet, which he used to see the top of the suspended stoplights and ceiling joists. An hour later, the two collected six audio and three cameras; all joined the others in the kerosene can, including those found and left alone.

A light sandwich and hot coffee perked up the two sleuths for their last sweep. Another hour passed, and two missed mini microphones and a camera turned up and filled the burn can.

Elie and Martin repacked the Humvee, adding some heavy winter clothing. The tedious task of downloading the computer files, photos, and drawings took over an hour; then, while Martin activated the eradication program, Elie gathered the papers, stuffed them into a certified burn bag, and took them to the incinerator, where she dumped the burn can full of kerosene and useless electronics on top of the paper. Then, smiling, Elie pushed the start button, starting the burn process. The incineration process lasted two hours.

The two fugitives couldn't wait that long, and once the fires burned brightly, Elie, now wearing military clothes, stepped from the Humvee, hopped into Martin's car, and fell in behind him as they headed for their attorney.

The attorney, Melvin J. Havelock, Esq., was a devout Christian and a member of the family church. He listened to the need for the name changes and said, "It will be no problem. We do these all the time, and our judge, Michael Candles, is also a church member and knows of your situation."

"Won't this place you in a dangerous position if the government finds out about your participation?" Elie inquired.

"No, our families and we are making our move, and this is the signal we have awaited. All is set."

Elie and Martin sat agape at the revelation.

An hour later, Elinore and Mac left the courthouse with the documentation to obtain the couple's new driver's license. Havelock told them to talk to nobody except Marge Deering. Mrs. Deering took the two to her office and applied sufficient makeup to hide their true features. After taking the file photos, Mrs. Deering cleaned the makeup away. Then took the images, which went on the replacement license.

"I thought these would have the made-up faces in the picture?" he asked.

"No, your face must match the driver's license if stopped. If the officer checks the record, he gets wants or warrants. Any investigator or electronic search will pass by your file folder because the picture on file doesn't match the name."

"Are you going to be safe doing this?"

"You must not remember me; my deceased husband was Thomas Deering. My current husband is Michael Candles, and we won't be here tomorrow."

Elie stood and hugged the older lady now that she recognized her. Martin joined Elie in thanking Mrs. Candles and said, "We'll meet again.

"Yes, we will, but enough for now; you are too busy to stay any longer; you have a wedding to attend. And remember, from here on, it's Elinore and Mac Cadin."

"Of course, it is," Mac said.

Ali and Mac called their parents and told them to meet them immediately where they sat Sunday morning and hung up.

Mac pulled the Humvee into a multi-level parking garage across the street from the church. They entered a side door on a pre-arranged set of bell rings. Pastor Mickey shook their hands, then looked out the closing door.

"The ceremony will take long enough for the night to fall. You are going to explain the change in your names to your parents first because they are losing their children."

"Understood." The two chorused.

Mac froze, "I have to go back and get the rings; they are in the Humvee.

Pastor Mickey's face softened; he smiled and said, "I have it on good authority; you won't need them."

Ali and Mac looked at the Pastor as if he had misunderstood what Mac said. "You will see, have faith," he said, then led them into the sanctuary.

The family and younger ones hugged and cried with their families, then Ali said, "I must explain something to you."

"Are you all right?" Lorraine asked.

"I'm fine; now listen; we were to develop a new power source with the fear of oil shortages and politicians messing up the energy available for the country. On the eve of that discovery, we both received a dream telling us to prepare to flee because of our work. God did not want man to have this power device; He had other plans."

"You told us that the other day," Lorraine said.

"Yes, since then, we had a visitor from Homeland Security, then we found the house, lab, and shop full of listening bugs and cameras. We destroyed them and all references to our work. Now we have changed our names and cut all connections to Elie and Martin Philips."

All the family members tried to speak at once. Mac held up his hands, "Listen carefully and memorize some words. First is servant; that is us. Then, when we call, all we will say is servant.

If you have a message, it must reflect a warning; anything else will jeopardize all of us. If we have news you need, it will be cryptic, and you must get with the other family and figure it out."

Mickey interrupted, "I will be there to help. But, enough, we have the ceremony to complete now, and I will visit with the families after the newlyweds depart."

The quiet, intense ceremony began, and Mickey prayed for the families and the bride and groom. When Pastor Mickey reached the part where the two exchange rings, he quietly said, "Stand where you are and pray for love between you and guidance from the Lord." Then he took three steps back. The two joined hands bowed their heads, and prayed from their hearts.

As the two families, the Pastor, and his wife, prayed, they heard angelic class voices singing and praising God. Then, looking up, and saw a mist, like a small cloud, appear between the two at the altar.

The sound of the voices emitted from the cloud, then reaching from the cloud, a pair of perfect hands bearing red scars where the spikes were driven through the Lord's hands clasped together as to pray.

Those in attendance seemed not to breathe as they watched the Lord's holy hands.

The Lord unclasped His hands, and in the reddened palm of His right hand lay a pair of interlocking golden wedding rings. The hands clasped again, and when opened, the rings were apart. The Lord placed the smaller ring on Ali's left ring finger. Then the larger ring on Mac's left ring finger. The nearly petrified couple trembled at the sight they were beholding. The Lord placed Mac's hand atop Ali's, and a voice more beautiful and soothing than the music said, "Fear not, for I am with thee," The hands withdrew into the cloud, which dissipated with the music.

The newlyweds drew strength from their faith, and the trembling ended. Pastor Mickey smiled and said, "My friends, let me introduce you to Mac and Ali Cadin."

Pastor Mickey, his wife, and the two families surrounded their children and, with tears of joy and wonder, celebrated the grandest wedding ever to be held in that church building.

With the ceremony completed, Pastor Mickey addressed those in attendance. "I want you to understand something. I normally wouldn't conduct a marriage ceremony under such short notice without exceptional reason. But, before you called, I felt the Lord's hand upon my shoulder; he instantly had my undivided attention. The Lord spoke to me in my mind and heart, telling me your predicament and part of his plans for you; that is why I knew you would not need to find the rings. Keep them; they are part of a God story. He commanded me to perform the ceremony, except for the part he conducted. There is more. The Lord wants you to go west and see Pastor Dick Johnson. He is a brother in Christ and one of my closest friends." He handed Mac a slip of paper with an address typed on it. "After seven days, you may proceed to your planned destination. There you will meet a friend, that is all I know. This is important, the Lord has given you a command, and you must follow it to the letter. Our time has ended for now. We will be together again sooner than you think. Now, go."

The newlyweds hugged their parents, showered them with kisses, then took their leave. Mac looked at the address in the Hummer and then handed it to Ali.

"California?"

SOCIALISM

CHAPTER SIX

DHS investigator Miles Vickers didn't trust Philips or his fiancée; although, at the same time, he had no proof, his gut feeling was that they had successfully developed an innovative energy source or had stumbled onto something that created power. But, in either case, they are hiding it. Why?

Vickers scowl projected a warning to all who saw him; 'don't play games with me,' as he walked faster than normal to the intelligence center. Then, using his identification card, Vickers entered the restricted, secure room.

"Eddi, has anything come up on the bugs or cameras?"

"Not yet; Philips and the girl changed clothes, and now they are reading material in their lab."

"All right, keep me posted if anything resembling a power plant shows up."

With his mind concentrating on the scientist, Vickers returned to his desk, where he went through Philips files again. The agent had a knot in his guts, telling him he had missed something. The sandy-haired agent grabbed his phone, making it look like a toy in his big paw-like hand.

"Morris, this is Vickers; I went through Philips' file, and there is woefully little information on him in his file. So check his phone records, and the girls, too, get a live tap for their cell phone lines. Then do an in-depth bank and credit check, along with owned property."

"Are we going to open a primary investigation on these two?"

"Not yet; my gut says yes, but I talked with them, and though I feel a distrust, there is no evidence they are other than what they appear to be. So, we'll hold on to the primary case for now; it may not be necessary."

"Okay, boss."

Vickers watch showed five-fifteen, and the last remnants of the office staff had left for the day. The agents called the intelligence room, where technician Jan Scroggins answered the phone.

"Scroggins," he said.

"This is Vickers; what's happening at Philips?"

"Not a lot, reading papers and then working on some electrical or electronic things. I haven't seen anything remotely resembling a power generator or device."

"Okay, make it standard-level surveillance; this might be a waste of time. If they crash for the night, you can shut down, and we'll pick it up in the morning."

"Yes, sir."

****

Miles Vickers walked into his office at zero-seven-thirty and immediately picked up his phone, calling the intelligence center.

When the tech picked up the phone, Vickers said, "Vickers here; anything on the Philips case?"

"We're having problems with the feed; I was just about to call you. All we're getting is white noise."

"Did you check the other bugs and cameras?"

"Yes, it's possible everything has gone offline."

"Has the power gone down in that area?"

"No, the high-power relay is working, but it's just receiving white noise."

"What do you mean all our bugs and cameras are dead?" Miles Vickers yelled at the surveillance technician monitoring the Philips' house.

"Listen to this," Mory May, the tech, switched through all the bug frequencies, and the roaring sound was static.

"What is that?" Vickers asked.

"You get that sound if the unit is offline or dead. I've tried to override their system and command them on, but the static remains."

"What about the cameras?"

"No audio static, but visual static, we call snow, and the sound is the same as with the bugs. Everything is dead."

"Get Todd Gable and his team over there; I want to know where the Philips and Canfield woman was ten minutes ago."

****

Ali and Mac left the house with only the clothes they wore, then drove to the suburb of Orland. The newlyweds briskly walked through the large Orland Square Mall, twenty-one miles from the DHS Headquarters. They purchased travel-grade clothing, including socks and shoes, then stopped in mall restrooms and changed. The clothes they wore went into the shopping bags, and Mac placed them into a charity collection station. From there, they took Highway 45 to I-80 and turned west.

****

Vickers hurried to his desk and sat before the open files on Philips and Canfield, looking for potential hiding places. But, first, he queried the tracker on the Philips car; it was stationary in a west-side neighborhood. Adding that to the mix, he came away baffled; there needed to be connecting information between Philips and Canfield in that area.

Grabbing his phone again, the agent called the on-call manpower room and had them dispatch two men to the car's location to check it and the area for the two people. His high blood pressure reddened his face as he slammed the phone into its cradle.

Vickers jumped at the rash ring of the government phone. "Vickers," he said with forced calmness.

"This is Hagar; we found the car parked in a low-rise garage. Whoever parked it here put it where no nearby residents could see it."

"Have it towed to our garage for an inspection, then write up a report to me to cover your trip; thanks." He hung up before the agent on the other end could say anything.

Before he could swear, the phone rang again. "Vickers," the agent growled.

"This is Gable; the house was unlocked, no cars around, and no people. Everything appeared to be in its normal place, and all the clothing was there. It's like the occupants left for the store and has not returned."

"Okay, your team bugged the place; see if your bugs and cameras are working; we have no signal here." The phone dropped casually into the cradle.

Ten minutes later, another ring, "Vickers."

"You're not gonna like this; the bugs and cameras are gone. We searched the property and found them in a home incinerator, burnt to a crisp."

Vickers seethed angrily, "Get a forensics team in there; treat it as a kidnapping of Martin Philips and Elenora Canfield by unknown agents."

"Do you think someone snatched them?"

"Personally, no. But we can put the highest pressure on finding them with that designator."

Vickers's sinewy muscles quivered with anger; he'd lost all track of Philips and Canfield.

The agent calmed himself and recalled the intelligence center.

"May."

"Mory, I apologize for jumping on you; I know you're doing the best that can be done. Has anyone checked the trackers this morning?"

"Not yet; we've been busy with the bugs and camera. Standby." Three minutes later, May returned. "We have two trackers almost on top of one another. They were in Orland, but now they are moving east on the city's south side."

"I'm going to send Shaw and Drew to apprehend them; they will contact you when they go mobile; I want you to guide them to the trackers; this is priority one."

"Yes, sir."

Vickers sat back, sipping his lukewarm coffee. The man let his mind roam over the known facts, and when he finished, he felt convinced Martin Philips and Eleanor Canfield had bolted. What bothered Vickers the most was the extent of the complete disappearance of the two; it smelled of professional help but from where?

The agent walked into the office next to his, "Myra, do you recall anything about Martin Philips or Eleanor Canfield?"

The forty-seven old veteran of twenty-two years of service with government intelligence agencies thought for a minute.

"I recall Philips being a mechanical and electronics engineer. And I believe the Canfield woman is his girlfriend and a nurse."

"Here is my copy of their file; I need a complete bio on them. Throw the file on my desk when you're finished with it, I'll be in the field, looking for them, and you can get me on my phone or the radio."

"Yes, Mr. Vickers." Myra Dickenson had a reputation for being quiet and conservative. But, unfortunately, her boss, Miles Vickers, rubbed her the wrong way. Vickers was driven by an evil streak and tinged with a lack of emotional control. Her late husband, Chad Dickenson, was the Chief of the Bureau when he passed away, and he wouldn't tolerate Vickers' character.

Special Agent Vickers returned to his desk; he knew he would have to report the scientist's disappearance to his superior, and it promised to get ugly. Taking a deep breath, he made the call, but to his surprise, the Chief had more pressing issues at hand with the threat of the Communists taking control of the country.

The Chief said, "This is your case; get control of it, chase your missing man down, then follow protocol."

The Chief had given Vickers a second chance, something that had become a sign of weakness and had fallen onto the trash heaps of history with the socialists in control. The agent knew he had more than a second chance to redeem himself. Instead, under Communist rule, he would end up on the trash heap of history as a lifeless body for failing.

The DSH agent headed for the Philips house, where he met with Todd Gable; and joined him in search of the residence. Two hours later, no valuable information turned up. Instead, Gable came across many documents, pamphlets, three Christian Bibles, and other religious material. Vickers told him to disregard them as evidence.

The lab proved to provide mounds of evidence of failed attempts to locate, create or develop a pioneering energy source which the socialist government could continue its attempt to conquer the world.

"Todd," Vickers said, "Could Philips have run because he had run out of ideas for the new energy initiative and was afraid of the consequence of failure?"

Gable looked around at all the failed attempts, "You may have hit on something there, Miles. These days, failure is almost a capital offense."

"That's what I've heard," Vickers said, his face a few shades greyer. "What's that at the edge of the lights?" he asked, pointing to the darkened area.

Both men searched for light switches, and when Gable found them, he turned on a series of overhead led lights which turned the area into daylight illuminance.

"This looks like an auto shop," Gable said aloud.

"Hey, Todd, look at this; I think it reels the ceiling back, but why?"

"Push the button; let's see what Philips built," Gable said.

Vickers pushed the green-covered button and immediately heard the start of electric motors and the whine of hydraulic pumps as latches released around the circular roof. The roof quietly retracted, and rays of sunlight filled the opening as the top continued rolling back. At the same time, a ramp rose from the floor to a mated attaching site at the edge of the portal.

The two men climbed a set of steps to the opening, then stepped onto the lawn. That's when they saw two sets of tire tracks in the short-cut grass leading to the driveway.

"Now, isn't this interesting?" Vickers mumbled.

Gable joined his boss on the lawn. "We saw many signs of intensive mechanical work and an automobile engine in the shop. There are also signs of manufacturing something, and several items I have provide no indication of what they're for or for what they could be used. We'll have to wait on our technicians to identify everything."

"Maybe he wasn't so innocent after all," the head agent said.

The on-site investigation continued, focusing on what Martin manufactured, if anything. Vickers talked briefly with the head forensic investigator and told the agent the investigation had just begun, and answers would be forthcoming.

Later, Vickers started an in-depth review of Philips and Canfield's personal and financial records at the office. Martin had managed his finances profitably and legally, drawing no scrutiny on himself. Although he was not a millionaire, he had accumulated sufficient funds to ensure a comfortable retirement under the older American capitalist economic system. But now, the government might confiscate that for redistribution before he would ever see a penny of it.

Elinore Canfield was, as Mrs. Dickenson stated, a nurse. She had accumulated modest savings but nothing on the scale of Philips. Nevertheless, her file revealed that her life held no secrets of wrongdoing, and she regularly paid her taxes with no issues. Elinore is Mrs. Clean.

'I'm missing something; these people are upright citizens, yet they destroyed government property in the bugs and cameras and may have deprived the government of a new energy source, then pulled a professional-level disappearing act. Nothing is making any sense. As an afterthought, it has to do with coming into possession or the creation of the energy thing. Again, why would they run from success?'

Vickers thought about possible answers to his questions.

'Would running save them from the government shutting them up by killing them for their success? Unlikely, the government would probably reward them as an encouragement to continue working.

Did some other governments offer them large amounts in return for their accomplishments and continued work? More likely, which implies they have succeeded.

Then there is the possibility that Philips and Canfield have acted like the infamous Rosenbergs of the 1950s by spying for a hostile country or group. One thing that is, without doubt, this is a mess.'

A light went on in Vickers' mind. In pre-intelligence training, an instructor said, "Nobody up and disappears; they change their outward appearance."

The agent prepared another attempt to locate the missing couple. He reviewed the available files on the two people, especially Philips. Nothing more emerged. The few items added to the files were past photos showing them in their younger years. The photos wound up as dismissed to a sub-file of material classified as unuseful.

Surveillance teams assigned to the Philips home watched twenty-four hours a day without sighting their prey. For the next two weeks, agents interviewed every doctor, nurse, and aide at the hospital where Elie worked. There appeared to be a discrepancy from the interviews; everyone knew Elie exhibited the highest nursing goal: helping the needy and injured or sick. She displayed compassion, and the Doctors often used her to give the worst news to family members. The interviewers found they would not find any dirty laundry on this potential suspect. Yet, Vickers still held that nobody up and disappeared without a good reason; there's a discrepancy somewhere.

Martin Philips' contacts consisted of other scientists with whom Philips communicated in his quest for the elusive power remedy. He had built a reputation of professionalism, was quiet-natured, a strong giver to needy causes, and most of all, developed the character of honesty and dependability.

When Vickers saw the reports, it added to his confusion. The parents of both suspects underwent interviews several times without gaining any information about the suspect's whereabouts. Trackers placed on their vehicles let the agents watch their movements, and when away from home a day earlier, two men at each residence bugged and set cameras in both their houses.

Daily, Vickers checked with the intelligence people, but the Philips and Canfields either told the truth or knew they were under surveillance because nothing additional was learned.

****

Norman and Lorraine Canfield found their first bug by accident. The device's antenna caught on a feather duster utilized by Lorrain as she dusted the upper vents in the living room. A hunt ensued, and they located listening bugs in every room of the house and the standard cameras in the kitchen, living room, and bedroom. In addition, Norman and Clarence communicated weekly with the burner phones and, in a cryptic burst, checked on any other information. Finally, Norman alerted his friend to their find. The two men agreed to meet after church with the Pastor.

Clarence and Darlene conducted their investigation, revealing a similar layout of surveillance devices. Neither couple disturbed the spy tools; instead, they altered their conversations and behavior to neutral, innocent people minding their lives. But they changed clothes in the bathrooms and gave the watchers little to report. They suspected their phones were bugged or tapped too.

During their meeting the following Sunday, Pastor Mickey said he checked his home and found no spy devices. He also said,

"If your homes had bugs, most certainly your vehicle has trackers and possible bugs, and check your clothing's liners and buttons; it's like looking for real bugs. Do you have a mechanic for your cars?"

"Yes, we both use an old friend."

"If you can trust him, make an appointment to change the oil and look for trackers."

"It's Mike Bragg, here in the church," Norman said.

"Good, I know Mike's a true believer, and he was in the intelligence corps when in the service, and he will know what and where to look for bugs and trackers. If you discover any, do not disturb them, do the same as you do at home, and we will deal with it soon."

Lorraine said, "I'm glad the Lord is with us; we would be easy pickings without His protection and yours."

"Thank you, Lorraine. Now we must return to our roles as dumb, simple people."

Pastor Mickey prayed with the foursome, asking for safety and comfort in Him. Then the meeting broke up, and the people walked out of the church, playing the role of unknowing members of the great mass of people.

As Vickers continued to run into dead ends and little if no information came in, his body and mind began feeling the pressures from his superiors. His mind ran through the events; *The socialist government had succeeded in removing the Constitution and Bill of Rights. Yet, government lawyers feared attempts to prosecute offenders and violating the two-hundred-sixty-five-year-old laws of restriction. Their rationale lay in the belief that such a move would invoke a massive uprising and an outbreak of civil war. As expected, far too many Americans retained weapons, despite calls by the socialists to confiscate all guns from the civilian population. But, on the other hand, I can do my job easier.*

Vickers thought with a smile; *'I don't have to abide by or worry about Miranda Warnings any longer, I won't have to kiss some judge's butt to get a search warrant, and now I can slap some doorknob in the head for being stupid, without repercussions.'*

The DHS agent drove to the Philips' residence, where a team searched for the missing couple. After talking with Special Agent Al Fredericks, Vickers walked among the searchers. Clarence Philips stood by, sipping his cup of coffee. He didn't offer any to the searchers or Vickers, showing his suspicious attitude for their intrusion.

Philips said, "If you tell me what you're looking for, maybe I can help."

"Where are Martin and Elinore?"

"Now, I can't help you with that because I truly don't know."

"Then you saw them before they disappeared?" he asked

"Yes, my wife and I talked to them as always; when we parted, I thought they would return home. Later, I tried calling him but received no answer."

"Is that his phone on the table?" he asked, pointing.

"Yes, it is."

"May I look at it?"

"Certainly, we have nothing to hide," Clarence said.

Vickers picked up the phone, checked the calls made section, and found Clarence's number, which showed no answer. Vickers showed the phone screen. The older man looked at the list of calls, and the corners of his lips lifted.

The agent asked, "Why are all the computers void of data, even normal data."

"I have no idea; I would think there should be many base and work files on those machines." Clarence pulled open a couple of drawers, "I can't explain the lack of files; I see some paperwork from a project they had been working on, but it's not much. I don't work here, and I have no idea what happened to it.

The DSH agent called for a computer expert, and after he arrived, he reported that someone had wiped the computers. "If we're going to stand a chance of getting any information, we'll need to take the hard drives in for examination."

Vickers turned to the elder Philips, who was not wanting to appear uncooperative and agreed. Clarence Philips knew Martin would ensure the drives contained no data or information.

"Mr. Vickers, I want to help all I can; I'm worried about Martin and Elie; they wouldn't just run off."

"Do you think someone abducted Martin and Elie?"

"I have no idea, but this is highly unusual and troubling."

Vickers's suspicious side believed the old man was up to his ears in it. *'I don't think the old man knows we've bugged his home, car, and clothes, but I have to admit, he's playing a good role.'*

"I'll add the possibility of abduction to the search parameters; that may help locate them. I'll try to keep you updated as much as I can, and if you hear anything, please call me," and handed Clarence a card.

Vickers gave the older Philips a receipt for the hard drives and a laptop and thanked him for his cooperation. After the government men left, Clarence ensured the lab and house were closed and secured, then set the alarm.

On the way home, Clarence decided to visit Mike Bragg, his auto mechanic friend. "I thought I heard a thump, any chance of taking a look at the chassis?

"Sure, the bay is open."

The mechanic pulled the car onto the lift and raised it into the air. Then, Clarence added, "You may as well give it a grease job, too, if you have time."

Clarence looked at the underside of the car. Philips was fastidious about his car's mechanical condition. While the mechanic went about his work, Clarence checked the frame and then looked above the fuel tank with a light. An oblong black container with an antenna at one end marked the tracker.

Clarence said he would return from the restroom in a minute. Once there, he called Norman Canfield and told him of his find. "I would have no doubt your car has a tracker as well."

"We'll act accordingly," then the line went dead.

SCOTTS VALLEY, CALIFORNIA

CHAPTER SEVEN

Still holding the slip of paper, Pastor Mickey gave her, Ali thought through the conversation with the Pastor, with his last words burning into her mind. 'It is a command from God and must be followed to the letter.' That ended any resistance she had toward the trip.

Mac looked through the latest edition of a Road Atlas, checking the existing routes. Of course, the quickest would be the interstate highways, but the police patrolled the roads, and occasionally, the DHS patrolled the streets to hunt the wanted. Then there was the weather. August is traditionally warm to hot, and it continued this year. Mac decided to take the major highway out of the metro area to the west. And by monitoring the state police and DHS frequencies, they could generally steer clear of authorities. Their greatest advantage came from keeping the Hummer from the knowledge of the DHS.

Ali had prepared sandwiches and snacks, allowing the Cadins to travel near the Illinois-Iowa state lines. After a brief rest stop, Ali and Mac crossed into Iowa and found a quiet motel to rest for a few hours. Mac made reservations at the motel chain's Council Bluffs motel. He planned to make a transition to night driving soon. The newlyweds spent an intensely quiet first night together.

The alarm clock rousted the two from a sound sleep, and they showered, then turned the Hummer westward toward Des Moines and then Council Bluffs. West of Iowa City, the newlyweds stopped at the Amana Colonies exit for lunch in one of the iconic Amana Colonies family-style restaurants. Mac had learned about the superb food and products manufactured by the Colonists. Heading the list of foods, he heard of the delicious American and German hearty and light portions, including chicken, hand-cut steaks, roast beef, sauerbraten, wiener Schnitzel cutlets, Amana brats, ham, catfish, shrimp, sandwiches, salads, chocolate, and coconut cream pies.

The Amana history of top-line affordable furniture and appliances was known worldwide. He often wanted to visit the Colonies, although now it wasn't the same world. However, they did enjoy the fine food always served in the restaurants at the highway exit.

Back on the road, Ali was intrigued by the carefully planted and maintained rows of corn and soybeans. The crops approached the last quarter of growth, and the corn stalks were eight feet in height; Ali and Mac had heard earlier that the farmers were looking at a bin-busting harvest. And with over four-thousand products and by-products coming from corn, it was matched by the oil-rich soybean crop to keep the farmers going through another brutal winter.

The sun was heading headlong toward the western horizon when they reached their motel in Council Bluffs on the banks of the famed Missouri River.

Two days later, they were driving south on California Highway 17 when they saw a sign announcing Scotts Valley ahead. As they were instructed to, Ali called the Johnsons a second time, the first when they started. Pastor Dick Johnson had previously received a call from his long-time friend Pastor Mickey Carvour, who filled him in on the unusual situation and how the Higher Authority directed him to send the newlyweds to Pastor Dick's for a week. Both men knew it was a command they would not fail. Dick guided the big military vehicle to his home beneath the thick covering of trees, which acted as a primary camouflage for the Humvee.

Pastor Johnson and his wonderful wife, Linda, met the couple as they emerged from the Beast. Linda, devoted as much to God as Dick, immediately took to Ali. Linda had iced tea and light pastries in the cool home's dining area.

Linda and Dick spent some time answering questions and asking a few of Ali and Mac. Dick inquired, "You say the two of you manufactured a new engine type in just a few days?"

"Yes, we were in disbelief ourselves. It takes years of design, redesign, and testing. This thing took off without serious problems, but that doesn't mean more redesign and testing isn't in the works."

"What did you do with it when you fled Chicago?" Linda asked.

"Come, we'll show you."

The four strolled out to the Humvee nested under a thick tree. Linda asked, "Where could you stow an engine in this vehicle?"

"Under the hood," Mac said nonchalantly. Then he released the latch and lifted the heavy hood to reveal the unbelievably simple designed engine. He took time to point out each major part and described its function.

"You drove out here from Iowa with that?" Dick asked in wonder.

"Yes, and without a single issue. Listen to this." Mac crawled behind the wheel and started the engine, which settled down in an almost silent idle.

"That's it?"

"Yes," Ali put in, "it runs like a dream."

"Did it provide enough power to get over the mountains without any strain?" Dick asked.

Standing next to his new friend, Mac said, "I suspect it has the power to pull a loaded semi-truck uphill with no effort. Of course, I have no idea of the engine's full capabilities, but from what I have seen, it could run the wheels off the Hummer."

"Wow, no wonder the government wants it as bad as they do. Have you heard the news today?"

"No, we monitored police and military movements all the way here to stay clear of them; why?"

"There have been terrifying developments handed down from Washington, and they aren't good," Dick warned. "The socialist regime has asked the new congress to pave the way for the Communists to take over the country."

"NO!" cried Ali. "The Communists have the bloodiest history of any totalitarian government in all of mankind. Without a degree of thought or regret, they will kill anyone to serve the state. The people have forgotten what they did in Poland, Hungary, the Baltic, and other eastern European states during the Cold War years. They have forgotten the millions murdered in southeast Asia and China at the hands of the Communists and the insane attacks on Ukraine."

Mac added, "What do they think will happen here if the Communists are given power?"

"Let's go back inside; you need to understand a few things, then it will become clearer," Dick said.

The four sat in the modest home's living room with iced tea to cool their throats nearby. They traded stories about the metro area, which Dick and Linda were familiar with when they lived in Rockford, Illinois.

Throughout the conversation, the hosts noticed the downcast air about Ali. "Ali dear," Linda got her attention, "Are you all right?

"Not really; I'm concerned for our parents; if the socialists turn, it will become an extremely hazardous environment for those of religious life and belief. Communist's history proves that out."

"Ali, that was one issue we discussed with Pastor Mickey. He has a congregation of such worries. All those who believe in God face the same threat Jesus said we would, and we accepted that probability. We all face the first death. The end of our days is nothing more than the transition moment to the presence of Jesus. As for fear of death, it is nothing. Tell me, what do you remember when the Pacific railroad tracks joined those leading to the eastern half of America in the 1850s?"

Ali's face frowned, "Nothing, I wasn't even born."

Dick continued, "That's right, you had no direct knowledge of that until learning about it in history after birth. Not one soul remembers the times before birth up to about three or four years old. As for death, it is written; *1 Thessalonians 4: 16-17; (16) For the Lord Himself shall descend from heaven with a shout, with the voice of the archangel, and with the trump of God: and the dead in Christ shall rise first:*

(17) Then we which are alive and remain shall be caught up together with them in the clouds, to meet the Lord in the air: and so shall we ever be with the Lord. (KJV)

"I remember that from Pastor Mickey's Bible Studies. Right now, though, I fear for our parents; I don't want them to suffer beatings or torture because of their beliefs; they are senior citizens and are becoming frail as they age. The same with Martins', I mean Mac's parents."

"Mickey is working on a plan to move the congregation somewhere safe. That's all we know. We still have more to do here.

God tried many ways to get man's attention and commitment to what is right. From Adam to the Great Flood, with nobody but Noah and his family surviving. Again, man failed to follow God's laws. And He dealt with them in Babylon. Then the Lord had to rebuke and punish evil-doers by destroying Sodom and Gomorrah.

Finally, after many generations of men committing sin, God had the Holy Spirit place Jesus in the womb of a Godly woman, Mary. Then, as an adult, Jesus traveled on His journey to save man during the last three years of His life. Jesus' efforts proved successful, and He declared in His last words, "It is done."

"However, Satan is most persistent and will not relent until Jesus puts him in the Lake of Fire. When He does, maybe the devil, who sinned with five 'I wills,' will be told, 'I AM, TRUMPS FIVE I WILLs. So, what do we do?" Asked the Pastor.

"Follow Jesus' lead and instructions?"

"Yes, and two of the important instructions are found in II Chronicles 7:14-15. The key verse is 15," 'and My people who are called by My name humble themselves and pray, and seek My face and turn from their wicked ways, then will I hear from heaven, will forgive their sin, and will heal their land.'

V15, 'Now My eyes shall be open and My ears attentive to the prayer offered in this place.'

We must pray daily and keep the faith until He comes for us, no matter what the situation until He comes for us."

"Pastor Dick, why are you sweating like a football player?" Ali asked.

The Godly Pastor removed his glasses and wiped the sweat from his brow and head, "When I get into communicating with Jesus, and He uses me, I sweat." Dick said with a smile.

"Ali, dinner time is coming; will you help me in the kitchen?" Linda asked.

Although they had just met, Linda and Ali had already become good friends.

Mac changed the direction of the conversation with, "Pastor Dick, what are the local churches like here?"

"Across the board," the Pastor said, "We have churches that claim to have Christian values the same as throughout the world. But unfortunately, the sad truth is that many churches fail that claim, such as five of the seven churches in Revelation chapters two and three.

To the church in Ephesus, Jesus said, "Nevertheless, I have somewhat against thee because thou hast left thy first love." The church had lost touch with God.

To the church at Pergamos, "But I have a few things against thee because thou hast there them that hold the doctrine of Balaam, who taught Balac to cast a stumbling block before the children of Israel, to eat things sacrificed unto idols, and to commit fornication. So hast thou also them that hold the doctrine of the Nicolaitans, which thing I hate."

For the church at Thyatira, "Notwithstanding I have a few things against thee because thou sufferest that woman Jezebel, which call herself a prophetess, to teach and seduce my servants to commit fornication, and to eat things sacrificed to idols. And I gave her space to repent of her fornication, and she repented not."

The message to the church in Sardis is, "Be watchful, and strengthen the things which remain, that are ready to die; for I have not found thy works perfect before God."

Message to Laodicea, "I know thy works, that thou art neither cold nor hot; I would thou wert cold or hot. So then, because thou art lukewarm and neither cold or hot, I will spue thee out of my mouth."

"What about the remaining two?" Ali asked.

"Neither Smyrna nor Philadelphia had a complaint against them," Pastor Dick stated, "God knew mankind would have issues since He gave them the right to choose, and Satan was the tempter. That's why Jesus came to our rescue."

"It all fits together, doesn't it?" asked Mac.

"Yes, despite the efforts of those who speak against God the Father, the Son, and the Holy Spirit."

"What a great sermon that would make, Pastor Dick," Ali said.

"I think Linda wants to show you to your room; I suspect you're tired from all that driving. Linda and I will be here if you wish to join us, but us old folks turn in by ten anymore."

"We'll get set in and would like to join you in prayer before we retire."

"Linda and I would like nothing better."

****

Pastor Dick and Linda had grown fond of the young newlyweds. Nine days after their arrival, their training in the intricacies of Biblical instruction ended, and the couple prepared for their dash to the home of Ali's paternal grandmother, located in rural Maine, along a waterway leading to the Atlantic Ocean.

According to Ali's parents, Myron Canfield constructed the tough fir house in 1906. Norman added, "The family had refurbished the house, replacing deteriorated wood and the roof in the late 1990s. One family member suggested selling the structure, but a large margin outvoted him."

Norman had given Ali the keys before the couple left for California. "If some unforeseen events befall you, head for this house. Here is a map; the home sits on a secluded property, surrounded and shaded by tall conifers. During World War II, the family painted the house in camouflage, and you have to walk or drive up to it before your aware it there. Best camouflage paint job ever done. Fortunately, the family voted on keeping it that way, so you may have to look for it. If you have gone to ground, into hiding, do not contact us, we'll be fine, and when it's clear, we'll call on a burner. We have to remain flexible and, for now, inconspicuous."

After praying with the Johnsons, Ali and Mac pulled the cover from the repacked Humvee and headed south on Highway 1 Cabrillo Coast Highway. Mac asked Ali to find a lesser-traveled road south to Interstate 8 in San Diego. Mac wanted to cross the country along the southern border, then catch Interstate 95 in northern Florida.

"Mac, I found Highway 1; it should be about right, except it goes through some dense population centers; I'll route us to stay out of metro areas and use more rural Interstates. The road system is extensive, and there are many good roads to get to Maine's Highway 1."

"That sounds like a good plan, you be the navigator and radio operator, and I can drive. One thing we want to do is plan a series of stopovers for rest and food. Once we hit the first one, they usually have a network at reasonable distances. When we stop for lunch, let's come up with some ideas for the security of this vehicle,"

"Yeah, I'm not in the mood for hiking," Ali quipped.

****

The hours slid by as needed; their bodies let them know when to stop. "This is a fairly good riding vehicle, and the mileage is great," Mac said, breaking a few miles of silence.

"I was just thinking of the engine not needing fuel. So I started messing around with applying this engine concept as a power plant for a boat. It would work like a dream. It's so silent; I bet it would make the ideal engine for a submarine, or upsize it, and possibly even a larger ship. Also, I bet it would make a good prop plane if the engine structure were designed and made of Magnesium or Titanium." Ali postulated.

"You're getting into this engineering stuff, aren't up?"

"Yes, and I don't understand it; I have never thought of being an engineer, but for some reason, I'm fascinated with it, and I can't seem to read or study enough on the subject. What's bothering me is concepts and solutions seem to pop from my mind, as if I had studied engineering all my life."

"Ali, let me throw out a question for thought," Mac asked.

"Have at it; I'm open to anything which might clear this up."

"You know, Ali," Mac began, "God works in mysterious ways and gives us gifts when we need them,"

"Are you saying the Lord is guiding us for His purposes and providing us with the necessary tools?" Ali asked.

"Look at the facts; I needed an assistant in getting this buggy ready for our flight. Where did you learn to solder like a pro? Or read a complex electronic blueprint that takes a trained electronics expert to understand? Or talk with me about mechanical engineering issues on my level?"

Ali's hand went to her mouth as she began comprehending what Mac said. "Oh my, it has to be a logical explanation. Oh, thank you, Lord, for those gifts, and may I use them for your glory," she uttered a light prayer. Then the woman sat in silence, wondering what gift she didn't have, but will need.

Mac drove the posted speed limit, and their trip proceeded without incident. Wisely, Ali scheduled their passage around population centers and skirted major cities, such as Los Angeles and San Diego. Four days later, the dirty Humvee drove into the State of Maine.

****

Clarence and Norman stood outside Mike Braggs Auto Shop with their wives alongside them, all four highly infuriated over the government's intrusion.

Norman whispered into Clarence's ear, "Let's go shopping; we'll get different traveling clothes, including socks and shoes, and change in the store fitting or restrooms after we pay with cash; then we can talk."

Norman repeated his whisper to Lorraine while Clarence did the same with Darlene. Then, Norman and his wife jumped into the Canfield vehicle while Clarence talked with Bragg.

A short distance from the auto shop stood a discount store. Norman wrote out a note in bold letters, 'NO TALKING,' and displayed it to each person.

At the discount store, maintaining their silence, the four friends purchased what they needed and, after paying, switched clothes, including shoes. The old attire was placed in large shopping bags and dropped into a recycling bin near the store.

Once well out of hearing distance, the tension dropped. Finally, Norman said, "The government has tagged us, and they will probably use us to gain control of our children. I'm not letting that happen."

Clarence said, "What's the plan?"

STATE OF MAINE

CHAPTER EIGHT

Norman continued, "I have been watching the news, and the socialists are moving closer to grabbing control of the monetary system. The part that bothers me is that the government has warned those travelers to begin heading for their home states. Next year, those who wish to travel across state lines must have written permission from the Office of the Czar of the Department of Transportation.

When these restrictions become effective, our homes, savings, and money are gone forever. So our first move is to get rid of the vehicle tracking devices, close our bank accounts, withdraw what cash we can, then CDs, close any IRAs or 401s, and take the paperwork with us. After that, we will have to liquefy each separately and at different locations while we drive to Maine."

Darlene began letting her emotions escape control, "Clarence, what are we going to do? Are we going to lose our home and everything?" A sob slipped from her quivering lips.

"Darlene dear, everything is going to be fine; we're going to have a lifestyle change; there is no escaping that. And we are going to have to play it loose to stay free, but remember what God has said three-hundred-sixty-five times in the Bible; "Fear, not, for I am with thee," or "Do not let your heart be troubled," and others meaning the same thing. So those of us who are called by His name put our trust in God, and He will care for us. That is His promise."

"Oh, Clarence, thank you, I couldn't do this if it weren't for you," she said, holding her husband's arm as tight as she could.

"We'll be fine, dear."

"Norman," Clarence turned to his friend, "What's this about Maine?"

"Remember I gave the keys to a house to Elie?"

"Okay, yes."

"That's where we're headed; Pastor Mickey and I prayed, and God wants us there. I don't know why, but there it is."

"That's good enough for me," Clarence agreed. Then the two women agreed.

"Are we going in one car?" Darlene asked.

"It would be best if we did, and we should sell both our vehicles and buy a used SUV; it will be better for traveling, and they are the most numerous vehicles on the road; it will make it easier to become just another SUV," Norman said.

Lorraine asked, "What about our friends at church; what's to become of them?"

Norman and Clarence looked at one another, then Clarence said, "We will see them again when I cannot say it's still in the works. Pastor Mickey has told us we are the vanguard for our church because the government has plans to end all religions in this country. That means the government will seize all church buildings, and it is unknown what may happen to the congregation or what will become of the church leadership, Pastor, and their families."

"This is insane," cried Darlene.

"It gets worse if the Communists do take over; they have a history of coming in with guns blazing."

"Why is God allowing this to happen?" Darlene persisted.

Clarence was ready for this question. "God has allowed people to have a choice and has bent over backward to ensure everyone knows right from wrong. He is sorting the wheat from the chaff. So what did God do with the refugees from Egypt when Moses led them out of Pharaoh's grasp, and they turned to the golden calf?"

"He let them wander in the desert for forty years," she said.

"Yes, and in doing so, He punished them for their sin. So then, when Eve gave Adam the fruit of the forbidden tree to eat, what happened?"

"God banned Adam and Eve from the Garden and caused women to have harsh childbirth."

"And what happened when Israel turned away from God on occasions?

"God allowed Hebrew enemies to disband Israel and disperse the people throughout the world, causing hardship and millions of deaths."

"Could you call that punishment?" Clarence pressed.

"Definitely," Darlene said.

"Hasn't the majority of the American people sinned and turned their backs on God? Then didn't the people vote in known socialists who made no bones about wanting to get rid of the Constitutional government for a disastrous social regime that hates Christianity?" her husband asked.

"There is no doubt about that."

Then Clarence said, "The Founding Fathers built this country based on the Judeo-Christian faith; even John Adams said, "Our Constitution was made only for a moral and religious People. It is wholly inadequate to the government of any other." And how faithful to God does today's population appear ?"

"The number of Christians is dwindling as we speak; the population wants to be secular or semi-religious as needed. But, of course, it all follows the Bible, doesn't it?" Darlene agreed.

"Yes, it does, and as followers of Christ, we do what he says."

"After considering the varied scenarios for our move, I believe the following actions are relevant. First, we cannot trust that the vehicles are free of surveillance; therefore, there is no talk about what we plan or do while in the cars. If we are separated and need communications, pull into a parking spot and use the burner away from the vehicle. The calling person dials the other's phone, then ends the call. The receiving caller parks and then calls the other person away from their car.

If need be, we'll go in different directions; we should arrange a meeting place before we depart. Be mindful of any followers."

"What do we do if we pick up a tail?" Lorraine asked.

"Try to lose them in traffic. They will usually remain two or more cars behind you. Try squeezing a turning light. What I mean is, if your approaching an intersection and the yellow light comes on, speed up a little and go through. A tail will have to stop behind others at the red light. Then you turn right for a few blocks before returning to your destination.

"Second, we cannot return to the houses; all is lost. From here, we go to our banking institutions and withdraw what we can and other securities. Then, we'll meet at the auto garage to remove the trackers. From there, we'll visit my friend, who will trade us a good SUV for our sedans which he will have ready for the trip. We will give him the trackers, and he will send them to California on a transport full of traded cars. If anyone has a better plan, I'm all for it," Clarence finally ended the conversation.

Norman said, "Let's make the banking withdrawal and meet at Bragg's Auto Repair."

Two hours later, Mike Bragg wrapped the two tracking devices in heavy aluminum foil and placed them in a car marked for a San Diego destination.

"When the driver arrives in Diego, he will attach the trackers to a couple of police cars."

Norman Canfield said, laughing, "That's the best disposition I've heard. But we had better head to Tommy's; it's getting late."

After a twenty-minute drive, the two sedans pulled into Tommy's Auto Sales. Norman and Clarence signed the titles, and the four friends thanked Tommy Morton, another church member, for the trade. Then Tommy said, "Marge and I will see you at the end destination."

Another round of goodbyes, and Clarence took the initial driver's turn. Then, he headed for the east entrance to Interstate 80.

Norman guided Clarence through the interstate maze around Chicago and onto Interstate 80 East. Their chances for a successful getaway increased with the different vehicle types; any lookouts would be watching for the old sedans. The group intended to remain on Interstate 80 until reaching the far western region of New York City, then turn north to Interstate 90 and eventually Interstate 95 north until they could get on U.S. Highway 1. That would take them to their destination in northeastern Maine. Driving and acting as tourists took four days, including stops for food and lodging.

****

Ali and Mac pulled off U.S. 1 and headed on the local roads not far from Jonesport, Maine. As they negotiated the gravel road, Mac noticed a silver-blue SUV half a block ahead, driving as if they were looking for a particular house.

Mac alerted his wife, "Ali, that silver SUV in front of us is turning into our lane. The lane is almost a quarter of a mile to the house and dips into a small valley almost to sea level; keep an eye open for unwanted visitors."

As the Hummer slowed to a stop around a bend in the road, they could see a house painstakingly painted in camouflage colors which nearly caused the house to appear as foliage. Nearby, another camouflaged structure sat closer to the bay's water level. It almost reached the measurements of a barn, except for having one level. Mac and Ali watched as four people stepped wearily from the SUV.

"Oh, my God, it's Mom and Dad," Ali squealed.

"There are my folks," Mac added.

Mac slammed the Hummer into gear and quickly drove to the SUV, startling the four older people.

Darlene immediately recognized Mac, "MARTIN," she cried and ran to her son, closely followed by Clarence.

That display triggered Lorraine and Norman as they saw Elie bounding toward them, her arms reaching out for her loved ones. The six family members held onto one another in almost steel-like grips, fearing another separation and everyone trying to speak at once.

Ten minutes late, with the six regaining their composure, Norman said, "Let's go inside; I need some coffee; the water should be on, and maybe there's ice in the refrigerator."

As the families walked to the front door, an animal scurried through the leaves and debris on the forest floor, causing Darlene and Lorraine to jump.

"It's only a rabbit, Mom," Elie said.

"Are you going by Ali or Elie now?" Lorraine asked.

"It depends on to whom I'm talking."

"What about you, Martin; is it Martin or Mac?" Elie's mother inquired.

"As with Elie, it depends upon who is asking. We have the identification for Ali and Mac if it's any government official. But, for family and friends who know us, it's Elie and Martin.

Darlene said, "I prefer the name I gave my son."

"I agree," Lorraine said, "We named our daughter Elie for Alinore."

Norman used his key to the front door, and upon opening, the clean, cool air testified to available power and working air conditioning.

Martin and his parents took in the magnificent workmanship in finishing the house's interior. A relaxing rustic-style interior greeted the families. In the basement, the utilities were up-to-date and functioning perfectly.

Elie immediately fell in love with the home. "This is gorgeous; who would want to live in a city when they had a house like this?"

Norman said to the family, "The house and property are paid for and are in my great-grandmother's maiden name.

"Oh, Daddy, please don't let anything happen to this house; it is one of a kind and the most beautiful and elegant home I've ever seen or even dreamed of."

"Well, my dear, your grandfather is the controller in this case. So, you will have to talk to him, "Norman teased. "In the meantime, would you ladies check the cupboards and refrigerator? We will need food for the six of us for the unknown future. Clarence asked."

"Clarence, I suggest we reassess that projection. I suggest that while the ladies take care of the immediate needs, we must find and line up food and supplies for about three hundred souls."

"What are you talking about, Daddy?"

"While you and Martin trained in California, Pastor Mickey, Clarence, and I met with the church board. Every member of our church is in the same predicament as we are. The board has done the same with the church savings; they also sold the building with a zero mortgage. As a result, the money needed for the supplies is available."

"And Elie, to put your fears to rest, as noted earlier, the house is in my great-grandmother's maiden name; therefore, our name is nowhere in the paperwork. A Christian lawyer worked to give us the survivor's benefits from my great-grandmother, my grandmother, thru my mother and father. Unfortunately, they have passed, and now it's in my legal name, Lorrain Mae Canfield."

"Elie's eyes widened, "That is amazing, Daddy, and you have one smart lawyer on your side."

"I have arranged to have an escrow-type account that automatically meet all bills. And an interest-bearing account paid into the escrow."

"You have planned this for some time, haven't you?"

"Yes, when the house and property came to me, I prayed about handling the transfer and end use for the Lord's glory. He answered my prayers in a dream, and here we are. This confirms that we are to relocate our church, and the people will arrive day by day. To that end, beginning in a couple of days, a structure of two stories will be constructed under the trees on the south side of the workshop. It will contain living quarters, baths, a dining hall, laundry, and a playground. The dining hall will be second for our church services.

The men will provide the workforce we will need for the next phase. I have not received any information on that; `I'm sure it will come as needed."

The women prepared dinner with the shopping completed and stored, and the two families sat together for the first time in several weeks. Their first order brought them into the presence of God, humbling themselves before the all-mighty High, blessing Him, and giving the Lord His due honor. Next, they thanked God for their freedom and present home. Then ask Him for forgiveness for sins they committed, especially those committed unknowingly. Finally, Norman prayed for the Lord to lead them or point them the way they should go, to follow His will. The family closed their prayers with praises and humility, followed by "Amen."

Then the family, who always knew the Lord acted on prayers in His time and expected the answers to their request to come as needed, were startled as the Lord gave his answer immediately.

First, a mist formed near the table, and in the fog, a bright ball of light; as it dissipated, they could see a figure standing before them cloaked in a white robe.

The families seemed frozen in time, hardly breathing, their eyes wide in astonishment and a touch of fear.

An unbelievingly soft, soothing voice came from the figure, "Do not fear me; I come from He to whom you pray. You asked for guidance and strength to follow the Lord, and He has granted your request. I am His emissary and will show you His will."

With a shaky voice filled with awe and emotion, Clarence asked, "What should we call you? What is your name?"

"The Lord has called me Timothy, so please, call me Timothy."

"Are…are you an angel? Asked Elie in a timid voice as she stared at the figure.

"So, we are referred to as such; we are servants of the Highest and do his bidding."

Lorraine gasped for breath and clutched at her chest, a possible sign of a heart attack. Then, as she fell against Norman, he cried, "Help."

Before the mesmerized people at the table could move, Timothy was beside the stricken woman, whose features were becoming pale and gray. Timothy placed one hand on Lorraine's shoulder and said, everyone, pray with me."

Everyone clasped the hand of the person on each side of them, and Darlene, sitting next to her friend, placed her left hand on Lorrain's limp, cold arm. Norman held his beloved wife in his right arm, and his left-hand clasped Elie's. The circle had been completed, and the white-robed angel lifted his free hand and prayed for the life of God's child.

A soft, loving voice drifted through the room, "Your prayers have found approval of the Highest."

Lorraine breathed air, her skin returned to its normal color, and she warmed to the touch. The families felt exhausted and drenched in sweat as tears of joy rolled down their cheeks.

Timothy gave thanks to the Highest for His mercy on behalf of the family. Afterward, the angel moved slowly among the people and instructed them on the desires of the Highest.

"Evening is here, take this time to sit quietly and know that God is with you, and He is here. Offer your prayers, and He will let his desires known to you. Then rest, for tomorrow, we begin to prepare for your move to a safer environment until the Lord offers His hand.

You have done well in this time of increasing danger, but remember, as a people called by His name, this is the way. So keep your eyes on Jesus, and you shall not lose your way. I will return in the morning, and we shall begin."

Without another word, the mist reformed, and Timothy disappeared with it.

The two family members surrounded Lorraine and questioned her about her experience, what it was like, and if she saw God.

"I don't remember anything," the confused woman said.

Norman took control, "Okay, everyone, let Mother get her breath back, and we'll explain everything a little later. Here, have a sip of water and relax; everything is fine," he assured his wife.

Two family members cleaned the dinner table and reset it for the next morning, while two removed trash and emptied the waste cans, and one couple washed and put away the dishes. Their efforts were spirited by recent encounters with their living God and his emissary, Timothy, a constant reminder of the power of the almighty.

The families reassembled in the living room, where they had a short discussion to attempt to answer what questions arose from the arrival of the surprise visitor, reading passages from the Bible that described angels.

Clarence took the helm and led the families into the intense prayers needed to help everyone resolve the heavenly event they witnessed, slowly making Lorraine understand what frightened her. Then, finally, she felt reassured that all was well.

When finished, the families felt relieved, and smiles blossomed abundantly at the prospect of the return of Timothy. However, the greatest gifts in the lives of the Philips and Canfields had to be described as those Jesus bestowed upon them; the immediate answers to prayer, the return of the Canfields wife and mother; and above all, the greatest of gifts, eternal life with the love and trust of Jesus, the Son of the everlasting God.

CHRIST BREAKS ALL BONDAGE

CHAPTER NINE

Blood-red rage coursed through Miles Vickers's veins at the notification that his surveillance teams had lost the trail of Philips and the Canfield woman. "Why are we paying these junior wanna-be agents? I've seen first-month recruits do better," the vengeful federal agent growled and cursed.

Vickers plopped into his chair and went through Philips's dossier for the fourth time. He wasn't sure what he wanted but would know when he saw it. The agent flipped through the first three sheets of data and stopped. He backed up one page, glancing a second time at the social and background attributes of Martin Philips.

There it was, under religious affiliation: 'Devout Christian.' The angry man sat trying to think of historical events of the Christian followers.

'In the 1860s, Christians ran underground railroads, shuttling runaway black slaves to the northern states. I wonder, is this possible today?' He thought.

Vickers opened his file on Clarence and Darlene Philips to page three, devout Christian.

Then the irate agent opened the Canfield file; devout Christian.

Further examination of their records showed they all attended the same church, raising Vickers's suspicions even more. *'Who is running that church?'* He wondered. With more questions than answers at each corner, Vickers asked his secretary to find out the name and address of the Pastor of Philips' church.

The agent's next move brought an analyst into the investigation with the responsibility of detailing the church, Pastor, and congregation, along with their histories, employment, and contacts. Vickers sat back, letting the facts of the case bounce around his brain. Then, everything began to circle that church, which had become the centerpiece of the expanding investigation and disappearances.

Vickers called the analyst, now assigned to a vacant office, to allow her to concentrate. "Jo, bring in another analyst and have her put together the histories of all the suspects and include the church pastor. That will take some of the burdens off you. Next, you better add a property search where they may hide."

"Yes, sir." The woman answered.

Agent Vickers turned to the financial report of Philips, and his eyebrows arched in surprise at the amount of money the scientist had in savings and investments. Then he noticed the date on the report; Fredericks made the report at the beginning of the investigation. He called Fredericks. "Al, this is Vickers; contact Philip's financial institution for an update on his funds." Then Vickers hung up before Fredericks could answer.

Ten minutes later, Fredericks returned his boss's call, "There is no money in the accounts; he took it all and closed all his business with the bank."

"How much did he have?"

"Over ten million, and several CDs. I did a trace, and he put the funds in an offshore account which we can't seize."

"Somehow, that doesn't surprise me. Check Philips parent's finances and those of the Canfields, including their daughter, Elinore."

"Will do."

'Well, it appears we have some absconders; the questions are now how many, where did they go, and what is their final destination?' Vickers thought to himself.

The agent called his sometimes partner, Todd Gable, "I have a lead; meet me at the car, and I'll fill you in."

"Okay."

As Vickers followed the traffic flow, he headed for the church building. During the drive, Vickers filled Gable in on the information and efforts involved in the case.

Agent Gable summoned it up, "It certainly looks as if both families may have or are on the run, and as you questioned, to where?"

Vickers found the door to the church unlocked and, when they entered, saw a man mopping the tile floor. Gable approached the sweating man, "Excuse me, sir, may we have a word with you?"

As the man turned around, he asked, "May I help you?

"Yes, we're looking for the Pastor."

"I'm Pastor Mickey; how may I help you?"

Gable looked surprised, "I thought you were the janitor."

"I'm many things, and one is a part-time janitor." Having served in the FBI for over 30 years, Mickey easily recognized the men as federal agents.

Vickers flashed his identification cards and badge, "You are the man we came to see; may we have a minute of your time?"

"Certainly, join me for a cup of tea or coffee?"

The six-foot Pastor led the two agents to his office and withdrew three bottles of tea from a mini refrigerator; then, he sat behind his desk. The two visitors sat in the soft visitors' chairs facing the man of God.

"Pastor, we're investigating the disappearance of Martin Philips and Elinore Canfield and were wondering if you have heard from them."

The Pastor looked as if he were thinking for a moment, "Yes, Martin and Elinore and their folks attended our service this past Sunday. They are wonderful members of our congregation; do you know them?"

"No, I'm afraid we don't, but we need to talk with them if you can help?"

"I have no idea where they may be at this moment, but if you can give me your number, I will ask them to call you; if I see or hear from them," Pastor Mickey offered.

"How about Norman and Lorraine Canfield and Clarence and Darlene Philips?"

"I talked with them on Sunday, but not since then. They are all retired; I suspect you may find them at home. I have their addresses if you need them."

"We have their addresses, but they were not home when two of our agents stopped by to find out if they heard any news from the young couple."

"I have no idea of their location at this moment, but I will try to contact them during the day and give them your number if you wish."

"We would appreciate that," Gable said. "Here is my card; you can call the office number during the day, and I'll add my cell number. If you hear from any of the Philips or Canfields, will you let me know?"

"I'll place your card right here, where it won't be misplaced," the Pastor said, smiling.

"How long have you been a Pastor?" Vickers asked.

Knowing the agent had probably completed a background check on him, Pastor Mickey suspected he was aware of his service time in the FBI.

"I've been a Pastor for about 30 years," the eighty-year-old Pastor said.

Back in their car, Gable asked, "Well?"

"He's lying through his teeth, but he did a good job covering it up. I saw the initials MP and EC on his calendar for Sunday afternoon. By the way, he never mentioned his career as an FBI agent." Vickers growled.

"I would have never guessed."

" I would be willing to bet he is the source of expertise in the getaway by the Philips and Canfields."

"When did you find that out?" Gable asked.

"When I saw his records, he would have the same information as our agents."

"Even after all this time?" Gable asked.

"It hasn't changed that much, mostly in the technical end, not hiding the devices."

****

Night settled across the eastern seaboard of the country, and the majority of the people had followed other parts of the nation in using as little electricity as necessary due to the extra excise tax increase to the cubic foot of gas consumed, and twice that amount in taxes on the heating oil most northeasterners used. The socialists claimed the tax was necessary to combat the climate change hoax. Some families were paying a thousand dollars a month to heat their homes in the winter. As a result, hundreds of thousands of citizens fled to southern states, bringing additional stress on already stretched resources in those states.

One forceful reporter pressed the formerly called White House Press Release Officer about the massive taxes the administration passed on citizens. The spokeswoman refused to address his accusatory questions. Then, while walking out of the New Peoples Press room, as the socialists renamed the room, two black-suited agents arrested the reporter for speaking against the government, and he hasn't reappeared.

The two exhausted families turned in as darkness grew on the Maine coast. They had followed the directions issued by Timothy on the cleaning and preparation of the large structure near the house. Martin had seen photos of wooden supports for a railroad-type bed leading into the water at low tide. The construction included a heavy timber structure that resembled a sled. But when he had the opportunity to look into the structure, he found it to be a long pier with bollards for mooring vessels.

Sleep came easily to the workers and staff. However, Elie felt no less exhausted, developing and heading up a small version of a medical clinic. All physicians had yet to arrive, and Elie took double responsibility in developing, stocking supplies, and treating the occasional injuries.

Deep into sleep, a dream came to the newly married couple. A soft but authoritative voice said, "Assemble two engines based on your design, which is with the blueprints and plans in the work area. You will install them in a shell of a craft when it arrives. Be diligent in your workmanship."

A bright sun peeked over the eastern hills of northern Maine after bathing the shores of the Atlantic coastline, bringing its brilliance into the bedroom of the newlyweds, Elie and Martin. Elie shook her head, and her pixie-cut blonde hair fell into place without a comb. Stretching, the young woman moaned with satisfaction, saying, "So this paradise and wonderful morning feeling is the icing on the cake of marriage your Mom talked about?"

"I'm the one who likes to cook and bake." Martin teased.

"You certainly make a fine sweet icing, Mr. Philips," Elie purred with a honeyed look.

"So do you, Mrs. Philips," as Martin stretched his waking muscles. "You're stuck with me; besides, I love you."

Following a few minutes of morning talk, the two sat facing one another and clasped hands. They opened their prayers, humbling themselves before the Lord, then gave God thanks for the bright day, the lives of their families, and freedom, then said, "Most of all, Father, thank you for your greatest gift, your Son, and His sacrifice for our freedom from the dragon. Father, we again invite you into our lives and ask you to reign daily in our marriage. Please give us the strength and guidance to be the Christians you want, and help us to lead others in glorifying you. Amen."

The three couples and the newly arrived family of four, who checked in the night before, sat at the breakfast table. Martin led the breakfast blessing on the bounty before them. The ten souls enjoyed the eggs, ham, coffee, and juice on which to begin a busy day.

During the table talk, Elie asked, "Martin, did you, by any chance, have a dream last night?"

"Yes, come to think of it, I did. Mine sounded like a soft voice, yet it had a tone of great authority. What did you learn?"

"So did mine," Elie agreed. " The voice told me to build two of our designed power devices, following the plans and blueprints with the turbine components. And to install them in the shell of a craft when it arrives. And the voice uttered an explicit instruction, saying, Be diligent in your workmanship."

Martin looked around the table. The youngsters looked bewildered, not understanding the adult words. But, on the other hand, the adults understood every word Elie said and turned toward Martin.

"That is exactly the dream I had, word-for-word."

Hushed words of amazement and awe came from the three sets of parents, for the first time fully realizing divine intervention was at work on this homestead.

Elie broke the awkward silence with, "Martin, it appears the Lord is making me an engineer as much as I'm a medical person."

Following the breakfast clean up, one of the workers at the facility took the newcomers to a family barracks to help them set up housekeeping. Elie and Martin walked about the grounds as several years had passed since they were last there. Elie noticed large panels atop the house and workshop in the area to collect direct sunlight.

"Are those for heating or electricity?" Elie asked.

"Both. I designed the water and electric elements a year ago when I took that short vacation. The panels are staggered between electrical and plumbing. All our hot water comes from the summer pipes; then they are shut down in the cold months. So, I use auto antifreeze with an exceptionally wide range of working temperatures.

The electrical charge from the panels doesn't go directly into the buildings but into those two bunker-like mounds. Those are insulated concrete structures built to house two submarine batteries. They are charged by the solar-generated electric grid and supplemented by the regular power company in the winter. That arrangement works well in that the power company, and I trade on which way the current goes. Usually, we balance out. You can't see it from here, but we have a windmill on the hill overlooking our northeast corner; all of its currents go to the batteries.

The batteries have a 440-volt output, but we use 220 volts, with four hundred amps. With that low draw, the batteries easily maintain a full charge."

"Join me, my dear; we must prepare that old SUV for the turbine drive."

Martin enlisted additional men and brought up a medium-sized tractor which towed the vehicle to the workshop. Martin caught a cloud developing in the corner of the shop, *'It must be Timothy,'* he thought. The angel appeared from the mist, a smile spreading across his unblemished face.

"I see you are already hard at work; how may I assist you?"

"Would you supervise the cleanup and any maintenance for the craft due in?"

"I would be glad to. Those crates in the corner contain the engines I told you about last night."

"I thought it was you who visited us."

The angel smiled and headed toward the overhead pier.

Martin wondered, *'Why have men constructed a covered pier when Timothy could arrange for divine help?'*

A small voice in Martin's head said, "Because He who made the stars wishes man to appreciate the labor of his hands, then man learns the value of self-reliance."

Martin smiled, "Thank you, Timothy."

"You're welcome."

Elie and Martin worked to remove the old engine from the otherwise well-preserved SUV. Then, Martin drove the Humvee into the shop and parked it near the SUV. The Philips engine presented much less labor to remove than the factory-installed big V-6 in the utility vehicle.

Noon came upon the working people before they knew it. The ladies set up a soup and sandwich table for the crews, and after Timothy blessed the food, the people sat, talking, smiling, and planning for the afternoon's work.

Forty-five minutes later, Timothy dressed as any of the workers and worked side by side with them, many of whom had no idea who Timothy was. Those who did said nothing but enjoyed watching the interaction. The crew returned to their jobs, with Martin and Elie heading for the shop.

By three PM, the SUV quietly purred, ready for its test drive.

Martin and Elie jumped into the front seat. Martin checked the lighting and electrical systems while Elie checked out the radio. After trying several frequencies, she turned the device off, satisfied that the radio worked as designed.

"May I accompany you," a voice came from outside the vehicle.

"Certainly, Timothy. It may seem like it's crawling with the speed you could travel." Martin said.

"Oh, I've often traveled by automobile in my position."

"That's wonderful," Elie put in, "it may give you an opportunity to see the beauty of God's forest handiwork."

"I always enjoy those scenes. God is the Master artist."

"Yes, He is," Elie whispered almost silently as Martin pulled onto the lane.

An hour after they left, Elie drove back to the homestead, delighted in the company of an angel. When they arrived at the house, she parked in the driveway and shut the engine off.

"Timothy."

"Yes, Martin."

"Do angels eat food?"

"Not as you know it. Our life comes from He, who created the universe, and we have no need for the food you must have."

"I was going to invite you to dine with us at a family-style eatery."

"I would enjoy accompanying you, but before we leave, I would like to show you something in the shop."

The three walked to the workshop, and when they entered, Martin and Elie stood stunned at the sight before them.

"Timothy, is that some type of submarine?" Martin asked.

"Indeed, it is," Timothy said. "It is large enough for Pastor Mickey's church to travel to your second home where there is freedom."

"But why a submarine? Why not teleport them to wherever they go?"

"As I said earlier, the value of self-reliance."

Elie asked, "Will we see the rapture at wherever we're headed?"

"The Highest One has not given the Son the order to summon those called by His name. And He who lives forever has all the martyrs in place for his plan. The ascension of those called by His name will fulfill a promise, and the church will participate, but not yet. And the dragon is moving to make martyrs of those not chosen. It will not be allowed. This vessel will move rapidly and silently to its destination, where the people will live in harmony until called. Several such voyages will occur from here, carrying the saints to their intermediate destination," Timothy explained.

Martin looked at the monstrous submarine. He had seen something like it in photos of American submarines. "Is this an American submarine?"

"Yes, it has the room for Pastor Mickey's church., and a few others."

"Where on earth did you get that? I'm not about to ask how you got it here."

"We found it lying around a shipyard at a place called Bremerton. It will meet our needs perfectly. Our staff refurbished it to hold up to four hundred people," Timothy said.

"How are we going to feed and care for that many people in a submarine? And will it go below the surface?" Martin asked.

"Martin, think about it. If our Lord fed and kept all those who came out of Egypt for over forty years in the desert, don't you think The Creator can care for a few hundred?"

"Ah, yes, point taken. One other question, and I'm sure of the answer, but will the submarine have to dive, and how deep can it safely dive?"

Smiling at the scientist, Timothy said, "The reason for the submarine is to escape. But, unfortunately, the heavy surveillance, tools of search, and weapons of destruction, coupled with intense paranoia, will drive the socialists and Communists to use them indiscriminately, as they have in the past.

I remind you that free people must use all at their disposal to remain free; if they do not, they will not appreciate freedom, accept the lie, and succumb to captivity. It is through Jesus that man will find liberty. And, yes, it will dive and can dive to three-thousand feet if needed.”

Martin thought for a moment, “There are those who suffer from claustrophobia, and the thought of diving to three-thousand feet could be disastrous for them. Therefore, I would ask you to avoid that attribute when discussing the submarine with the church.”

“I’m sure we can cover that issue easily enough,” Timothy assured the scientist.

LOS ANGELES CLASS SUBMARINE

CHAPTER TEN

A straight line west southwest from the Christian's Maine homestead, DHS agent Miles Vickers enjoyed the warm colors of autumn's flowers and trees. But, unfortunately, the days were now shorter as the sun dipped to the south due to the earth's orbit around the sun, and cooler temperatures floated south from the Artic air flow in Canada. The results would create cold, snow, and ice. None of which would improve Miles Vickers' disposition.

Several days passed without inquiries from Vickers' supervisor on the missing families of Philips, Canfields, or the church congregation. Instead, Vickers felt the unsaid pressure, increasing his blood pressure and decreasing his civility toward his co-workers.

The agent reread his copy of the case. Eddi Cox ran every conceivable search on everyone in the case, yet it appeared as if they had vanished into thin air. Even the federal intelligence agencies grew tired of Vickers' quest.

He called his partner, Todd Gable, "Todd, grab a pad of paper and a pencil and join me for some brainstorming."

Two minutes after the call, Gable walked into Vickers' office and pulled up a chair. "Miles, are you okay?"

"Do I look okay?"

"No, you look like hell. Miles, your face is drawn, and there are bags under your eyes, not to mention you've turned into a crab."

"I don't need your analysis of my health, Todd."

"Yeah, you do. Listen to me; I'm not exclusively your partner; I'm your friend. If I weren't, I wouldn't worry about you."

"I'm sorry, this case is driving me nuts; my instructor in missing persons told us people don't just disappear; they move. So the big question is, 'where' did they go?"

"You remember in our investigation class, the instructor, what's his name, Alex who?"

"Alex Chalmers," Gable answered.

"Yeah, Chalmers, he said if you run out of leads and nothing turns up in two days, start at the beginning, right at the initial scene; you missed something."

"Come on; there's nothing here; let's get back to Chicago."

When they arrived back at the Chicago field office, Vickers and Gable bounced the case back and forth, watching to see if anything fell out. Then Gable asked, "Did you ever find out why someone burned our cameras and bugs?"

"I have a theory on that," he chuckled. "I was reviewing the interviews of friends and relatives of the Canfield woman, and the information suggested she is a feisty one. So when she found the camera in her bedroom, she got mad, probably thinking we're voyeurs or perverts, and wanted to tell us where to go."

"We're not voyeurs and certainly not perverts. At least I'm not," Gable sniped with a laugh.

"Come with me, Todd. We're going to begin at the beginning, the Philips house."

"I agree, we haven't a clue, and if we don't come up with something, Meyers will nail our hides to the wall as an example of failure."

The two agents began a painstaking search of the large home and workshop, with Vickers electing to take the house and Gable starting in the shop.

A local beat cop tripped to the residence and stood by to ensure the city would not fall into a legal claim of theft or vandalism. But instead, the cop watched the agent more out of curiosity about what the DHS agent was hunting.

Vickers first searched the smaller bedroom; he looked between the mattresses and under the bed, where he found the normally present dust bunnies. Then, looking around the woman's bedroom, Vickers saw a book on the end table beside the bed. It was a Bible; he opened it and flipped the pages for any notes. The agent noted that someone underlined many passages to emphasize a point or verse. In addition, a woman's handwriting made notes in the margins throughout the Bible. Vickers didn't know why, but he put the Bible in a tote bag he found. Next, the agent checked the closet, finding petite woman's clothing and several same-sized white nurses' uniforms. He made a mental note to have the hospital staff reinterviewed to determine if Canfield had made any contact with them.

The agent moved to the master bedroom, showing regular use. Using the same search routine, he pulled a pillow off the bed and was about to throw it in a corner when a piece of paper fluttered to the floor. Opening the folded paper, Vickers looked at a drawing. It was a rough pencil sketch showing something circular mounted on a block, with lines, which could be wires, coming from both ends. To his layman's eyes, it appeared to be some electronic component. The drawing went into an evidence bag.

Vickers turned up nothing substantial, then saw another Bible on a nightstand. As he found in the Canfield Bible, there were no paper notes, but more passages underlined and plenty of writings in the margins, particularly in the last book of the Bible, the Book of Revelation.

Vickers looked at Revelation's first page and saw someone had drawn a red box around verse 3. An arrow pointed to words in the margin; 'The only blessing in the Bible to read a book.' The man wrinkled up his nose, "That makes no sense," he muttered. That Bible went into the tote bag with the other one. The investigator noted that all the waste baskets held clean liners.

Agent Vickers moved on to continue his search pattern. He moved to the kitchen, his first stop, the waste basket. Four pieces of paper lay in the bottom of the thirteen-gallon trash container. The agent laid them on a counter and found two pieces matched to make one sheet. When placed together, a note read, 'Pastor Mickey, 10:30.' The remaining paper was blank. Vickers put the two pieces into a plastic evidence bag he pulled from a small stash he carried into every scene he visited. Other than the paper in the trash, the kitchen turned up spotless. The investigator moved to the living room.

Vickers recalled from viewing the surveillance footage that Philips and Canfield often rested on the sofa, so he made that his first stop. Vickers pulled the seat cushions from the couch and checked the surfaces for signs of hidden zippers or cuts to hide anything. The seats were found intact. Then the inquisitive man searched the area below the top cushion and discovered a folded church program of the service, dated eight weeks earlier.

Vickers mumbled, "That's the last service before the people disappeared." He put that into an evidence bag.

The remaining rooms and bathrooms failed to yield anything of value; however, the house looked as if the occupants had stepped out to pick up some groceries at the store and would return at any time. "It's as if they disappeared at the door," he muttered.

Vickers walked to the entrance of the workshop. He could tell the shop was organized and probably exceptionally clean on any workday, but now searchers had left it a mess.

"Gable, you in here?" the agent called.

"I'm over here, Miles," a voice answered from a dark area where the retracting roof rested in the closed position.

When Vickers found Gable, he worked through a large trash bin. "Going into dumpster diving, now?" He asked.

Gable laughed, "A good investigator sometimes finds the most valuable evidence in the trash."

"That's true; what did you find?"

"So far, one item which stands out as different."

"Okay, knock off the suspense, whaddaya got?"

"A map of Maine."

"That's a big state with huge areas of forests and thousands of miles of coastline; I hope you have some markings on it."

"I haven't looked that close yet. It's in a bag on that big table."

Vickers meandered over to the table, sitting under the bright led lights. He picked up the sealed evidence bag. The folded map showed the coastline, but the information panel obscured the contents. He flipped the package over and saw the heavily forested interior of the state.

The search continued for another hour before the agents called it quits. While sitting in their car, Vickers and Gable discussed the relevancy and value of their findings.

"I like that map," Vickers said, "It's the first inkling of where those missing people might be. And that note somebody wrote looks like a solid lead. Let's drive by that church the

Reverend Carvour runs, the last time we were there, I came away feeling he wasn't so clean, and now I'm sure of it."

At the now-closed church, the agents showed no surprise. Then they drove around the building and spotted a single vehicle tucked into a parking slot near a door.

Gable crawled out of the official vehicle and tried the door; finding the door unlocked surprised the man, and he waved at Vickers. The two guardedly entered the church, not sure if anyone remained behind. Then, the two heard the clang of metal on metal as if two buckets banged together. The two split up to cover one another and reduce the possibility of a single person taking them out with little trouble.

The source of the noise emanated from the kitchen area. Vickers cautiously looked into the kitchen and saw the Pastor cleaning one of two buckets. The agent waved to Gable, who joined him.

They backed up to the door leading into a dining hall next to the kitchen, and Miles called out, "Pastor Carvour, are you here?"

"In the kitchen," came his answer.

"How ya doin, Pastor?" Vickers said, trying to sound friendly.

"I'm fine; what can I do for you, gentlemen?" Pastor Mickey's response sounded normal, but Vickers' intuition spiked. Although the Pastor's voice was normal, the tenor sent an alert as far as it could be heard. Carvour's wife, blessed with acute hearing, picked up the warning in the next room. The strong woman steeled herself, then headed for the kitchen.

"Hello, any problems here?" she asked.

"Oh, no, we're from Homeland Security and following up on some missing folks," Gable offered as the Pastor's wife moved to his side.

"Have you heard from the Philips or Canfields since our last visit?"

"No, I haven't; how about you?" Mickey asked his wife.

"No, I've been around the house or here for the past couple of weeks." Then, turning to the DHS Officers, she continued, "As I recall, the last time they were in our church had to be, what, Mickey, six or eight weeks ago? And since the congregation up and left, we haven't had contact with anyone."

"What do you mean, 'up and left'? Gable asked.

"Two Sundays ago, we had our normal congregation, about three hundred, and everything appeared normal. We haven't seen them since. I was fearful the rapture occurred, and we missed it, but there are other worthy Christians around, and they're still here. So, I have no idea where they went, and everyone I speak to says they haven't any idea either."

"Pastor," Vickers piped up, "When did you last visit with Martin Philips?"

Pastor Mickey paused and appeared to check his memory but arranged his words to avoid untrue statements.

"Yes, we talked about the church service and what part he could play in it. Martin is a dedicated member of our congregation."

Vickers became serious and official, "Pastor, you and your wife will have to accompany us to our office. We still have much to discuss, and this is not the place, and time is against us. We want to get you home before it gets too late."

Mickey smelled a rat, but there would be no way the couple could resist the more powerful and armed men. He silently prayed as handcuffs went on Mickey and his wife.

"Sorry about the cuffs, but our regulations require them for your and our protection," Gable said apologetically.

Mickey asked, "Would you lock the building, please; the keys are in my pocket."

"Sure," Vickers said, surprising everyone in the room with his soft voice.

The lady asked, "And could you grab my purse? It's in the next room, on a counter."

"I'll get it," Gable said.

The ride to DHS headquarters took forty minutes in Chicago's traffic. Once the four people arrived, the two detainees sat in an interrogation room with windows, allowing the officers and staff in the DHS office to observe them. Although Gable removed the cuffs, they couldn't leave; Gable had locked the door from the outside.

"What are you going to do with these people, Miles?" Gable asked.

"We're going to keep them until I'm sure they are telling the truth about the disappearance of that entire church congregation."

"I know with the changes in the law, you have the authority, but is it the right choice, or even smart?"

"Whaddya mean? Who cares about two old people?"

"That couple is not afraid of you or the government. On the contrary, everything about them says they have horsepower beyond your wildest dreams," Gable warned.

"That's their problem, and we have ours. But, in the larger scheme of things, they don't even count."

"You're the Case Officer; it's your choice," Gable relented.

"You're damn right it is." Then Vickers, his anger welling up in him again, grabbed his keys from the desk and pushed past Grable.

The agent watched his senior officer stomp toward the interrogation room and open the door. Then, a split second later, he appeared behind the tempered viewing glass.

"All right folks, this is a 'come to Jesus' meeting, and your gonna sit here until you tell me the truth about those missing people," Vickers growled in his toughest voice.

Nothing happened. Mickey and his wife sat looking at the angry man with bland looks on their faces. "Did you hear me?" Vickers sounded more intimidating.

Mickey looked at the agent, his eyes only seeing a man in need of Christ, and answered, "Are you getting enough sleep, Miles?"

Vickers stepped back, *'How did he know my first name?' sizzled in his head.* But then, Vickers had to ask, "How do you know my first name?"

Pastor Mickcy dccidcd to play along with the agent's tactic but use a more patronizing response. "Miles, I know many things, one of which is the agony you're suffering over this case." Mickey felt his love's hand squeeze his leg as a warning not to pull this tiger's tail too hard.

"What are you talking about? I don't have any problems with my cases."

"I know your supervisors are applying pressure on you to find out where people are going, and your frustrations are nagging at you."

"You don't know anything about me or my job. So stop trying to throw smoke and mirrors into the mix, and I'm asking the questions around here."

A small voice whispered in Mickey's ear, "It's time to remind him of God's promise."

"Miles, you know God loves you, and He sent His Son to save you from your sins so that you can stand before him, free of sin, and join the ranks of His Saints."

"Stop with the preaching."

"I don't preach; I tell you what Jesus needs you to know right now."

"I don't believe that religious stuff; it's just for weak men and old women."

"Are you sure? Do you honestly think you can afford to take a stand on that logic?" Mickey prodded. More squeezes.

"Who are you?"

"I'm Mickey Carvour, but you should ask God who He is."

Laughing, Vickers joked, "Okay, God, who are you?"

A soft, commanding voice above the three people said, "I AM who I AM, Miles."

The sardonic smile on Vickers' face fell away as the agent looked at the ceiling, checking it in every direction, looking for the speaker he knew wasn't there.

"What kind of a joke is this? Are you some kind of a ventriloquist?"

Mickey sat in his chair, moving his head in a negative gesture.

Miles Vickers' smile changed from sarcastic to questioning with a taint of fear. Then, not sure what he heard, he left the room, and the 'lock-on-closing' latch clicked into place.

Agent Vickers quickly walked to Todd Gable's deck. "Did you hear that booming voice?" he asked Gable.

"What voice? It's noon, and everyone except one or two agents has gone to lunch."

"How could you not hear that voice; it came from above us and rattled the glass," he exaggerated.

"Miles, are you all right? You're white as a ghost," Gable asked.

"Don't say that," commanded Vickers.

"What?" Gable returned, "Ghost?"

"Don't say that again," Vickers said, his voice two octaves higher. Then he turned and left for his office. Todd Gable watched his senior officer walk away, and questions of the man's sanity crept into his mind.

In his office, Vickers dropped his Glock into the holster on his belt, then looked at the glass window of the interrogation room. Vickers' eyes simmered with hate at the perceived taunting he underwent in that room. Then he bolted from his office, heading toward the interrogation room.

Gable looked up to see his senior partner holster his gun and hurry out toward the door. The look on his face scared him, and he called to two other agents nearby, "Hurry, we have to stop Vickers."

Fortunately, the angered agent fumbled as he tried to get the correct key for the interrogation room, thus allowing his fellow agents time to reach him as he opened the door.

Vickers had wrapped his hand around the butt of the Glock when he heard the yell of Gable, "DON'T DO IT, MILES."

Sweat beaded on Vickers' forehead as he turned toward the familiar voice. "Stay out of this, Todd."

"What's that?" the agent behind Gable asked, pointing toward a rapidly expanding cloud of mist.

Everyone in the room and those who could see through the large window also saw the aberration forming. Vickers froze in place, fear clutching his chest, as a six-foot human form seemed to materialize within the mist. When the figure of a man appeared as the fog disappeared, everyone could see the man was clothed in white robes.

Gable asked, "Who are you? What do you want?"

"I am Timothy, and I'm here for Pastor and Mrs. Carvour."

Vickers snarled, "Get out of here, you monster; they are our prisoners."

Timothy stepped forward to stand next to the bewildered couple, "Come," Timothy commanded. Mickey and his wife stood, their eyes wide open in trepidation, and stood in front of the mysterious being.

Vickers' rage peaked, and he drew his Glock, but before it cleared the holster, a pair of eight-foot powerful, white wings sprung from behind Timothy, wrapped themselves around the couple, and drew them tightly to him. Timothy lowered his head, his eyes riveted on Vickers, when a soft voice said, "No, Timothy."

Timothy straightened up, and a mist formed around the three in his group, then they disappeared.

A second later, Vickers straightened up, and he seemed to realize he had drawn his weapon. Then, in a flash, he dropped the gun into its holster and looked around, confusion clouding his mind.

"What's going on here?"

Todd Gable stepped up and asked, "Miles, what happened?"

"I dunno, why am I up here; I was at my desk, reviewing my case; I just got here a few minutes ago."

"Do you know what the time is?"

"Yeah, probably eight-fifteen; why?"

"Miles, it's thirteen-thirty; we went to the missing people's church to interview the Pastor and brought them back for interrogation."

"What, how can that be?" Then the man looked around, glanced at his watch, and said, "I'm not feeling too good."

HOMESTEAD

CHAPTER ELEVEN

"Miles, every person here has seen or knows of the appearance and actions of a person or being which resulted in the possible kidnapping or jailbreak of two people we had in custody. Nobody is blaming you for what happened."

"I know." the slowly recovering agent murmured. "I'm not concerned about that, but I am worried about my loss of memory covering the time we returned here and the end of the event in the interrogation room. And by the way, does anyone have any leads on where the Carvours are hiding?" Vickers asked.

"Nothing, it as if they up and vanished as that church congregation disappeared. And we have no idea where they went or how they got there," Gable said. "Here, he left this calling card," as he handed Miles a white primary flight feather over two feet long.

"Todd, I have a nasty headache; I'm going home if you need me."

"I can take you home and arrange to drop your vehicle off at your apartment."

"I think I can make it with no problems; I'm feeling better by the moment except for the headache," the agent pleaded. I should be better by morning and get here on time. If things get worsc, I'll call you."

"All right, Miles, be careful; I'll call later to ensure you're still kicking." Gable jested.

Thirty-nine minutes later, Miles Vickers entered his apartment on the third floor of a brown brick building facing Lake Michigan.

Vickers wasn't always a cynical anti-religious man. On the contrary, he came from a middle-class family devoted to the Christian faith through the Swedish Baptist church. His troubles with religion came after his indoctrination by the destructive socialist government, which stressed fidelity to the party and its agenda to the exclusion of all others.

The agent's mind-altering encounter caused Vickers repressed religious beliefs to struggle for freedom. Socialism's basic structure is the antithesis of religion and liberty. As an afterthought, Vickers decided to talk to the DHS Chaplain while they still had one.

Miles Vickers brought the Bible he picked up at the Philips house to the Chaplain's office. Their first order of business had to do with the interrogation room incident.

Rev. George Harrelson asked, "Tell me, Miles, how many people were present in the interrogation room when the figure appeared."

"Six, Agents Todd Gable, Randall Oxnard, Jamie Lovell, and myself. Then we had two people in temporary custody for questioning," he reviewed his notes, "Mickey Carvour and his wife. Pastor Mickey Carvour is, or was, the pastor at the southside church whose congregation disappeared."

"As I understand the situation, your supervisors have pulled any records, tapes, videos, or other reports and slapped a classified tag on them. That's troublesome; it reeks of fear."

"I can relate to that," Vickers agreed.

The Chaplain asked for Vickers's statement beginning at the start of his day. Miles filled him in on his movements and whom he talked with and saw. "I sat down at my desk to review the case of the missing church-goers, then I seemed to wake up with my service weapon in my hand and Todd yelling at me. Later, Todd filled me in; I must have blacked out for about five hours. I don't do things like that," Miles said. "Todd told me the figure appeared, wrapped big wings around the two prisoners, and gave me a vicious look. Then, I heard a voice, such as I had never heard before; speak from the ceiling. That's when they vanished. I have to admit; it spooked me."

Chaplain Harrelson thought a moment adjusting his thoughts. "Miles, Christians believe God made angels function as messengers, small orders to complete, and a host of other duties. In times of imminent danger, humans have believed that angels have saved lives, a toddler seemingly pulled from the edge of a cliff or riverbank, where they could lose their life. Likewise, angels are commonly blamed for saving military personnel from certain death.

Could this figure be an angel; we'll probably never know; however, I wouldn't bet against it. You say he gave you a vicious look; explain that if you will."

"When this figure, angel, or whatever it was, stepped toward me, I started to pull my sidearm. What happened next took less than a heartbeat. "He mumbled something, then these huge white wings, at least seven or eight feet long, seemed to jump from behind him, wrapped themselves around the prisoners, and pulled the Carvours to him as if he was protecting them."

Vickers stopped and thought to bring the greatest accuracy to his next words. "Then, the aberration lowered his human-appearing head into his chest; his eyes stared at me under the shadow of his eyebrows. I felt as if there was a laser dot on my chest, then that soft, powerful voice began, 'No, Timothy.' The figure raised his head; a fog formed around them, and they vanished."

"That is quite a story; I'd like to interview the other members of DHS on what they saw."

"You will have to ask the director about that; I understand a shroud had dropped over the entire episode. The Philips couple we seek is connected to the church where Carvour preaches. That is why we wanted to interview them in private," Vickers said.

"One of the angelic duties is to act as a bodyguard on selected people. That would explain the defensive posture of the angel, which protected the Carvours."

"That could be, Padre," Vickers agreed. "I recovered this from the Philips house under a search warrant, hoping it might provide some information on the Philips's location." He handed the Chaplain Martin's Bible.

The Chaplain looked at the front pages, then opened the sacred book and flipped through the rest of the thin, strong pages. "It appears Mr. Philips is a serious Christian. He has attended Bible studies and probably classes on books or stories. Mr. Philips's Bible is heavily notated, and passages are underlined and colored for further scrutiny. It appears much of his work is in the Book of Revelation, and he possibly could be among those we refer to as 'End Timers.' That one believes the final days of the church are close at hand and are preparing for the rapture of God's people."

"We've seen these crazies before," Vickers said, "And every one of them was wrong," The agent said.

"I have seen that too, but the true believer doesn't know the time or date the rapture will occur; they prepare and wait diligently. The Bible says, ***Matthew 24:36. 'But of that day and hour knoweth no man, no, not the angels of heaven, but my Father only.'***

"Not even Jesus knew the time or date," the Chaplain explained.

"Now, how is that possible? If Jesus is God, the Son, he would know that."

"First of all," Chaplain Harrelson answered, "At that time, Jesus was in His ministry and human form, and He couldn't have known it. If He knew and answered, he could only do so as the Son. And then His ministry would have ended in failure, and salvation could not be possible. That is why Satan tried to tempt Him in the desert."

"That's pretty heady stuff, Chaplain."

"Yes, it is. And in the Book of Revelation proves you cannot read the Bible as you would a novel. You must study it, word for word, the personages, the times, the people. The Bible is symbolic, and the answers to the symbols can be found in their initial use. That came from a Minister who studied the Book of Revelation for over fifty years, and he continues to find corrections in his conclusions."

"I can see it is a lifetime endeavor," Vickers commented. "By the way, here is a calling card that visitor left behind," then he handed the Chaplain the two-foot-long white primary feather.

"Todd Gable found it after the angel left."

The Chaplain acted as if he feared touching the feather after hearing of its origin.

Vickers retrieved the Bible; he wanted to see if it might hold an answer to his primary question. He left the Chaplain's office and checked his watch. Where did the time go? It was quitting time, so he went to the garage for his vehicle and headed home.

****

Martin and Elie walked around the monstrous vessel; it rivaled the size of an American WWII destroyer. The submarine was securely moored to heavy bollards set in cement. There were two wide gangways from the concrete pier to the main deck.

"Martin, this is perfect for boarding; all the people need to do is walk aboard. However, I fear the elderly may have problems getting into the bowls of the sub," Elie said.

Timothy answered the woman's concerns, "For those who cannot negotiate the ladders, there is an elevator system inside the sail. We want to keep this vessel under the roof until it sails and as soon as it returns."

Thinking ahead, Elie added, "Speaking of spies in the sky, we better plan on a night launch and submerge at the earliest opportunity."

"Yes, that is our plan," Timothy said.

Elie smiled at his soiled robes, "You look as if you enjoy working with mechanics?" Elie asked.

"I do enjoy it; I didn't believe we had that in us." My singular problem is that Gabriel gives me strange looks if I'm not sparkling white. Our Creator chuckles about the whole thing.

Elie and her husband broke into ear-to-ear smiles. Timothy cocked his head to one side, "Have I said something amusing?"

Elie took any concern from the angel, "No, Timothy; we never thought about our Creator smiling or chuckling."

"Our God has a wonderful...how would I say it? He has a wonderful sense of humor."

"Martin assured the angel, "Timothy, it gives us great happiness to know of the humor God has. His wisdom is infinite."

"I find the Father and the Son, and Spirit; enjoy the giggles and laughter of babies and everyone else. I believe He has given His children that blessing because it resets their emotional health, and he delights in seeing happiness. Now, your concerns about the passengers boarding. As I explained earlier, we redesigned the vessel as a covert transport for the people to appreciate what was happening. The pressure hull is now one piece. The sparse openings are the three hatches on the main deck; two allow entrance into the twin living and communal spaces. The third is for the control station in the conning tower and leads into the central pressure hull. All sensors, cameras, and electronic gear are connected to an integrated system to maintain maximum hull integrity, including the propulsion system."

Martin added, "That's where we come in, build and install the new power devices on the three mounts."

"Yes, one each for the engines and one for the ship's internal power."

Martin asked, "May I ask about the engine design?"

"Certainly, Martin."

"We have no idea how you altered this vessel, and even if our engine design is compatible, how can we plan anything?"

"The Master designer has considered all that. I have a set of plans you call blueprints. I believe you will find your work boring," Timothy said. "All communications are in English. The Captain will have a," he looked at his notes,…. "Helmsman and his assistant steer and send speed orders from the bridge. All an engineer will be required to control is the speed. He turns a dial to increase or decrease ordered speed, according to a speedometer."

"What about diving this monster?"

"A man will control the depth from the bridge, but I have no idea how that will occur. I'm sorry, but Engineering is not my primary responsibility, and I lack the special vocabulary needed for that field," Timothy explained.

"That's all right, Timothy; we will figure it out. Can you tell me where Elie and I will find our quarters?" Martin asked.

"Certainly, follow me," and the white-robed being took the couple aboard and down to the second level below the main deck. On their right and left sides, as they walked toward the stern, lines of doors ran to a distant bulkhead. "These are cabins, each large enough to accommodate a family of five. If a family is larger, we only have to remove a bulkhead, and we have a larger cabin. There are cabins on the other side of this boat. In the middle, after the control tower, are four eating spaces, each with cooking areas."

"This is fantastic, but I have a few questions; could you answer them?" Elie asked.

"What are they?"

"I'm sure some of our folks suffer from claustrophobia; how will we be able to help them?"

"Jesus will calm their fears, and each cabin has, on the exterior bulkhead, what appears to be a window, and calming sea life swimming by."

"Then there is food, milk, and a wide need for hygiene supplies," Elie pressed.

"Each side of the vessel has a supply counter, and our passengers can find all needed items there. As for food, remember, our Lord fed five thousand on fish and bread. So, he will see to the needs of the people," Timothy said.

"My apologies, I forgot my place."

"No, not at all. Our Lord delights in those who worry about the welfare of the needy. They are the movers who care for the people and are blessed for their efforts."

"Thank you, Timothy, you're so kind," Elie praised Timothy.

Timothy's head bowed as if to express shyness at her words.

"Come," the white-robed Timothy directed. "I will show you where you must construct your engine."

The end of the short journey brought the three to a bulkhead hatch that bore the title "ENGINE ROOM." Elie and Martin entered and looked around, noting the use of led overhead lighting that made the space look bathed in sunlight. In the central area, a large machine had the label 'DISTILLER.' Martin said, "Our fresh water."

"Yes," answered Timothy. "With the removal of the original engineering plant, we have plenty of space for refrigeration, air conditioning, heating, and freshwater supplies in one central area.

Over there," Timothy pointed, "Are three generators awaiting their power source. Those are in the crates where you will find them," again indicating.

Along this bulkhead is the mount for the engine power unit. As you can see, it is constructed to accept the frame of your engine."

"Are there any tools here?"

"Yes," Timothy motioned for the two to follow. "All the tools you will need are provided in this caged area. The engines and auxiliary systems should work maintenance-free for the short time we need them. However, these are made for man to operate and may need repairs, but that is unlikely."

"Thank you, Timothy; we would like to begin our work at this time if you do not need us."

"I was sure you would want that, but do not forget the mealtimes; you will eat in the house for now."

"Thanks again, Timothy."

Martin saw a metal table bolted to the deck. He rolled the blueprints out on one end. The first order of business centered on electrical generation. There were several sheets of instructions and blueprints on the construction and installation of the power unit. He handed Elie half of them, and they headed for the crates.

Once opened, they found a smaller version of the turbine they put in the Hummer. It was light enough for the two of them to carry the two steps and set the turbine in its bearing cradle. First, the end flange is mated with precision to the generator shaft flange. Next, they installed a dozen provided high-torque connecting bolts and nuts in the mated holes and torqued them to the specifications listed on the blueprint. Finally, Elie installed the bearing caps and torqued each bolt appropriately. The woman could not help herself and hooked her index finger around the last bolt and pulled. To her surprise, the shaft turned with almost no resistance.

Elie turned to see Martin watching her.

"What?" she asked.

"Wondering about the lack of resistance?"

"Yes, it makes no sense. How will it create electricity with no brushes?"

"It's a brushless system, all electronic. And there are no reduction gears, thus almost zero resistance." Then the two installed the safety covers.

Martin and Elie finished mounting the control and governor features, and it was completed. Two hours later, all three generators sat ready for their test runs. But, first, Martin called the man who acted in the Chief Engineer's position, Jonathan Nicholas.

Nicholas brought an electrician along, and the four people went over the procedure outlined in the assembly instructions, finding them short and directly to the point.

One at a time, the generators were started and allowed to run for half an hour to warm up, giving the crew time to check every bearing temperature and adjust the oil temperature. Everyone expressed surprise and was awed at the silent operating generators.

"Wait until the electrician places a load on them; they will howl," Nicholas said.

"Martin said nothing; he doubted they would make much noise since there was no reduction gears to howl or brushes to hiss.

More noise came from the closing of the switch that loaded the generator than the unit created. All three generators gave off an almost unheard hum of the spinning shafts. When the electrical loads were applied, the generator RPMs dropped two a minute. The control system compensated by opening the screw-controlled throttle a tenth of a turn, and the generator settled to thirty-six hundred RPM.

Nicholas called the bridge and had the shore power disengaged. A small adjustment automatically occurred, and the almost silent generators ran perfectly.

The four crew members found and pulled up chairs to take a break while the first test run continued. Each person recorded bearing and RPM readings in the required four test runs and filled in a dozen additional conditions in the logs Nicholas created.

Nicholas made another call, and a thirteen-member crew entered the machinery space. The man in control of the unit set up a four and eight watch, four hours on watch, eight hours off watch, the same as in the American Navy.

The day's work had ended in success, and everyone formed a circle and thanked the Lord for leading them.

NORTH AMERICAN COMMUNIST PARTY

CHAPTER TWELVE

Work on the sub continued, with the Philips constructing and installing the frightening simple engines. Unfortunately, without testing the full capabilities of the toy-like power devices, their speed and maneuverability remained an enigma. Other engineers worked feverishly checking the communications on dozens of internal circuits.

Meanwhile, the first church members began arriving, and Norman, Lorrain, Darlene, and Clarence relocated the arrivals to the newly built structures. Arrangements for bedding and other needs came from the supply office at the end of the barracks.

****

Miles Vickers's reawakening of his spiritual life began to stress his lifestyle with the difference between his hardcore secular existence and that of a Christian. As a result, the man fell into a dream-filled REM sleep the day after his encounter with Timothy.

A soft, commanding voice whispered in his ear, "Miles, Do not fear the voice, but embrace it. First, read the introduction of the Bible; it will explain its cryptic nature, then read Hebrews, chapter eleven, and learn what faith is."

Vickers's woke with a start and sat upright. He looked around, half expecting to see that angel again. However, his Spartan apartment did not provide an easy hiding place, easing his initial fears. Miles flipped on the bedside lamp and saw the

Bible he had taken from Philips' home. The message whispered into his ear, still resonating.

Another voice spoke to the confused man, "What the hell are you doing reading that book? Get rid of it; before it gets you in trouble at work."

Vickers shook his head, thinking, *'Am I going mad? What's with these voices? One says read it, the other says don't, and why shouldn't I read it?'*

He looked at the Bible's leather cover, and in addition to identifying the book, Vickers noticed the lack of an author. Instead, there were some lines saying, 'Red Letter and Concordance, then Scofield Study Bible. After reading the introduction and instructions, the agent learned that the red letter meant Jesus's actual words appeared in red letters. Likewise, the Concordance lists earmarked references of importance and where to find them in the Bible.

The reference to Scofield Study Bible is the editor's name and a study system he created. *'This might come in handy in trying to understand these writings,'* The agent thought.

The last item which caught his attention, Vickers, read that over two-thousand years were spent writing the Bible as he saw it. So, first, God caused a man to write what he instructed, then years later, another did the same.

That made no sense; the history indicated that forty-four people took part in writing the sixty-six books of the Bible, and they, for the most part, did not know about the earlier writings or those that followed. Even worse, they came from different parts of the world and probably couldn't pass a modern school's third-grade test. Yet the writings are in perfect harmony and without a single contradiction from the beginning to the end. How is that possible?

Vickers reread that part, then the answer stood out, "God caused a man to write," God is the author.

The agent sat back, his mind spinning with the words, but his doubts evaporated when he flipped through the Bible; it was the only possible answer. Vickers recalled reading a Sherlock Holmes story, and the author, Arthur Conan Doyle, said, "When you have eliminated all which is impossible, then whatever remains, however improbable, must be the truth."

Vickers turned to the eleventh chapter of the Book of Hebrews, where he found a wealth of information on faith. Even with his head swimming with wisdom, he felt better and continued to read. He cross-referenced verses for clarification, and the words became clearer in his mind.

Miles took a break and glanced at the clock, which blared zero-three-zero five. He set the Bible down and lay back on his pillow, not knowing when he fell into a deep sleep with no dreams or nightmares.

Miles reported to work on time the next morning; the air in the office building was foreboding, and nobody talked or joked as they once did. The agent chalked it up to fear or the knowledge that an angel had snatched two prisoners from beneath their noses.

There was also a possibility that the mood resulted from the upper echelon having exploded into a rage over an inexplicable event. But, whatever happened, he would hear about it soon.

Adrian Gibson, DHS' Chicago Agent in Charge, didn't bother knocking on Vickers's office door. His reputation as a highly competent commander was regularly succeeded by his arrogance and lack of candor when dealing with his agents.

"Well, what's your story, Vickers?"

Miles laid out what He and Gable accomplished and the unexpected event in the interrogation room. Too many people saw it, making alterations foolish. He kept it in the mysterious and unknown category. Gibson's record confirmed that anyone who mentioned an angel or religion could result in a few free, unpaid days off, not to mention a meeting with the psychiatrist.

The top dog huffed and puffed, then stamped out of Vickers's office, knowing he couldn't place blame on the agent. Miles grinned with a small measure of inner pleasure at tweaking Gibson. But on the other hand, it served to aggravate Miles' stress levels. Vickers didn't fear Gibson but never let his guard down with the dangerous man.

As Gibson passed through the office door, he growled, "I'm taking over the investigation."

The straw felt like a ton of bricks. Vickers saw his career crumbling before his eyes. He knew he had to work for at least another month to keep his pension intact, and he had worked too long, much of it under the worst supervisors; then, he would at least have that to support him if he couldn't find other work. The agent looked at his hands, shaking as if he had Parkinson's disease, and the sight drove the icy shaft of fear into his heart.

The once proud Special Agent, Miles Vickers, made his way home without seeing the road or traffic. His only thoughts centered on the safety he felt when the door locked behind him, keeping the wolves of insanity at bay.

Falling to his knees in dire despair, Vickers could hardly focus on the floor. The shattered man crawled to his bedroom, his mind searching for some way to keep his sanity going to ensure he would survive. He instinctively knew the answer could show itself in one place, the black leather binding entitled: The Holy Bible.

Somehow, Miles Vickers, still crawling on his knees as a defeated man, found his way to the bedstand and reached for the Word of God. Vickers knew the passage he needed was in the Book of John; finally, he saw it. He wiped his eyes, which blurred his vision. ***John 14: verse 6: "I am the way, the truth, and the life; no man cometh unto the Father, but by me."***

Still, on his knees, Miles prayed, crying to the Lord, "Lord, I am a sinner who persecuted those who followed you, and I was wrong. But, Lord Jesus, I need you in my life; I know I am nothing without you. I pray you will have mercy on me, guide me to do your bidding, and use me in any way you wish. I pray for guidance to honor you and learn how I may serve you."

Miles broke down, his emotions pouring from him with the dark sins of his past. Finally, the man sobbed, Lord, help me to be a Christian, a follower of you, the true living God."

An hour later, Miles lay exhausted, drenched in sweat as if he had shoveled a ton of grain. Yet, he felt better than he could remember. Then, the same soft voice sounded in his ears, "Miles, I have heard your cries of pain and found them true. Your sins are as far from you as the east is from the west, and you will be known as Ethen from this day forward." More tears, these of joy, fell from the reborn man.

Ethen stood and gathered clean clothes, then showered. He never felt cleaner. Then looking at his face in his mirror, the born-again man stepped back. Looking again, he saw a different face, still his, yet different, and he noted his blonde hair was now soft and white.

****

Adrian Gibson sat in his office, adorned with the blood-red flag of the oppressive government behind and to the right of the head of the Chicago region DHS Office of Homeland Security. The blood-red flag with the silver rendition of the Homeland

Security Seal in the upper left corner called the 'canton' provided Gibson a contrasting background. But, when viewed on a TV screen, it projected a chilling effect.

Gibson made one call, and a dozen calls returned from senior officers at each level in the impossibly complex hierarchy of the politician-in-charge, who reported solely to the President. In addition, Gibson fielded calls from the White House regarding the unprecedented event.

In the Oval Office of the White House, President Charles Sanders, a staunch supporter of a Communist government in the former United States, sat behind the office's iconic Resolute desk with his smug, self-gratifying gaze drifting around the famous room. He visioned himself at the peak of every political effort in the world. He was now the leader of the once most powerful nation in world history. But then, the soft sound of the phone alerted him of an intruder into his glorification of accession.

"Yes," he answered. "Put him through." After the secretary forwarded the call, President Sanders said, "Hello, Adrian, how are things in the 'Windy City'?

"Well, sir, until yesterday. I take it you heard about our visitor?"

"I heard about someone or thing kidnapping two prisoners, but little else."

This time, Gibson told the President the story without embellishments or limitations. He ended his report with an expressed opinion that the unknown subject had all the appearances of a celestial nature.

"You are aware the official party line is that such beings are myths and conjured lies, aren't you?"

"Yes, Mr. President, I am only reporting the known facts as we know them today; further investigation should clear the matter up."

"Very well, find out what it was and deal with it; you will receive written authorization from me to use whatever force you deem appropriate; just make it quietly disappear. Am I understood Agent Gibson?"

"Understood, Mr. President."

"You have my direct line; keep me in the loop."

"Yes, sir."

Gibson sat stunned, then fantasized; *'It would appear he had become a President's man, but it's only confirmed by his continued use of me for personal missions.' He thought to himself.*

A thousand miles to the east, President Sanders began thinking, *'I should be able to use this incident to complete the takeover of the former United States and bring everyone under the control of a Communist government.'*

'Since several people at DHS witnessed the event in Chicago, it wouldn't fly to pass it off as an aberration or intoxication of a mind-altering chemical. We should make the official position of the party that a being from another world had finally made contact with the earth. The North American Communist party will lead the way in protecting our world with the help of Russia and China.

Then, Russia can reacquire those states that comprised the old Soviet Union and restore it to its former glory. And at the same time, China will finally have an unprecedented opportunity to gain control of Taiwan. After that, it will only take a small amount of pressure for others to cave in, and worldwide communism will become a reality.'

Sanders grabbed a pen and paper and put his plan on paper. Then, he reached into the lower drawer and withdrew a security folder, the large red letters spelling out its classification: ultra-secret- compartmented.

Thoughts of worldwide domination with him in control clouded his judgment.

'As for Adrian Gibson, the Special Agent in Chicago will become the point man for now, and I must move him up the food chain. I need to involve my number two man if Gibson will have to become the instigator of this scheme because it went south.'

****

The Agent-in-charge of the Chicago Office of the DHS meticulously read and committed to memory the witness reports. It struck him that those reports were highly suspicious because each one almost mirrored the others as if one author dictated them all. So Gibson changed tactics and began searching the reports for leads Vickers failed to follow up on or failed to recognize as crucial.

While reviewing the witness backgrounds, the head agent noted the lack of identification of both families' parents, grandparents, and great-grandparents. Gibson grabbed his phone and called Todd Gable.

"Gable, I'm putting you in charge of filling in the missing information in the family trees of Philips and Canfields, including the property they own. Better get started on it immediately; the higher-ups are pressing for details," he lied. "Pick a partner for this assignment; I want two brains working on it, don't leave anything slip by you."

"Right away, sir," Gable grumbled.

The top agent made a second call to the intelligence center. "Let me talk with Myron Greyson."

"Greyson speaking, sir."

"This is Gibson; I take it you are aware of the little episode in the interrogation room, are you not?"

"Yes, sir, I have our people trying to locate any vehicle, aircraft, or other means of transportation involved. In addition, I have one man dedicated to working with astronomers to determine where the mysterious person originated from."

"Good, keep them on it full time; if you need manpower, call me, and I'll get them for you."

"Yes, sir."

Greyson scratched his head. Eddie Cox asked, "What's up, Myron? You look like you like someone handed you a death wish?"

"It could be that bad, but you are getting involved. You're to find the vehicle that spooky aberration arrived in and where it originated from."

"Oh joy, thanks a lot. Now we aren't looking for a needle in a haystack, but a needle in the universe."

"Yeah, I know, and I'm sorry about that; the orders just came from Gibson himself. You better contact your brother at NASA."

Meanwhile, Gibson had his secretary type up the orders to the agents as needed to accomplish the demands from the top dog.

As an afterthought, Gibson grabbed his phone again. "Shaw, you and Morris recanvas the neighbors of Philips and Canfields and look for any relative information and possible hideouts."

"Yes, sir."

Then, the DHS head stopped by his secretary's desk. "I hate doing this, but this now goes to the top. Beginning today, this office is on twelve hours, off twelve hours, seven days a week." Gibson said, "All vacations and time off are canceled."

The woman looked at Gibson, unsure if she should feel sorry for him. "Yes, sir, right away."

As the top agent left the secretary's office, he thought, *'I'm going to have to deal with Vickers; that man has started coming apart.'*

A promise of early snow made itself known to the 'Windy City' As an icy blast of arctic air pushed its way south down the length of Lake Michigan. The thirty-degree temperature began to drop toward the predicted five degrees above zero, and twenty-five-mile-an-hour wind gusts made the weather feel worse.

"Mother Nature has a mean streak in her," muttered Gibson.

A radio meteorologist forecasted cold air but no snow. The agent laughed at the broadcaster's accuracy as snow flurries whipped about the car in the wind, confused by buildings and alleys.

After a hot shower, the agent grabbed a hoagie and a beer from his refrigerator. Then, as he chewed the day-old bread, he flipped on the TV and switched the tuner to a news channel. There was a ten-second blurb about a bright light in the Federal Building, but the story petered out without additional information. Hoping the story would die by morning, Gibson shut the television off along with the light and fell immediately into a restless sleep.

****

Adrian Gibson woke with a start. Then the agent squinted at the clock, the numerals glaring four-fifty-five AM. Gibson refused to try picking up a few more winks after a night filled with unintelligent nightmares. Following another shower to clear the night sweat away, Gibson dressed and headed for his car without eating. Although light snow still blew around, there was no accumulation. So instead of eating at a restaurant, he stopped by a fast-food joint for a breakfast sandwich and coffee, which tasted old and burnt; the agent threw it into the trash and grimaced at the pimpled-faced kid in the pay window as he pulled away.

A block from the Federal Building, Gibson saw a throng of news reporters meandering around the entrance to the building. *'Those idiots got into some bad habits under the freedom to do whatever they wanted amendment. But that's gonna change pretty fast,' he thought.*

The DHS man in charge pulled into the rear parking for the building and headed for his office. Unfortunately, he no sooner hung his coat on an antique coat tree than the phone started ringing. It was some reporter sniffing around for information from an unnamed source. Gibson slammed the phone into its cradle and blocked all incoming civilian lines. His supervisors were the sole people who could call in, and within five minutes, the phone rang again.

"Gibson speaking," he growled.

The agent's attitude changed immediately. "Yes, sir, I'll prepare a response right away; yes, sir, it will be ready for the nine AM news briefing."

After reviewing the overnight reports and the special dispatch from Washington, Gibson had put together a statement for release at zero-nine-hundred hours. He spent the remaining time before the briefing polishing his statement.

Special Agent Adrian Gibson took a position behind the podium in front of a room full of reporters and TV cameras. Behind the speaker was a briefing stage, with a large banner bearing the new seal of the DHS and, to his right, the red flag.

"Ladies and gentlemen, The light observed from the sixth-floor window came from a visitor who abducted two prisoners from the room. The visitor information is in the official release on the subject. A full DHS investigation is underway, and information will be forthcoming," then he stepped away from the podium and lights without answering any questions.

A follow-up speaker from the State Department took the podium, and a flurry of questions flew at the woman. She expertly fielded the questions with respectful and intelligent answers that told the reporters nothing.

Gibson, to his delight, made it to his office without an ambush by reporters, but his phone rang on his entry.

"Special Agent Gibson, speaking."

"Agent Gibson, this is Senator Robert Michaels; I'm on the Senate Intelligence Committee. Congratulations on the fine briefing; concise and to the point. And most of all, saying markedly little of the subject matter. Keep it up, and you can find a good job as the Briefing Officer for us."

"Thank you, Senator, but my forte is investigations of national security interests. Besides, communications were my worst subjects in college."

Following the small talk, the Senator asked, "What do you make of this so-called visitor?"

"Sir, we have little doubt that whatever appeared before came from another world and made off with two prisoners for reasons unknown at this time."

"I see," the Senator said, "Did you see this visitor?"

"Yes, sir, I was there."

"Give me your honest opinion."

"I believe what we saw came from another world. It became angry when we tried to restrain the two prisoners and lowered its head. The eyes looked as if they glowed, and I expected to see fire erupt from them until I heard a voice say, 'No, Timothy.' I can tell you this, I, nor anyone else there can tell you what it was, but there is no doubt about its reality, and we were helpless against it."

"What about a Biblical figure, say an angel?"

"Anything is possible, but I am an atheist and don't believe in Bible stories, even though others here are Christian and believe it to be an angel."

"Very well, I'll wait for your call; meanwhile, I'll try to hold off the media scare here; call me with something soon." Click.

NORTH AMERICAN COMMUNIST PARTY

CHAPTER THIRTEEN

A quiet time descended upon the DHS office, giving Gibson time to organize the rest of his day. The first order of business had to be Vickers. Gibson ran a thought through his mind, *'With the heat on, Vickers had become a liability.'*

Gibson's letter of censure outlined Vickers' unprofessional handling of the Carvour interviews, subsequent arrest, and later the fiasco in the interrogation room. Vickers was the agent in charge, therefore, responsible for those failures. However, the protocols required in such contacts had been created not for standards of professionalism. But to protect the command structure from political and adverse legal action under the old government.

Gibson's recommendation included a letter of censure in Vickers' personnel file and a transfer to the Sturgis, South Dakota office as a single agent appointment, attached to the Rapid City Office. The transfer is effective twenty-four hours from the date of notification. The senior agent planned to have Vickers served with his transfer orders the following day.

****

At the Christian Homestead in Maine, the final steps for the first transfer of Christians from the late United States to an undisclosed location drew to a reality. But, for their security, the people were told that they were to prepare for year-round warm weather and would be kept in the information as it developed.

Martin and his bride, Elie, had moved their warm-weather and long life/rough service clothing aboard the submarine. Now they spent time packing the tools and electronic equipment needed for the survival and daily life of the church congregation. Other members would bring woodworking tools and other metal-related tools.

The morning sky was brooding, and to the northwest, it grew much darker. However, it wasn't because there was a shortage of light, a storm marched in their direction, and the weather forecaster predicted the collision of the cold north air and a warm southern front laden with moisture to the north of the homestead with up to nine inches of snow in the offering. Martin and Elie went to the work area, and to their surprise found the submarine gone.

Almost in a panic, they spotted Timothy and told the angel what they discovered.

Smiling, the friendly angel quietly said, "It was moved to a safer location a short distance away. We will see that you will get there safely."

Carpenters had built a covered walkway from the barracks buildings to the house. They connected it to an original tunnel system built as an escape route between the main structure and the long work building a hundred-plus years earlier.

****

Adrian Gibson flipped through reports from the investigation into relatives of the Philips and Canfield. Then, Gibson took a second look at Canfield's family tree, finding a great-grandmother who passed away before the Philips issue developed. The search for property ownership by her name showed no property in her name.

With a whisp of fear for an incompetence charge, Gibson found her maiden name, which disclosed that the woman still owned about twenty acres of land in Maine on a tributary leading to the Atlantic Ocean.

Gibson's mind clicked, *'A tributary leading to the Atlantic?'*

Then he muttered, "I'll bet a thousand dollars that's where the absconders are, and they will try to escape on a boat." After noting the address of the suspect property, the agent consulted his list of aviation assets in Maine. DHS maintained An air detachment on the Air Force Base at Bangor, Maine.

Gibson grabbed his phone and called the DHS duty officer at the Bangor base. "This is Special Agent Adrian Gibson, SAC, Chicago. I have a Top-Secret mission, Authority NACP-1. I need a two-man detail flown to the area of Jonesport. I will send the address via TTY. Identify occupants and forward a list to this station by TTY ASAP."

"Yes, sir," the young operator said. Then the phone went dead.

Special Agent Charles Novak contacted the resident SAC and read him the message. He said, "I'll be right over, get a chopper and crew together for a sortie."

Agent Novak had the duty flight officer set up the crew and helicopter for the mission, and he prepared the fifty pages of paperwork such a mission would entail.

****

Church member Don Fugate began his fifth trip from the covered dock. Dawn had come and gone; now, the sun, slowly orbiting much lower in the south, was about to be overcome by thick, gray clouds. The air temperature failed to rise more than five degrees from the previous night's low and stood at thirty-four degrees. Winter was coming to Maine.

Pastor Mickey, who joined his parishioners, began the orderly trek and boarding the transfer boat. All the while, Timothy watched the progress of the church, which reminded him of a similar movement of humanity in Egypt more than thirty-five hundred years earlier.

The passengers crammed themselves into the spaces below the main deck to escape the cold breeze while the boat sped for Steele Harbor Island, a tree-covered but otherwise desolate offshore island of thirty-five-foot elevation of standing rock. Wind gusts of thirty miles an hour rocked the boat as the vessel rounded the island. Fugate increased the throttle setting and the boat's bow bit into the waves with saltwater spray coming over the main deck.

A short distance later, Fugate turned to port, bringing the boat into Lower Herring Cove, which gave immediate relief from the cold wind. As the passenger boat approached the end of the cove, a painted steel door slid on suspended rails to open a passage of twenty feet. Don Fugate masterfully motored past a black hull barely visible in the dark cavern, then turned to his starboard to moor the boat port-side to a dock.

The whine and growl of working rollers signaled the closing of the sliding door, which, when closed, appeared as part of the landscape with the careful camouflage painting.

Once the big door latched shut, overhead light flashed on, bathing the submarine pen in a pale light. The lighting afforded the passengers their first glimpse of a three-hundred-two-foot submarine that had appeared the night before. All the passengers had yet to see such a boat but knew of them from the news, books, and movies, yet they had no concept of the size of the vessel. The adults gawked at the undersea craft, daughters hugged close to their mothers, and boys could hardly wait to get aboard.

The passengers boarded the black tile-clad vessel in a quiet, orderly manner. Those who could descend the ladders were sent aft; the remaining passengers used the small elevator in the sail. When the last of this initial voyage stepped on their deck, the hatches clanged shut and secured. The elevator was raised into its storage cradle in the sail, and that hatch was then closed and secured. The hatch indicator lights in the control room turned green, indicating all access ports were watertight, save one—the bridge.

The boat's Captain, Bradley J. Holeman, rose to the rank of Captain, USN, and commanded two Los Angeles class submarines with combat encounters with Russian attack submarines. Captain Holeman, a widower, was known as a devout Christian.

Standing atop the sail on the small bridge, the OOD and a talker began taking the sub toward the Atlantic Ocean, and a short hundred-ninety-one miles eastward on course one-four-four-point five degrees to the Continental Shelf. The boat cast off, and the Captain ordered all ahead five knots and gave the helm their heading.

In the engine room, Chief Engineer Jonathan Nichols nodded to the throttleman, who looked at him when the bell sounded. Mike Webber, a former destroyer throttleman and under instruction by Martin Philips, increased the throttle a notch on each engine, raising the RPMs slightly, and the twin screws easily pushed the boat forward.

An unseen mist formed in a far corner of the roomy space; Timothy, in Seamans's clothing, stepped up to the engineer. The generators are at less than a whisper, yet they propel four thousand tons or more at almost six miles an hour."

"Yes, Timothy and I have no doubt they could push this boat faster than the safety limit of the bow."

Timothy bowed his head in prayer, then looked up, "I have discussed this issue with our Master designer, who said he would repair it and add a governor to restrain faster speeds."

Turning to the angel, Nichols asked, "What is our maximum allowable speed?"

"Sixty-five knots," Timothy mentioned.

"Oh, that's all?" Then he picked up the phone. "Captain Timothy informed me we have forward speeds up to sixty-five knots; then a governor will not allow any increases."

"We will make good time then," The unflappable Captain quipped.

Wind speeds had increased since the boatload of Christians entered the shelter of the cove, and the temperature dropped to freezing.

"OOD increase speed to twenty knots."

"Aye, sir."

The submarine developed some rolling and pitching as the wind and waves came at them from the port side. Not wanting the passengers to become ill, he ordered the topside crew below deck and secured the bridge cover. The hull hatch was sealed with a slight increase in air pressure within the boat.

"OOD, how much water is beneath the keel?"

"Three-hundred-fifty feet, sir."

"Submerge the boat, OOD, take us down a hundred feet; we should hit the shelf in about five minutes; once we're over deep water, dive to five hundred feet, maintain twenty knots."

"Aye, Captain," Delbert Ackerman replied. The OOD also had LA class boat experience and one cruise with the Captain. OOD Ackerman checked the clock on the gauge board to determine the dive time. Then he double-checked the "Christmas tree," the traditional name of the access indicator board, finding all green.

A few seconds later, "Board is all-green, Helm, increase depth to one hundred feet, at fifty feet per minute."

Once the sail sunk beneath the water's surface, the submarine's ride became much smoother, but with a slight hint of a roll.

The OOD called the sonar hut, "What is the depth to the bottom?"

"Over six thousand feet, sir."

"We have crossed the Continental Shelf, Helm, increase depth to five hundred feet at fifty feet per minute."

"Aye, sir."

The boat silently disappeared from the turbulent world above, where the Christian's enemies searched for them. At five hundred feet, the passengers no longer felt movement; and the soft whir of vent blowers and lights indicated life carried on, ensuring them that all was well.

Captain Holeman turned on the 1MC, the shipwide announcement system. "This is Captain Holeman; we have completed the beginning of our first exodus of Christians from the former United States. Although we won't be heading for the land of milk and honey, we will be going to Western Australia, whose government has welcomed us, and representatives will be on hand to assist everyone in finding shelter until the families can get set up in homes. Food and plenty of sea life are available to support everyone. The population is Christian; we will begin to integrate with the Australians, who expressed open arms for God's people. Americans are in the minority, and we must respect the Australian people and their government. Our countries have long been allies, and despite occasional bumps in the road, our histories have been good.

This, for the most part, will be our home. No doubt some of you may elect to move to more populated cities, but that is your decision. Most families will come to assimilate into the Australian culture in Broome. The area is primarily Christian and has a rich open-arms history. The people have respect for other cultures, and we must return the custom to co-exist. We are God's people, and He has commanded us to love our neighbors as we love ourselves.

There are vast areas inland to build homes; the beginning will require patience, stamina, determination, and asking the Lord for help.

We will provide additional information during our voyage. If a question develops, do not hesitate to ask any crew member. Captain out."

****

A message arrived at the office of Marjorie Allensworth, one of the families electing to remain in the greater Chicago area. A contact working in the Homeland Security office discreetly advised Marjorie that SAC Gibson learned of the Maine property and had planned on raiding it.

Marjorie contacted the caretaker Robert Hazen, who set into motion a pre-planned action that transferred the property ownership to the Jonesport Public Schools for the market price.

The transfer occurred overnight, and the school owners immediately dispatched work teams to modify the buildings to the school's needs. The first projects included a large sign and flagpole at the driveway entrance. The sign identifying the location of the school offices and the flagpole flew the flag of the State of Maine.

At the same time, the movement center of operations transferred to the underground facility at Steel Harbor Island. After years of quiet excavation and preparation, the facility could hold and care for three hundred people per group. It would officially begin the gathering of Christians for transport to towns and cities in Australia. They would bring a force of trained and experienced engineers, operators, designers, fabricators, and the Christian ethic of hard and honest work.

****

Lieutenant Harry Blackman devised a flight plan to recon the estate Agent Gibson gave him. Part of his planning included the current and forecasted weather, which created concern and would ground all aircraft. His call to the meteorologist confirmed that all aircraft in the imminent storm path had been grounded.

The recently promoted Lieutenant wasn't looking forward to telling the SAC of Chicago's office that he was going to wait. The man's lack of empathy, manners, and temper was notorious.

Blackman's call, fortunately, caught Gibson in a conciliatory mood, and the SAC said he would be happy to accept any help he could get.

Gibson called his secretary, "Mary Lou, are any additional reports on the Philips church case pending?"

"Just a second, sir." A quick review of the recent reports filed by the several agents she worked with failed to expose either Philips or his church's name. The Christian woman picked up the phone and dialed her supervisor, "I checked all pending reports, and it appears you have everything current."

"Click," the rude hang-up wasn't missed.

Going back to the proven technique of reviewing everything from the beginning and looking for missed evidence or information, helped the agent when he pulled a series of aerial photographs of the property.

In the back of his mind, Gibson knew he wouldn't get a team onto the property or in the house until the storm passed. The delay allowed him the time to review the case.

Looking at the half dozen eight-by-ten color photos, he noted the road leading to the house could be either crushed rock or twin strips of concrete. The ladder was less likely due to cost and time. In either case, traffic use could not be determined.

"Clark," he bellowed.

"Yeah," the unimpressed agent responded as he appeared next to Gibson's desk.

"Pull up a seat; I'd like your input on what you see and don't see in these photographs," Gibson ordered.

Tom Clark pulled up a chair and took the first photo while Gibson prepared to note Clark's comments.

The agent studied the photograph from side to side, then top to bottom, verbalizing every feature he saw. Agent Clark went silent, causing Gibson to look up and watch as the man pulled a folding fingerprint glass from a pocket. He flipped it open and again scanned the photograph.

"The house has been painted in woodland camouflage, similar to Army vehicles. And there is a large rectangular outbuilding to the north side, with what appears to be a covered walkway between it and the house."

"Why covered?" asked Gibson; there are plenty of evergreen trees covering the area, so the wind would not be an issue for a short walk unless it's to reduce snow accumulation,"

"It could also be an attempt to keep passage out of sight," the agent offered.

"Good point; that's why you're here."

"But what's in the building is the real question. Is it a warehouse or a barracks?" Another look at the building revealed nothing of its contents until Clark saw the shadows of what appeared to be swings, merry-go-round, and other playground equipment.

"People, it's a barracks; there is a playground next to the building with signs of moderate use, indicating either refurbished equipment with average use or older equipment with light use. The building shows signs of recent construction."

"Good, keep going."

"The house chimney appears cold and without recent use." Agent Clark slowly looked at each side of the structure. "There are a pair of white tubes or pipes protruding from the south side of the house, with what appears to be steam coming from the longer one. They have an efficient HVAC system in operation; that's probably why the chimney is cold."

"You have earned your pay today, Clark. Thanks, I think I can handle it from here."

Clark left, then Gibson grabbed a magnifying glass from his desk drawer and began scanning the long shed or building south of the house. Further close examination of the structure showed it was camouflage painted in the same forest woodland scheme as the house and barracks. But, of course, nobody paints their home in camouflage unless they don't want it seen. And the property is still in Canfield's grandmother's maiden name. "Good job, Canfield," mumbled Gibson.

'This must be the center of the absconder's operation, but where are they headed?' Gibson wondered. When he looked at the south structure, he noted water ran up to and into the end open to the tributary. "They're escaping by boat," he said.

Gibson's next move was a call to the Maine Department of Homeland Security. He asked for an old colleague he knew was in the office.

"John, Gibson here; how ya doin?"

"Great, how about you?"

"Been better; some politician is pressuring me over a few absconding Christians."

"I'm not even going to ask what that's about."

"You're better off if you don't. But I do need a little help."

"Sure, but please don't get me involved; you know how I feel about politicians."

"I won't, but I need the Coast Guard to check and keep an eye out on any boats running escapees." Gibson filled his friend in with the information he needed.

"I know the Commandant at the Coasty station in Jonesport; I'll give him a call. I doubt they will go out now; we have a strong storm inbound, dumping an estimated nine inches of snow on us."

"So I've heard ask them to check if they need any time on the water after the storm."

"Will do."

"Thanks, buddy; Black Label as before?"

"Sure, why not? I'd better get busy writing up the request; I'll call if anything turns up."

"Thanks," the line clicked into silence.

'I wonder if they will bag the spaceman?' Gibson thought.

CHAPTER FOURTEEN

The passengers asked if the submarine could be named *'The ARK.'*

The Captain approved the request without questions.

Two days from the submarine pen, the boat cruised at twenty knots to avoid drawing attention to its presence. The passengers and crew had become accustomed to the steady hum of the fans and felt no pitching or rolling surface vessels endure. Moreover, the special design of the enclosed external motors quietly gave off less than a whisper-like drone at their speed and transmitted no noise to the hull, its occupants, or any potential listeners.

"OOD, increase speed to twenty-five knots at one knot per minute and notify the engine room we will work up to thirty knots over the next half hour."

"Aye, sir."

Seconds later, "Captain, the engine room acknowledges your message."

"Very well, initiate the order for the increased speed.

"Helm," the OOD said, "Increase speed one knot per minute to twenty-five knots."

"Aye, sir, "Increase speed one knot per minute to twenty-five knots," the Helm responded, and he changed the speed demand in compliance.

Five minutes later, nobody on the boat knew they sped through the water at twenty-five knots.

Half an hour later, the OOD asked, "Helm, feel any vibrations on the wheel?"

"Negative, sir."

"Sonar, we are at twenty-five knots. Are there any noise transits?"

"No, sir," the sonar watch reported.

OOD Jack Morton reported, "Captain, we are coming up on thirty minutes since going to twenty-five knots."

Captain Holeman said, "OOD, increase speed by one knot per minute to thirty knots."

"Increase speed by one knot per minute to thirty knots, Ayea, sir.

Everyone in the control room watched the pit log repeater increase slowly to thirty knots.

"Captain," the OOD called out; we're at thirty knots and holding."

"Very well."

In the engine room, Martin, Mr. Nichols, and the engineers moved over all the machinery with stethoscopes. After several minutes of listening to bearings, pumps, the main turbine, and the hull, they stood in awe at the silent operations of the plant.

****

"Comrade OOD, sir, I picked up what could be propeller cavitation, but I only got a split-second of transit, then nothing. The contact is bearing forty-five degrees, at twenty-eight kilometers, and moving southeast. I need a second contact to give you an exact course. Identification, unknown."

"Well done, Comrade sonarman. Try to acquire the source, and the Captain will decide what to do."

The OOD called the Captain in his Spartan quarters, "Comrade Captain, we have a possible contact. Do you wish to investigate?"

"What would you do, Mishka?"

"Why I would investigate; it is an unknown contact, sir."

"You have the conn Mishka; investigate."

"Helm, come to zero-five-zero, speed twenty-five knots. Sonar, we are pursuing to investigate your contact; find him."

"Aye, sir."

The attack submarine swung around and headed for the *ARK*, turning up twenty-five knots within two minutes. Captain First Class Eduard Valentin Sidorov stepped onto the control level, and the OOD brought him up to speed on his action.

Behind him, the Political Officer stood back and watched.

"Comrade OOD, you will prosecute the unknown vessel, and if we do not have its sound identification in our files, you will have it recorded."

"Yes, Comrade Captain.

As the sub approached the suspected track of the unknown boat, the OOD queried sonar.

"Comrade OOD, there is no sound in the water at this point."

"Is your equipment working?"

The worried sound technician said a minute later, "The sonar is working perfectly, sir."

"Helm," the OOD said calmly, come to zero-four-five degrees, increase speed to thirty knots."

The Political Officer began to butt in, and the Captain said softly, "Igor, the man must learn by doing his job; I suggest he be allowed to do it."

"Your right, Captain; I was going to ask him the possible political nature of the boat we are chasing."

"Right now, that would be a little premature, as we started this on a possible propeller cavitation and have not yet identified it as a boat."

"That makes sense, Comrade Captain; please continue."

****

"OOD, "Sonarman David Haskill called out, "I thought I heard something out there; I recommend a 'Crazy Ivan."

"Another boat?"

"Possible."

"Bo'sun, IMC.

"This is the Captain; we are going to investigate a possible noise and make some severe maneuvers. Everyone, sit on the floor, lock arms and brace your feet on a bulkhead if possible.

Ten seconds later, the Captain ordered, "Helm come starboard ten degrees and dive to six-hundred feet.

The deck tilted, and the bow dropped as the boat rapidly closed six-hundred feet.

"Captain, there is a boat astern at about two miles; speed is estimated at thirty-five knots." Seconds later, "Conn, Russian Yasen astern."

"Helm, center your rudder, speed forty knots."

The engineers looked at one another and turned the throttle open one click every fifteen seconds. A minute and fifteen seconds later, the *ARK* bulled ahead, opening the distance between them and the Russian attack submarine.

****

"Comrade Captain, it is a boat and has two screws."

"Can you identify it?"

"No, sir, it is not in our reference banks; I recommend we ping it."

"Do it."

A deep growl emanated from the bow of the Russian boat and chased the *ARK*.

"Captain aren't you going to shoot at it?" the political officer asked.

"No, they have not made any aggressive moves, and it has two screws."

"Two screws?"

"Yes, an American submarine is unlikely, as they have one screw. However, our navy has submarines with two screws, which may be one of them."

"Sir, sonar reports the mystery submarine is speeding away at forty knots."

"Impossible," the Political Officer said.

Captain Sidorov stepped to the sonar station, "What is this report?"

"Sir, I regret to inform you that the mystery submarine has left the area at forty knots; it is confirmed on our computers."

"Comrade, I will need a detailed written report of this incident. Your supervisor will assist you if you wish."

"Thank you, Comrade Captain," the frightened sailor said.

Seeing the stress on his face and hearing it in his voice, Captain Sidorov looked at the young man. "You have nothing to fear, Comrade; you did your job perfectly. Make your report."

"Yes, Comrade Captain," the relieved sailor said.

****

Half an hour later, after returning the *ARK* to one-two-two degrees, the Captain asked the Helmsman, "How are we doing?"

"Excellent, sir; it's almost as if we're sitting still."

"That's what I'm wondering about. OOD, check on the engineers; I want everything double-checked. We're way out on an unknown limb here. To my knowledge, no sub has gone this fast."

"Aye, sir."

"Engine room, Philips speaking."

The OOD passed on the Captain's concerns.

In the engine room, Martin said, "Hold on a second."

"Jonathan Nichols speaking, sir."

"Jon, this is Jack, Captain Holeman is concerned with the quiet and smooth operation of the boat, and frankly, so am I. I'm not used to a pillow-soft ride like this."

Nichols laughed; "None of us are. I've made a dozen checks in addition to the hourly readings and readings by the men. This plant is as quiet as a tomb, pardon my pun, and we are traveling at forty knots according to the pit log, with all readings normal."

"That's all I needed to know, thanks." Then, turning to the commander, the OOD said, "Sir, we are at forty knots, and all readings are normal and constantly checked."

Captain Holeman smiled, "I'm sure glad the modifications and work were done by the best mechanics and scientists outside of this world."

The Captain called the Navigator, "Chet, recalculate our position and ETA at Broome at forty knots if you will."

"Aye, sir."

"Bo'sun, 1MC. "This is Captain Holeman. May I have your attention? We successfully eluded a Russian submarine patrolling the area, that's why we needed to make severe maneuvers. Now, we are again headed for Broome at a greater speed. Ladies and gentlemen, you're traveling faster than anyone before you in a submarine. We are moving at forty knots: that's forty-six miles an hour, a record. However, that is not our mission. Our mission is to get you safely to Broome.

Australian authorities will meet us at the pier, and my information is that you will be taken to an interim lodging facility for processing. The Australian government has granted all Christians and those of other faiths who wish to ask for political asylum citizenship after ninety days. In the meantime, everyone will live here under a regular visa.

At this point, it is clear that the North American Communist Government will imprison or execute any Christians caught. Unfortunately, everyone was warned that this situation had occurred before in history, and the people ignored it. Unfortunately, it is now a reality in what was America.

Work with the authorities, and we will live to see a brighter day. Captain out."

****

Adrian Gibson spent the remaining hours of the morning preparing the probable cause and search warrants for the property in Maine. The primary support for the warrants were hostilities against the socialist government, a clear threat to the regime's national security, and absconding with national secrets and devices of power generation.

Gibson took it to the local Ministry of Justice, and following a review, he stood before a judge, who asked, "Do you swear?"

Raising his hand, Gibson said, "Yes, your honor, I swear everything in the application and warrant is true and accurate."

An attorney representing the State asked to be heard.

"Granted," the judge said.

"Your honor, The sensitive issue of the unknown and suspected alien and its power in breaking free the prisoners remains under investigation. Therefore, we request that the court seal the documents in the interest of State Security."

I Concur; these proceedings and documentations are now sealed until the State needs them."

"Thank you, your honor."

Following a brief discussion with the State's Attorney, Gibson returned to his office to complete the paperwork for the Air Force assistance and the raid by the local office of Homeland Security.

Gibson called his supervisor and brought him up to speed on the case and he expected a call from the senator.

"Yeah, that guy has been sniffing around here; he's looking to further his political career at our expense. So therefore, I want you to use a lot of discretion and caution when dealing with that guy; he's a political rattlesnake who will throw anyone under the bus to further his ambitions."

"I got that right off the bat," Gibson said.

The Chicago SAC made a copy of everything and walked it to the Officer-in-Charge office, where Roxanne Stewart reviewed the reports, charges, and warrants.

"How sure are you that we're dealing with a supernatural being or extra-terrestrial?"

"Absolutely convinced; I saw it with my own eyes, and there was nothing human about it."

"Very well, I trust you know our careers will be on the line with this one."

"Yes, ma'am," Gibson agreed.

"Good luck, bring back something with tangible substance."

Gibson turned to leave, his teeth tightly clenched in determination to capture all the people at that compound, dead or alive, preferably alive.

****

True to predictions, the snowstorm hit the Maine coast, dropping almost nine inches of the powdery white stuff across a large swath of the coastline. The staff remained from the first shipment of refugees, and after an hour and a half, vehicle and pedestrian traffic moved with respectable ease around the property. The long shed and covered pier area escaped the snow removal activities. The singular contents of the shed, the transfer boat, sat on blocks to keep it from sustaining winter ice damage. While on the blocks, the spring will bring an overhaul to the handsome craft.

Adrian Gibson met with the men and women of the assault team in the DHS gym at the Bangor Air Force Base. Largely composed of selected former special forces operatives, most women served in the Army Military Police, and all carried the combat veteran status.

Captain Norman Haggard directed the attention of the newly named Storm Troopers to an uncovered terrain-less map disclosing the target house in the center.

"Lieutenant Michaels, Dorman, and Carter will supervise the assault on this house and attached supply barracks. The company will divide into four sections. Michaels will lead the south force, Dorman the gravel lane assault, and Carter will come in from the north. Everett Newsome will bring the fourth group up the tributary from the mouth by boats and insert their men into the covered shed from the water. We do not know if the shed is a landing or a small shipbuilding and launching site.

All attempts must be made to capture the occupants alive, but self-defense counter-fire is authorized. We have evidence that the occupants are radical right-wing mercenaries and are expected to be armed. Therefore, caution is in order.

Gibson took over the briefing; "Air cover will consist of a pair of armed Apache Helicopters, as needed. In addition, each ground team will have an armored Humvee with a mounted M-60 machine gun on top."

"Agent Gibson, isn't that a bit of overkill firepower?" Senator Robert Michaels asked.

"It is needed for self-protection, Senator. These right-wing radicals have known connections to armed right-wing revolutionaries."

"It was my understanding that all individuals were prohibited from owning or possessing any type of firearm," the Senator asked.

"That's true; the problem lies with those who hid weapons for revolutionary attacks. It takes time to root all those weapons, and it is not uncommon for the revolutionaries to put up a fight."

"I see," muttered the Senator.

"Senator, this is standard support procedure; in recent past stand-offs, our people only carried their sidearms until we began taking casualties. In addition, we have received information that the revolutionaries have made plans for a counter-offensive against the government, and we expect they have automatic weapons. That will not be tolerated, and the criminals will be dealt with in a proper manner."

The teams reviewed the targets, their approach, and their takedown procedures during the remainder of the day. A four-man team left early to carry out pre-attack surveillance. Then, with the heavy layer of snow on the ground, the team parachuted from five thousand feet into the nearby timber in an attempt to avoid footprints left from a march.

****

An alien visitor had become Washington's open secret. The possibility that the visitor could be an angel was quickly crushed under official actions. First, the government refused to validate such a being because to do so would validate God, whose existence the government refuses to accept because communism is the antithesis of everything God represents.

In place of the angel theory, the government floated a story that the light observed from the Federal building window was, in effect, a pioneering and classified welding technique. When that excuse failed to pass muster, the alien visitor developed. The government began feeling the power of the media to produce the so-called visitor until a visit by the head of the Ministry of Information who used intimidation to convince the press of the errors of its ways.

During this time, Ethen, also known as the former Miles Vickers to the unsaved, had no doubts that Timothy was an angel and one on a mission from on high. His contact with this created being was the catalyst in opening his heart to the Lord.

Ethen contemplated requesting a transfer to Kansas or Iowa to allow his mind and soul to heal from the years of abuse he absorbed in Washington. The job's characteristic changing of the agent's distinguishing traits for the worse cost him his marriage. His wife divorced him and found a better life in Missouri with their two children.

As Miles Vickers, Ethen never developed a strong spiritual relationship with God, and the years in DC exacerbated any chances of redemption. Now, with a better life before him, Ethen needed to get away from evil's playground and return to God's fold. The man looked for a place of peace until he was transferred.

****

Early morning was shattered by the start of two Apache war machines and the warming-up period. Two heavy-hulled boats of the DHS seaside assault force were lifted by CH47 helicopters to Sawyer Cove at Jonesport for launching toward the target property. At the DHS office on the Bangor Air Force base, three heavy combat trucks warmed up for their ingress into the expected combat zone. The land transport left early because they had the furthest distance to travel.

By zero-nine hundred, the force stood ready. SAC Gibson held the mike to his lips for a short time, then calmly said, "Execute, execute, execute."

The idling trucks and boats roared into life, charging for the quiet, sleeping homestead. The two boats slowed as they entered the dark, sheltered landing, where they looked about the empty work and mooring spots. A spotlight lit the transport boat, leading the troopers to it. The blue and white boat sat silently on the support blocks. Two soldiers went aboard and returned empty-handed.

"There is nothing in the boat; everything is spotlessly clean." One trooper called to the assault boat captains.

"Everyone, head for our secondary target," sending the men across the snow to the side door of the house.

Lieutenant Dorman arrived at the front of the house and took up defensive positions awaiting the troops to arrive on the flanks. Dorman acknowledged that the boat troops were at the side door.

Gibson pulled up in a Humvee and stepped out. He waved at Dorman to breach the large house.

The central unit made a combat entry into the house and was startled to find eight people sitting at a long table with breakfast before them and saying grace over food.

Reverend Richard Johnson, newly arrived with his wife, Linda, from California, looked up at the men and smiled.

"Gentlemen, I'm Chaplain Dick Johnson, and you are just in time, care to join us for breakfast."

Dorman's mouth slammed shut. "I'm sorry to disturb you, but we're looking for Martin Philips."

"Martin and a group of folks went for a boat ride, and we haven't seen them since. I and my family," he waved his arm about the table, "Just arrived from California. We were contacted by Mr. Wagner, the house's caretaker, and asked to sit and clean the house and buildings. Is there anything we can do for you? We have hot coffee if you would like a cup."

"You said you are a Chaplain, a Chaplain of what?" Dorman asked.

"I provide Chaplain services for the California Highway Patrol, the Sheriff's office in Coon Valley, and for the military personnel in the area, that is, until we were asked here."

Gibson stood in the background, taking in all the information. There was something in the kindly man's voice that rang true. For one thing, their vehicles arrived just after the snow ended and bore all the stickers and license plates from the far western state.

Dorman asked for the Reverend's papers and looked them over. Everything was up to date and complete. He handed the documents to Gibson, who double-checked the information and then made a quick call.

When he hung up, he quietly said to Dorman, "Question him again on the time they got here, who they were with, if anyone, and who was here when they arrived." Then the SAC stepped out the door, meeting Lieutenants Michaels and Carter.

"We're too late. They fled by boat before the current occupants arrived, and they're telling the truth about not knowing where the absconders went.

"Sorry to drag you and your men out on a dry case." The dejected agent knew he was in for hot questioning when he returned to Chicago, but it wasn't the first time.

AUSTRALIAN CHRISTIANS

CHAPTER FIFTEEN

Agent Gibson, are you going to set up surveillance on this place after we're done?

"No, the ones I want have disappeared. I couldn't justify the manpower or logistics for such an operation at this point. So let them be, as long as they don't cause trouble."

"Yes, sir," Dorman said. Then, the trooper turned to the other two Lieutenants, let's get these people back to base and stand down."

****

Reverend Dick Johnson watched the black-clad troopers mount up and drive off. "Dave, drive into town for a gallon of milk, and while you're out, see if their spies are left behind."

"Yes, Dad; anything else needed?"

"No, I believe we have what is sufficient to clean up for the next group; they should begin arriving in a day or two. I have no idea when the submarine will return. Our people on Steele Harbor Island will let us know when it gets in and when she can head south again."

After Dave left and the rest of the family was busy cleaning the breakfast table, nobody noticed the mist form in the corner of the room.

The messenger, dressed in working man's clothing, stepped up to Dick, "Pastor Dick."

"Dick Johnson about jumped out of his shoes from the start. "You're awful quiet for a big man. And whom might you be?"

"I have been looking forward to meeting you; I have heard of your devotion to He who created us, I am Timothy."

"Your reputation precedes you, Timothy," Out of habit, Dick held out his hand.

"I have never shaken hands before; this will be a wonderful lesson for me," the angel claimed.

The two shook hands, and Timothy, smiled, "It is a pleasurable sensation to feel your truth, honesty, and devotion to our Creator."

"You could feel that? Dick asked.

"Yes, and our Father is pleased with you."

Pastor Dick stood, stunned to silence, with his wide grin and sparkling eyes, looking at his first angel. Then, coming back to reality, Dick asked, "May I introduce you to our family?"

"I would like that."

Following the introductions, Dick and Timothy walked toward the door, "I am curious; you did not tell anyone who I am, and I sense a strategy behind it."

"Each human must be seen as who they truly are, not as whom you may wish they are."

"My Creator was indeed correct, as always; you are a wise man, and one of my responsibilities is to learn about you and the Christians in your flock. Thank you. I will start cleaning the barracks if you need me."

"We will be there shortly."

Dick and Linda Johnson called their flock together and headed for the next-door barracks. Richard brought a disc-playing radio and set it up with a disc of favorite hymns and music.

Dave returned from Jonesport's small grocery and joined the work party in the barracks. Dave said, "According to those I spoke with, the soldiers drove straight through town without stopping. I learned that the townsfolks are close neighbors, and outsiders are quick to be noted. By the way, there are some nice-looking churches in town; maybe we can get a chance to attend some of their worship."

"We will, even if it means making time available. Nothing must stand between the Lord and his people," the Pastor confirmed.

****

Pastor Mickey finished his sermon, thanking the Lord for his bounty and protection. Before closing the service. He reminded the congregation of their responsibility to reach out to those who do not know the Lord or have no church and to be open with members of other Christian congregations."

In the normal chaos of the people departing the service, Mickey shook the hands of the third couple from another church in Jonesport.

"Pastor Mickey," James Hitchfield began, "Mrs. and I wish to thank you for your sermon and fine words. We found your sermon to be timely in the current events, and we want to welcome you and your flock to Broome.

One of the standards for immigration to Australia is that the immigrant must have a self-supporting endeavor, be a teacher, or have other positive attributes, but not come here thinking Australia will support them."

"I'm glad you brought that up. This next week we had planned to set up a meeting with the Shire's councils and Broome's leaders. Our church council has worked with the Australian Embassy personnel to identify any people in our church does not meet your health requirements. After several inoculations, our people have been pre-screened and approved for permanent Visas.

As for skills, every family has one or more members who are trained and skilled workers. No family will be dependent upon the government for any assistance. We have experienced dental Doctors and technicians, including two qualified dental manufacturers. We have no less than seventeen Medical Doctors in various fields and twenty-eight trained, skilled, and registered nurses, including two trauma and three surgical nurses.

We have skilled construction people, electricians, welders, and two experts in metal molding, construction, and finish carpenters. Then there are painters and half a dozen interior decorating specialists. There are two certified divers and over a dozen applicants in training. The list is even longer, and more trained and capable Christians will be coming."

"Thank you, Pastor Mickey. I was told you were an FBI agent. Is that true?"

"Yes, it is I was a field agent; that is where the true FBI agents are at their best. I was never a supervisor; I turned the supervisor position down twice and was a field agent for over thirty years.”

“Tell me, Pastor; you weren’t involved in any political Tom Foolery, were you?”

“No, I retired years before politicians weaponized the agency.”

“Yes, all citizens looked up to the FBI as the quintessential law enforcement agency in the world until the politicians ruined it.”

“Every field agent and the former agents agrees with you,” Mickey said.

“Pastor Mickey, it is a pleasure to have you and your church come to Broome and our Shire. We look forward to having you integrate into our community and, if you wish, seek citizenship.”

“I’m certain many will; our homeland no longer exists,” the Pastor said.

“I’m sorry for that; we face the same enemy here.”

“Don’t let them gain control; it would be a disaster for everyone.”

“Yes, Australia’s leaders are quite knowledgeable on their tactics, determination, and intentions. However, they will not succeed.”

Finally, the congregation and visitors departed for their homes and other destinations. Mickey, his wife, and their adult children walked the short distance to their temporary residence, enjoying the warm morning sunshine.

Lunch and a church council meeting covered many subjects, including a proposal to build a desalination plant at the city limits to provide additional fresh water during the dry season.

When finished, the council planned to meet with the Shire and city leaders with their plans for homes, small businesses, and a list of skilled and unskilled labor available. They also had a list of proposals to benefit all the residents of Broome.

Time had become an issue because the church expected another Christian group to arrive within three or four weeks.

The Australian leaders expressed their gratitude for the quality of people the Americans who arrived. Their pre-transit preparation surprised the rough-hewn Australians. The American church leaders presented a bright future; however, it would take more than words to convince the experienced town and Shire leadership to accept them as equals.

****

In Chicago, during the after-action debriefing, the lack of timeliness and surveillance carried the tags as the cause of the mission failure. Hindsight is always easier than proper preparation to place blame where it is wanted. Ethan sat at the back of the room, avoiding all attempts at being involved in the case. Thinking about the timing of his dismissal, he wondered if the celestial powers had anything to do with it. At a late morning break, Ethan took advantage of the minor chaotic gathering in a foyer to leave and head for the plane which would take him to Rapid City.

Another attendee, the former Senator Robert Michaels, hobnobbed with other guests saying, "Now that we have solidified our hold on the government, the right will never see a presidency again. In fact, with their Constitution and so-called Bill of Rights trashed, the former Congress and Senate are empty seats. We have voted to tear down all the big government sites, the Capital, Lincoln, Jefferson, and Washington monuments. The White House will become the North American Communist Seat for the use of the President, who will be named shortly.

All religious movements are now banned, their properties and buildings will be torn down, and useful buildings will be built in their place. In addition, anyone caught wasting their time in clandestine meetings will be apprehended and sent to Siberia for re-education training.

All those who engage in offenses against nature will be imprisoned where they can't spread disease. Drug merchants, dealers, and users will be executed on apprehension. That is what it will take, then we will have a decent civilization, unlike what the unruly charlatans that sat in Washington before we took over implemented.

There will be no scummy-looking individuals with loudspeakers stirring up trouble and riots." All looters, arsonists, robbers, and the like will receive significant prison sentences. Abortionists, their helpers, and hags seeking them will…let's say, disappear from the streets."

One DHS listener noticed a red lapel pin with a gold inlaid hammer and sickle replacing his Senate pin. Special Agent Ryan Ferris drifted away from the one-time senator, serious concerns flooding his mind. Ferris had already decided to leave DHS, he was a Christian, and the DHS would lead the federal agencies in ferreting out and firing any religious people, and that is if they were lucky.

His supervisor was out when he arrived at his DHS office. Knowing several of the people in the office were now quiet Christians, he called for them to meet in a small conference room, which he swept for listening devices.

When the last person he contacted arrived, he locked the door and had them cluster around him in a tight circle just inside a chair and table closet. He gave them the bad news in a low, almost whisper voice. Looks of fear and anger distorted the people's faces.

Many wanted to find a way out of the country while they still could, remembering the horrors which occurred along the Berlin wall, from one end of German to the other. And the murders by the Communists in Hungry, Poland, and Baltic states.

"Get to your Pastors. Hopefully, they can help you with what you need. But, no matter what happens, you must not deny the Lord; to do that will blot your name out of the Book of Life, from which there is no return."

One young Christian woman asked, "What do you mean?"

Ferris explained, "The Lord says not to fear the first death. The first death is what all living things face. We will go to our graves. But when the Lord comes again, he will restore us before Him. Then there will be judgment; we must all answer for our unforgiven sins. The Books will be checked, and if a person in the Book of Life denies the Lord, their name will be blotted out, and they will go to the Lake of Fire for eternity.

"Yes, it is a narrow path we have chosen to follow, but the Lord will help us if we ask and let Him. And the rewards are beyond your dreams."

"How do you know that?" She asked.

"Spiritual verities are not discoverable by human wisdom. *1st Corinthians: 2- 9-10 'But as it is written. Eye hath not seen, nor ear heard, neither have entered into the heart of man, the things which God hath prepared for them that love Him. But God has revealed them to prepared man. Verse ten: But God hath revealed them unto us by His Spirit: for the Spirit searcheth all things, yea, the deep things of God.'"*

"Ryan, where is all this leading?"

"I don't mean to frighten you, but you have seen what has happened to our country. It has fallen almost to the bottom with what I have told you. So, all I can offer is to take your family and head north to Canada; they have a socialistic way but are still democratic and have the throne of England. Once there, ask for asylum from religious persecution. I would suggest seeking passage to New Zealand, Australia, or another UK destination, but not England or any of the Islands, as they are too close to Russia. There is one possibility, select one trusted, strong Christian and have him go to the church and speak with Pastor Al, he may be able to help—one last word. Remember, keep the faith, and keep your eyes on Jesus. We are all going to die the first death, but I, for one, will not deny my God. Now do what you must, and may our Lord go with you and keep you close to Him."

The quiet group broke up, and in minutes the office was vacant.

****

Two men knocked on the door of the camouflage-painted house and were waiting for a response. Then one, Reverend Joshua Manning, said, "Listen, I hear hymns." So the two men followed the sound of music to the barracks, where they found the Johnsons and Timothy singing and cleaning.

Linda Johnson saw the two men first and instinctively knew they were no threat. "Hi," her cheerful voice rang out in the empty room, "What can we do for you?"

"We would like to talk to the Reverend Dick Johnson, do you know where we can find him?"

"Certainly, he is my best friend and husband; come with me." In the next room, Dick and Timothy checked some minor damage caused by child play. "Dick, these gentlemen wish to speak with you."

Linda returned to her chores, and Dick held his hand to the two strangers, followed by a smiling Timothy. "What can we do for you?"

The men told their third-hand story, and Dick turned to Timothy, who closed his eyes to speak from his heart to the Lord.

The two strangers watched, unsure of what was happening or if they had come to the right place.

Timothy opened his eyes, "Pastor Dick, our Lord has commanded that all who are called by His name are to seek passage here. Therefore, our new visitors are to assemble here immediately and take shelter in these barracks. Then, after dark, I will lead them to our jumping-off facility, we will walk across the ice to the station, and the people can stay and rest there. Then he addressed the two men.

"Gather your flocks and tell them to pack a three-day change of clothing and personal items, and nothing else. Then you will contact this man; he will bring you here on a bus. None of your church is to contact non-believers or those whose beliefs are unknown. To do so will jeopardize your safety. We will make the trip in two days when the ice is thick enough to walk upon."

One of the two, a layman, asked, "How do you know these things?"

"My friend, I have a feed on the weather as far as it will affect us. My source is very accurate."

The man turned to his partner. Pastor Brett, I'm not sure I can do this; these people are crazy. I'll see you at church on Sunday." Then the man left, muttering to himself.

Pastor Brett started to follow him when Timothy said, "He will be fine for a while; you must let him leave."

"I must stop him; I know he is short-fused and cynical, but he means well."

Pastor, you believe in angels, don't you?" Timothy asked.

"Yes, certainly, they are God's messengers and, at times, our caretakers; why?"

"What do you think they look like?"

"I have no idea, there have been thousands of pictures, drawing, and figures depicting angels over the centuries; it is hard to say what they look like," the Pastor explained.

"Show him, Timothy," a soft, smooth voice came from the ceiling.

The Pastor looked up for the speaker and, finding none, suddenly got frightened. First, he looked at Dick, who smiled in enjoyment, then at Timothy, who said, do not fear; his work clothes vanished, leaving him suspended a foot off the floor in a white robe and eight-foot wings extended.

The Pastor fell backward onto a pile of cleaning rags. Timothy knelt beside the fallen man, and he awoke, his eyes wide in fear.

"Do not fear, Pastor Brett, I will not harm you."

The man stuttered at first, then took a breath and asked, are you a real angel?"

"I am."

"Is this a dream?"

"No dream," said Dick; "I'm too sore from cleaning to be in a dream."

"Pastor Brett," Timothy addressed the almost dumbfounded man. "I am here to supervise the movement of those Christians who will leave this country. Are you and your flock wanting to leave?"

"Some of our people heard of ugly things in store for those of religious beliefs, and the speaker suggested leaving while you can."

"I know, and he spoke the truth. There are two possible ways to flee: to come here or drive north to the Canadian border while they are still open. You may, of course, choose to remain at home, but you know that and what is coming."

"If you're an angel, surely you know when the rapture will happen, don't you?"

"Review the Book of *Matthew, Chapter 24, verse 36, 'But of that day and hour knoweth no man, no, not the angels of heaven, but My Father only.'* No, Pastor Brett, I do not know," Timothy said.

"What must I do to help my people?"

Timothy smiled, "Now, you are thinking and acting as a shepherd. Tell your flock to pack clothing for three days and necessary personal items, nothing more. A bus will stop at your church in three days, be ready."

"Pack clothes for three days and the necessary personal items; meet the bus in three days at the church," the Pastor repeated.

"What of my friend?"

"He does not remember this day."

****

The *ARK* sped toward their pen at thirty knots following a proven safe passage for submerged boats. Unknown to her crew, a U.S. boat interested in the *Ark's* speed tagged along about five hundred yards behind.

Captain Thomas Latham checked with the sonar shack for identification. "Sir. We have no references to this boat in our banks. I don't think it's Russian because there are some noise transients that are consistent with a *688 Los Angeles* class. The confusion is the lack of other transients we have on file."

"How about a modified boat?" The Captain asked.

"Certainly possible, sir. However, nothing is coming in that trips the identifiers in the computer. I can tell you this is the most noiseless plant I have ever heard of. Another thing, this boat has two screws."

"Is there any engine noise at all?"

"The closest is a weak level hum coming from the port and starboard sides. Possibly a nacelle housing an electric motor. But, at thirty knots, a motor at that speed would give off a higher pitch and volume."

Captain Latham stood, silently thinking. "We would almost have to see it out of the water to figure this out. Let's see if we can figure out what we're dealing with, then take it from there. I'll check back in an hour."

The hour elapsed in an amazingly short time, and the sonar shack had no answers.

"OOD, send the crew to General Quarters and sound the collision alarm. Three minutes later, the *SEAWOLF* class boat pulled alongside the *ARK* at five hundred yards to the starboard.

"Captain Holeman, we have a *SEAWOLF* class boat five hundred yards off our starboard side."

A slightly garbled underwater voice bounced off the hull of the *ARK,* "This is the *USS SEAWOLF* off your starboard side. Please identify yourself."

"Now, what do we do, Captain?" the OOD Asked.

"That's Tom Latham's boat. He's a good friend and a man of the fold." The Captain picked up the mike to the underwater communications.

"Tom, this is Brad Holeman; how did you find us?"

"By a low-power hum from a motor; otherwise, you're a hole In the water. I thought you retired."

"I did."

"But you're in a dead quiet 688, and that has to be something very special."

"Yeah, special, it is. Let's talk privately; check the surface and we can go to hard wire."

"Roger that."

The surface of the sub-tropical Atlantic was glass smooth. The two boats surfaced and rigged a ship-to-ship sound-powered phone line.

"Okay, Brad, how did you get that 688?"

"My boss did the procurement; I'm just the driver."

"Brad, we've been friends for over twenty years and were Godfathers to our kids; what have you gotten into?"

"How secure is your line?"

"Hold one."

"It's just you and me, Brad."

Captain Holeman told his friend what he needed to know about their operation. Then he asked, "Have you any news on current events at home?"

"No, we're blacked out."

Brad explained the takeover of the socialist government and the complete turnover to communism. And officials promised to destroy all religious organizations and imprison those who didn't go to reeducation camps in Siberia.

"So, what's your part in all this?"

"I'm taking those Christians who want to leave to a fresh start."

"Kind of like an underground railroad, then?"

"Exactly. Are you and Sandy still going to the base Chapel in New London?"

"Yes, and we have missed you, but now I understand. Do you have the same cell number?"

"yes, but be advised, all calls are now monitored, remember, we now have a paranoid Communist regime running the country, and nobody or rank is of any security."

"I understand; I'll be in touch."

The line was broken, and after retrieval, the two submarines dove and went their separate ways. As they did, both Captains lapsed into deep thought.

INDIAN OCEAN AT BROOME. AUSTRALIA

CHAPTER SIXTEEN

At the first meeting of the church body, the leaders formed a committee to work with the city fathers on projects and other needs the city would require in providing services to an increased population.

Chief Electrician Marvin Davies said, "On the engineer's drawing boards lay plans to generate electrical power, and desalination plants, including using old ships for electric energy and water supply. Other areas needing discussion are carpenters, bricklayers or stone workers, plumbing, medical, and additional workers. In addition, questions about permits and required minimum standards must be addressed for them to meet the city's ordinances.

One primary concern is developing housing and where the city fathers wanted this to occur, and we will need to appoint the first Planning and Zoning Coordinator. In addition, stores, transportation, and repair facilities, and how we can work them into the city's overall plans, need clarification. Another concern is the strain placed on the underground aquifer feeding Broome, with possible methods we have looked at to help maintain and increase the abundance of fresh water."

Elie took advantage of the engineering lull to find employment as a nurse in the Broome hospital. In outlying towns, medical services were always in need of trained and qualified personnel. The church council's reliance on the engine, Martin understood, was not for man. He needed to speak with

Timothy and get guidance from above on handling it. The issue became problematic with the suspected need for more energy.

Martin felt the potential issue surrounding the special engine may become detrimental to the Lord's command; Martin excused himself to find solitude where he could lay it before the Lord.

Not expecting an immediate response, Martin jumped when startled by the voice behind him, "Martin, is everything all right?"

"Oh, Timothy, I wasn't expecting you so soon."

"I didn't mean to frighten you."

"No, I'm fine, but I need guidance on a serious issue."

"I know, the use of the engine. Is there a way to disguise or prevent anyone from seeing it?"

"From our people, yes. My chief concern is a state official snooping around and demanding to see what we use for seemingly unsupported electrical generation. If coming from a vessel, we can easily deflect questions. However, security becomes progressively weakened if the unit is mounted publicly or on private property."

Timothy took the issue to his higher authority, then turned to Martin, "You may rest assured, there will be no unauthorized individuals checking on the power supplies."

"Thank you, Timothy, and give my thanks to God."

"You're welcome, and our Lord would prefer you thank Him in your prayers."

"Of course, I knew that when I said it."

Martin returned to the committee meeting and took his seat.

At an appropriate opening, Martin asked for the floor and was recognized.

"Ladies and gentlemen, thank you for your attention. The water issue is easily solved by salvaging fresh water distilling plants from decommissioned military and civilian sea-going vessels. Our designed engine can supply the necessary heating and electrical needs to make the distillers operational reasonably at well below the costs of building a new one. With it, we can help provide the city with water, and the overflow is then diverted to the aquifer."

"An interesting solution," Noel Lancaster answered. "Would you like to head up a committee to assemble the proposal?"

"I would, however, I am already committed to the construction and supervision of development, research, and construction of the engines we use, along with the development of the proposed distilling sites."

"You are and will be a busy man, and thank you for your service to our people," Lancaster said.

"Not to seem snobbish or conceited, but we must consider this not for our people, but the people of Broome, which now includes us."

"You are right, Martin; thank you for reminding all of us of that fact. And for the record, you are neither snobbish nor conceited, my friend."

****

Following the encounter with the *USS SEAWOLF,* the *ARK* approached its pen; the radio operator contacted the pen control center.

"Steele Control, this is the *ARK*; we request mooring directives."

"*ARK*, echo, one victor."

In return, the radio operator answered, "*ARK*, November 58 indigo."

"Welcome back; wait for the full opening of the door, then moor starboard side to your previous location."

A half-hour later, with the Captain on the sail bridge, the first line recorded the end of the submarine's first mission.

Captain Holeman left the sail and headed for the hatch leading to the forward half of the main deck. He made his way past crewmen installing the stanchions supporting the safety lines.

Pastor Johnson met the Skipper on the pier. "Welcome home, Captain, it's good to see you again. I trust you had a quiet trip."

"Thank you, Pastor, and Pastor Mickey asked me to say hi for him, he is very high on you and your family. He, his wife, and family await you in Broome; I believe you will find that community an excellent place to live."

"I've heard there are intensely poisonous snakes there."

"There are snakes on every landmass in the world, with the exclusion of the Antarctic shires, Ireland, and a few other small islands. And yes, Inland Taipan snakes are around, but they are quite shy and try to stay clear of humans. They prey on small mammals and keep them in balance with nature. Snake bites are rare these days, and we have a ready supply of antivenom in the event of a bite."

"I would hate to see a grandchild bitten by one."

"I agree, but, as I said, snake bites are rare, especially in towns."

"I can live with that."

"Good, If you would have the people gather their traveling clothes. We will be settling in a tropical environment, and you will not need more than a sweater in the cooler evenings in June through August."

"That's right; the weather patterns are reversed here and there."

"Yes," the Captain said, "Broome is in its summer season now."

"Thank you, Captain; our people will be ready to board at your command."

"Very well, we will need the first day to load supplies; if you can, would you round up about a dozen strong young people to help load the supplies? So, our men and women can get them properly packed."

"That won't be a problem; when would you like them here?"

Captain Holeman pointed to the three flatbed vehicles pulling up to the pier, each stacked with provisions.

"I'll begin fetching them as soon as I get to the phone."

The afternoon sun closed on the horizon by four PM, but the pen's closed doors hid the waning daylight. The crew didn't have to wait long before the working party arrived. Under the supervision of experienced former sailors, the provisions found their way to the appropriate storage sites below decks.

The families set up lines to help the needy members easier boarding through the sail elevator while the others utilized the ladders.

By eighteen-forty hours, the passengers were setting up their temporary quarters and preparing for their new homes. Captain Holeman and the crew prepared to get underway on the sail bridge at eighteen-fifty-five.

The sun dipped below the treetops, and the pen doors opened after the operations crew ensured no boat or air traffic was in the vicinity. Then, the Captain expertly maneuvered the big submarine out of the pen and cove to the open waters of the Atlantic.

There they met the *SEAWOLF*. As the boats passed, semaphore flags were used for communications. Following a brief flag conversation, Captain Holeman contacted Pen Control.

"Pen Control, *ARK*."

"Pen Control."

"Have companion headed for you; I vouch for him. So now we are two."

"Pen Control copies, have a good trip. Pen out."

Captain Holeman watched through his binoculars as the great doors opened for the big sub.

"Captain, we have three hundred-plus feet beneath the keel."

"Very well, Check with the board."

The talker said, "Board has one red, our hatch, all others green."

"Very well," the Captain acknowledged. The six-foot-tall sailor looked three-hundred-sixty degrees through his binoculars and found no contacts on the winter ocean.

"Radar, sitrep."

"We are clear to our limits, and the weather holds us to eighty miles."

"Very well, shut it down and stow all electronic scopes and shafts. OOD, you have the conn, take her down to two hundred feet, at fifty feet per minute."

"Aye, sir."

The bridge team disappeared below the lip of the open bridge, and the covers slid snugly into their slots. As the Captain dropped into the control room, a crewman sealed the hatch, changing the red light to green on the board. The sound of released compressed air came from forward of the sail, sending a spray of water-saturated air two hundred feet into the air, and the bow nosed a little deeper into the icy water.

The dive provided a gentle dip forward for the passenger's comfort, and then the boat leveled at two-hundred feet below the surface. Once the sub crossed the Continental Shelf, the order to dive to five-hundred feet repeated the process. Six minutes later, the boat leveled off and turned to the course of their first run.

"OOD, increase speed to forty knots; use the standard acceleration chart."

"Aye, Captain," he repeated the order and then complied.

The captain gave the crew and passengers the same information the first group received. Then everyone settled in for a boring trek toward the 'Downunder.'

"Captain," a voice came from the adjoining passageway.

Captain Holeman went to the hatch, "Ahhh, Pastor Johnson, stop up to see the control center?"

"Yes, it fascinates me how a submarine works."

"I understand you do a lot of Chaplain duties," Holeman said.

"Yes, for law enforcement and military."

"We can always use a Sky Pilot here. Could I interest you in conducting services as needed?"

"It would be an honor, Captain. Let me know when and where. Here is our cabin and phone number; I look forward to helping wherever possible."

****

At six-hundred-thirty-seven miles southeast of Steele Island lay the Akula submarine commanded by Captain First Class Eduard Valentin Sidorov, not unlike a spider resting in its web.

The Captain pulled the boat-wide communications microphone from its holding clip. "This is the Captain, our brief time near the surface allowed us to gather our download from Polyarny.

One of our Yasen boats encountered an unknown submarine with two screws, which did not match anything in our data banks. That is not unusual, as our navy constantly designs unusual and better boats. In this case, Polyarny says that the submarine is not ours. That only leaves the Americans who can build a vessel capable of forty knots. We will intercept that boat, provided we can pick it up. Then we are instructed to force it to the surface for inspection. Captain out."

"Officer of the Deck, take us to one-five-five meters, then go search quiet until we hear this American boat. And you might listen for Los Angles class submarines"

"Yes, Comrade Captain."

****

Captain Holeman's 688 cruised at forty knots in a southeasterly direction. The boat's noise signature remained lower than its contemporaries with the redesigned drive systems in place.

"Well, Captain," OOD Jack Morton said, "We're on our second trip to Broome; what do you think of the *ARK*?"

"To say impresses would be an understatement. I never expected I would command a submarine at these speeds. We knew it would come sooner or later when I was on active duty. I never thought I would become part of it. And to think, we still have twenty-five knots available to us."

"Are you going to try for the high-speed record?"

"No. First, we aren't in the navy any longer, and second, our modifications make this another class boat. A third factor is that no navy witnesses are recording the event."

"I know, and they are so picky, too."

"Mr. Morton, you have the conn; I'm going to tour our craft, then be available in my cabin. I'll call when I arrive there."

"Yes, sir."

With but a soft whir from the ventilation fans, the submarine silently glided toward the mid-Atlantic. The OOD checked their position regarding crossing the equator and found they had forty-one hundred miles to travel. A quick mental calculation told him it would take about three and three-quarter days.

Captain Holeman strolled along the starboard cabins, hearing children's laughter at play. Normally on a submarine, such a tour kept the commander looking for anything which could threaten his command. On this vessel, that still prevailed, as with every ship's commander at sea. However, he felt more like a shepherd on the previous and current voyage, and it felt good.

"Mrs. Hamilton, how are you today?" He asked a slim woman of forty, who was taking her son and daughter to the new land.

"I'm very well, Captain, thank you, and how are you with your boat?"

"Pleasantly surprised, this vessel was one of the best submarines built; however, the addition of a second screw and we believe the redesigned engines make it the fastest boat in the world. And so far, it has been a pleasure to command; it is exceedingly responsive. And better yet, it allows me to tour it more often and meet our guests.”

“Would you mind if I tag along? I try to walk every day, but that hasn’t been the case the past few days with all the preparations, travel, then getting aboard.”

“Not at all; I would enjoy your company.”

“Oh, Captain, you would have no trouble meeting nice young ladies in your position.”

“Contrary to belief, the Captain’s lot is largely lonely.”

“What about your family? Certainly, they provide a comfortable environment for you?”

“Normally, that is the case for the most part, but I lost my wife to cancer two years after we wed.”

“Oh, please forgive my intrusion; I had no idea.”

“That’s quite all right; Emily past several years ago, and I guess you can say I married the Navy.”

The two walked in an awkward silence, then Captain Holeman asked, “May I ask about your family?”

Helen Hamilton let her chin sink to her chest, then straightened up, and she announced, “My husband, Michael, was murdered in a shooting at a daycare center a year and a half ago.” Then she took a deep breath to settle herself down.

“Now, it’s my turn to grovel and apologize for bringing up a painful event.”

“No need, Captain; you had no way of knowing any more than I.”

“Are you getting along all right?”

“For the most part, yes. Sometimes the holidays get a bit difficult, but that too is easing with time.”

“I can appreciate that, but as you say, the holidays can be rough. May I ask if you plan to walk daily? Maybe we could get our legs stretched at the same time?”

“I’d like that, and my name is Helen.”

“Bradly, but I like Brad.”

“Brad, it is.”

“Here is the engine room; I usually stop by and talk with the men to let them know I appreciate their efforts.”

“Am I restricted?”

“Not at all,” Brad opened the hatch and allowed Helen to enter the surprisingly quiet space.

“This is extremely quiet for an engine room; I would have expected a much greater machinery noise,” Helen stated.

"You can thank the hand of the Lord for that. He is a master mechanic."

Brad pointed out the four generators with the covered engines, then showed Helen where the freshwater is produced, and all the pumps and auxiliary machinery quietly worked.

"Captain, er…Brad, I see the generators, but where are the engines?"

"Excellent observation, Helen. This generator on the starboard side provides electrical power to the starboard motor, which is mounted on the hull's exterior. The generator on the port side," where he pointed, "Provide the electrical energy to the port motor, or as we call them, thrusters."

"Interesting, and what does that generator service?"

"That is the ship's power supply generator. It provides electricity for all of the submarine's internal needs." Brad explained.

"That small unit does all that? I'm at a loss here," the red-haired woman said. "My brother was an engineer on several ships, and he would tell me all about the engineering workings of steam-powered ships. It got to the point I would dream about being in an engine room. But this does not fit the normal engineering plant, even for a submarine."

"Helen, I'm impressed; I had no idea you were so knowledgeable of mechanics and marine engineering."

Helen's shyness showed itself in the slow creep of reddening at her neck and working its way upward.

"I used to be a tomboy and liked working on lawnmowers, then eventually graduated to auto mechanics. And my brother's information naturally stuck."

"Where is he now?"

"He is working as a mechanic in the oil fields of Oklahoma, the last I heard."

"When we have time, I would like to sit and talk with you; it would be a great change from these characters," he pointed at the Chief Engineer, who stuck his tongue out, bringing a laugh from Helen.

Brad showed the interesting woman a turbine, still in its crate, and explained the mechanics of its operation.

"Brad, I thought that was impossible."

"What is that?"

"An engine that creates more energy than it needs to run is in perpetual motion; it will rewrite the laws of physics."

"Yes, it would if man got it, but this is the jewel God has prohibited man outside the Christian world to have access to. I would hazard to guess that because the history of man shows their desire to turn such things to evil ends, and this would be a game changer."

"That certainly makes sense," Helen agreed.

"What are the known limits of output?"

"That's the secret we don't have an answer for. It may be high enough to power an aircraft since it powers this craft. But, maybe more than that, we don't know."

"With what you said, how fast can it drive this sub?"

"We are limited to sixty-five knots by the nose structure of this boat. And that's almost seventy-five miles an hour."

Helen's hand covered her mouth at the revelation of power a few steps away.

"Captain, please come to the conn," came over the 1MC.

Captain Holeman grabbed the handset of the sound-powered phones. "What's up?" He asked the talker.

"Sir, we have a tail; Sonar said it sounds like an Akula. It isn't the boat we ran into on our first run."

"I'm in the engine room; I'll be right up."

"Come along, Helen, I need to get you to your cabin, and I need to get to the bridge."

"You go ahead; I'll make it all right."

"I'd like the pleasure of your company that far."

"Then, let's go."

When they reached her cabin, Helen said, "I enjoyed our walk, Brad, and look forward to the next one."

"As do I; maybe we can have dinner some evening."

"Maybe we can," she said, flashing him a smile that said yes.

The Captain reached the conn and announced his presence. "What do you have, Mr. Morton?"

"The Akula has asked for our identity and demanded an inspection."

"What did you say?"

"Het."

"I didn't know you spoke Russian."

"Just to say no."

"Let's get our passengers in their quarters and maintain quiet. Also, give them the speech we used on the last run when we first ran into that other character. We may have to leave him behind as well.”

A slightly garbled foreign voice bounced off the hull, “I say again, identify yourself, and be prepared to be boarded.”

The Captain picked up the underwater microphone and said, “This is a privately owned vessel in international seas. We have violated no international Law of the Sea. You have no jurisdiction here, and if you are a pirate, you are out of your league.”

“If you do not surrender, we will fire upon you.”

“Well, Mr. Morton, tell everyone to hold on tight; we are going for a ride. That boat carries the Type 533mm torpedo; we can outrun it, but not by much. Better pray for help from our Maker, or we may see Him before we think. Helm, all ahead flank, sixty-five knots.”

“Aye, sir,” a strong voice answered. But it wasn’t the watch Helmsman. The Captain turned and saw a white-robed Timothy smiling as he ordered the commanded speed.

The submarine lurched forward like a race car that was given a nitric oxide boost.

****

“Comrade Captain,” the Russian sonarman called, “He is gone; he accelerated to…to sixty-five knots and is gone.”

“Torpedo room, prepare to fire two Type 53 torpedoes.”

“Control room, tubes one and four are ready for launching.”

“Launch the torpedoes at two-second intervals.”

BROOME, WA

CHAPTER SEVENTEEN

"Comrade Captain, what have you done? You had no authority to attack that boat," the Political Officer screamed. "Moscow will have your head."

"They refused to comply with my orders; I have the authority from Polyarny."

"It is a terrible mistake; it could bring retaliation."

"From whom? They claimed it to be a private adventure; we have it on tape. I doubt whoever they are could mount any attack we can't evade or withstand. So, the issue is closed; the boat will sink without a trace."

****

Captain Holeman watched the *ARKs'* speed rapidly reach sixty-five knots, then called the former torpedo room, where many passengers huddled in concern at the sound of water rushing past the hull.

"Forward cabins, crewman Henry speaking."

"This is the Captain; how's the bow holding up?"

"All dry here, a bit of rushing water past the hull, but dry."

"Good, we'll maintain this speed for the time being, that Akula fired a pair of Type 53 fish at us, and we're leaving them behind."

"I'll speak with the passengers and keep them calm," Henry said.

"Great, I appreciate that."

"Aye, sir."

Captain Holeman turned to Timothy, who stood at the helm, smiling like a kid at the circus. "Timothy, we have much to thank the Lord for this day. He again saved His people from the clutches of evil."

"Yes, Captain, He has, and Our Creator appreciates your thoughts and praises. By the way, the Most High approves of you and Helen."

Brad dropped his head and offered a prayer of gratitude to the Lord for his approval. Then he heard a voice, "You're welcome."

Brad looked around, then at Timothy, who smiled and said, "Well done, Bradly."

For the first time, Captain Holeman couldn't find the right response. His mind blurred with the thought of God and an angel speaking to him. His emotions slipped into overdrive, but he fought off the urge to let his feelings have an outlet while at the conn.

"Thank you, Timothy," Brad croaked out. "OOD, maintain speed and course for ten minutes, then bring us to nine-hundred feet, same course, and go silent. I'll be back by then, if not before."

"Aye, Captain."

Brad headed for Helen's cabin; upon reaching it, he knocked lightly on the door. The red-haired lady, looking ten years younger than her age, smiled when opening the door. "Come in; we must talk."

"I have no more than a few moments and must return to the control center; we aren't out of danger just yet."

"I know; I wanted to tell you I had a visitor."

"Timothy?"

"Yes, and he had some startling news for me, and I admit, it was great."

"Me too. To give you the short version, our angel said we had been approved. That comes from the Highest level."

"Yes, I know."

"I know it has been a woefully short time for us, but I want you to know how serious I am. Will you marry me?" Brad asked.

"On authority and approval of my Lord, I will most certainly marry you; for some reason, I've known from the first moment I laid eyes on you while we were boarding that somewhere down the line, we would be together." She raised on her toes and gave him a light kiss, "Now, go be a sailor and get us to Broome; I have a feeling we are going to see a wedding there."

Brad hardly noticed he made it to the control center but put on his business mask when he entered the tense conn. "Report."

Mr. Morton's relief, OOD Carlton Devers, announced, "Captain on the bridge. Captain, we have left the Akula far behind, and the torpedoes are no longer in pursuit."

"Very well, Mr. Devers, take us to nine hundred feet and rig for silent running."

"Aye, sir."

Captain Holeman pulled the 1MC microphone, "This is the Captain. In case you are wondering, we encountered a Russian submarine whose commander wanted to board and inspect our boat. I have no doubt he intended to take everyone and this boat to his home base, where we would be detained, and the boat's secrets revealed.

"I will not allow that to happen. We have a superior speed which took us away from the Russians. They fired two torpedoes at us, but like the previous torpedoes, they were left behind. We all owe our lives to God for His gift to us. We have dived a little deeper and are going to what we call silent running. All passengers, please remain in your cabins, and lay down for a nap. It will be quiet and still, so that should help. Captain out."

Brad turned to Timothy, "Can you put the children to sleep with happy dreams while we disappear?"

"I will be glad to help." He said a second later, "The children and adults will be asleep peacefully once the sub reaches the ordered depth."

"You're an angel, Timothy."

"I know," he said, smiling.

"Mr. Devers, if you please."

The 688 dropped at fifty feet per minute, and eighteen minutes later, the boat leveled off at nine hundred feet, slowing to twenty knots. After that, the unique lack of noise came from the twin motors on each side of the hull, giving off a low-level hum that could not be detected ten feet away. Other than that, the *ARK* became a hole in the black water.

Brad asked the Navigation Officer, "How much water will be beneath us between here and Australia?"

After consulting with the track and depths, Mr. Charles, 'Chuck,' Praxton said, "We will have from eight to seventeen thousand feet below us to within a hundred miles of the Australian coast, and there are no seamounts on the maps."

"Thank you, Mr. Praxton; that sounds like smooth sailing."

"Anytime, sir."

In the sonar shack, the Captain said, "Keep a sharp eye on the passive array. I doubt we'll run across any submerged traffic, but I'd rather not discover their presence after we hit them."

"Yes, sir, and we agree, no bumper cars down here," the man in charge joked.

"OOD, have the crew, except the watch, turn in. They may as well take advantage of the quiet while they can."

"Aye, sir. And you?"

"I'll take a walkabout and maybe have a late dinner in my cabin, ask them to hold off securing until I check something."

"Yes, sir."

At Helen's cabin, Brad gave a light knock to avoid waking the children. The door swung open, and Helen stepped into the narrow passageway. Usually a bit shy, she felt no problem wrapping her arms around Brad's waist and quietly holding him securely to her. Brad responded, his big arms folding protectively around the great woman now in his life, feeling as normal about their grasp as if they had always been together.

After a minute of comfort, Brad asked, "Can you get away for the quiet supper we discussed?"

"Yes, my sister will watch over the children."

"You can tell her she can rest too; Timothy assured me everyone would be resting the night through."

Helen returned to the room, reappeared, slipped her arm around his, then strolled toward his quarters. At his cabin, the Captain took Helen's order and had the gally crew make two servings. After they served dinner, the Captain told them he would clean up, and they could turn in.

Following their meal, the two engaged in some small talk; Helen asked, "Do you think our lives will be guided from here on out?"

"I believe we will always need God's laws and guidance, and at the same time, we must use good judgment in our gift of choice."

"I agree? We seem to have been given a path to follow since we boarded?"

"The Lord has given us the right to choose our path. He has indeed given us laws to live by and rules to guide us from day to day. But we can follow our path if we want to. However, the Lord has given us the blueprint to live by in the Bible and trusts us to follow his wishes. Along with that, He knows we will make mistakes; that's why Holy Spirit is there to guide us, and Jesus is there to forgive us for our weaknesses. He knows we are weak and will make those mistakes, but as long as we follow the eleven commandments and ordinances and follow His daily guidelines, He is a forgiving God because He loves us."

"I thought there were Ten Commandments?"

"John 13:34 quotes Jesus, "A new commandment I give to you, that you love one another, even as I have loved you, that you also love one another."

"Now Jesus said that to His disciples, and aren't we, His disciples?" Asked Brad.

"You're right; Jesus even called it a new commandment."

The two continued their discussions for another two hours, then Brad said, "My dear, I have to return to work, but I need to get a little sleep first; let me walk you to your cabin."

As they strolled along the narrow passageway, they continued to trade ideas surrounding their future life together. Finally, Brad gave Helen a light kiss at her door and said, "Have happy dreams." They parted, and the sailor headed to his cabin to clean up the supper table and then had no problems falling asleep in his happy mindset.

The following morning, Captain Holeman ordered the boat to five hundred feet and maintained its course to an area two hundred miles off the northwestern coast of the 'Downunder' continent. The boat rose to periscope depth, where the Captain checked for other vessels. Finding none, he raised the radio mast and sent a burst message to Steele Island, outlining their voyage and encounter with the Russian Akula. Then he downloaded waiting mail.

Another burst went to the Australian Navy, alerting them of their presence, destination, and cargo. It was acknowledged with welcome and expected arrival information.

"Mr. Ackerman set our depth at two hundred feet and prepare to surface one-hundred-forty miles from Broome. And maintain a course of zero-seven-four-point-five degrees, twenty knots."

"Aye, sir."

"Captain, may I remain on the helm to dock?" a familiar voice asked.

The Captain looked at the duty Helmsman. "Sir, Timothy has passed all the requirements of a Helmsman, sir, and is the calmest Helmsman I've ever encountered."

Smiling, the Captain nodded his approval saying, "Of that, I have no doubt."

The three-hundred-sixty-two-foot submarine sailed smoothly at two hundred feet, and five hours later, "Mr. Ackerman, would you call Chaplain Johnson to the conn?"

"You wanted to see me, Captain?" The senior Chaplain asked upon arrival in the conn.

"Please, stand beside me, we will be surfacing shortly, and I thought you might enjoy your first look at your Australian home."

"Very thoughtful of you, Captain; it will be a once-in-a-lifetime event for me."

"Mr. Ackerman, make all preparations for surfacing."

"Aye, sir. Bo'sun on the 1MC, make all preparations for surfacing."

"Aye, sir." The call went out, sending the crew to their maneuvering stations for surfacing and entering port."

"Mr. Ackerman, we will moor to the jetty where the landing party awaits; you have the conn."

"Aye, sir."

"Mr. Ackerman, prepare to surface. Sonar, check for surface contacts."

"Conn, sonar, no surface vessels within fifteen miles, clear to periscope depth."

The OOD ordered, "Bring the *ARK* to periscope depth."

Compressed air forced water out of the bottom flood holes, and the lighter buoyancy raised the boat. As soon as the periscope head appeared, the Captain checked the immediate surface area for boat traffic. Seeing none, he nodded to the OOD.

"Surface, surface, surface." The alarm was sounded, and additional air flowed to the dive tanks, bringing the boat to the surface; then, the trim tanks were adjusted to level the vessel.

The hatch in the sail popped open, and the assembled lookouts scrambled up the ladder and opened the sliding bridge cap, then took their watch positions to observe everything around the submarine.

A talker, the Captain, and Chaplain Johnson followed the men up to the top of the sail. The Chaplain looked around the horizon, then at the bow to the stern of the sub.

"Oh, wow, I never dreamed I would have a sight such as this," the senior pastor said, his eyes wide, like a youngster who walked onto a ship for the first time.

"Captain, do you ever get used to such a grand view?"

"No, I never have. And there are sunrises and sunsets you can only dream of and see in photographs others have taken. The beauty takes your breath away."

"I can believe that," Dick Johnson said in a soft breath.

"Pastor, may I have a few moments of your time?"

"Certainly; what can I do for you?"

"It won't be right away, I don't think, but I would like to talk to you about a possible marriage."

"I think I can probably take care of that. When you are ready, call me. I want to sit and talk with you and your lady beforehand to ensure you're right for one another."

"That's a good idea, but this is something a bit different. You know Timothy, don't you?"

"Yes, an interesting individual there."

"To be sure. Would you have any problems if he were to sit in on your interview?"

"No, not at all; an emissary from on High would be a blessing."

Before we head back to Maine, maybe we could get together."

"I'm at your service, Captain."

"Good, now the harbor is not far ahead; enjoy the show."

"I'm looking forward to it."

Mr. Akerman joined the people in the tight confines of the sail, and a lookout said, "Pastor Johnson, we have room up here in what we call the forest. There is an open platform to stand on, and we will strap you in the safety harness, so you won't fall. The view is superb up here."

A few moments later, the Sky Pilot had one of the best viewing positions on the boat. He thought, *'I sure hope Linda doesn't see me up here; I would be in a heap of trouble.'* Then he softly giggled to himself.

Mr. Akerman expertly moored the sleek submarine to the jetty. Then Dick noticed the flagstaff at the back of the sail. Normally the Stars and Stripes of America would be flying there.

But, no longer a valid national ensign, in its place flapped a white ensign, with a dark blue field with a red cross in the canton—the Christian flag.

Several buses sat on the pier as the submarine approached. Once secured to the jetty, two brows were lowered aft the sail to allow traffic to and from the two hatches into and out of the boat.

The crew took great care in escorting the passengers along the narrow deck to the gangplanks to avoid them going over the vessel's side.

****

Homes built by the earlier settlers had been constructed rapidly before the current passengers departed Steele Island. This allowed many families to move into homes, some of which only needed additional finishing touches to be considered complete.

Another priority issue was educating the newcomers about the potential danger of snakes and spiders, particularly the Funnel Spider and poisonous snakes. The newcomers heard both creatures tried to avoid humans, but individuals insistent on pestering either could receive a life-threatening sting or bite. Fortunately, antivenom was kept available for any rare bites.

In conjunction with Australian laws and local guidance, elementary and high schools were on drawing boards and grounds prepared for the structures when approved.

Several manufacturing and sales shops sat in various stages of development. However, careful attention has been given to ensure that needed products were purchased from established local businesses first, thus developing a non-threatening commercial atmosphere and strengthening relations between the Australian population and those who came to join them.

One area that rapidly flourished was the molding and machining of various sizes of engine turbines with standardized couplings according to projected energy requirements. Martin and Elie worked full-time, six days a week.

The trucking industry of Australia came to the rescue by transporting large amounts of raw and finished materials to the shops and stores in Broome with the recent and projected population growth.

The best growth for all showed on Sundays, where mixed crowds attended services in newcomer and local churches. But, of course, such mixing is not without the occasional disagreements, in which both sides quickly resolved their differences, and those involved slapped backs and laughed about non-issues, becoming a bickering point. In short, Broome was a small quiet town before the newcomers arrived, and everyone worked hard to keep it that way.

After minor repairs, the *ARK* saw a scheduled return to Steele Island in two weeks. Brad and Helen's relationship quickly solidified, and they called on Pastor Johnson to conduct his interview. The betroths, and Timothy dropped by the Johnson's home, where Linda had set out some tea and a tray of fig and coconut cakes mixed with apple and cinnamon cakes.

After an opening prayer, Pastor Johnson said, "I understand you wish to marry, is that correct?"

Helen and Brad agreed that was their wish, and Timothy sat quietly, taking in the questions and answers.

"Helen, tell me about yourself. Where are you from, and about your children, have you talked with them about your desires and how they may affect them?"

Helen laid out her life in a thumbnail sketch and then covered her happy marriage and the loss of her husband. She devoted her life to her son, Ian, age eleven, and Edith, twelve; like her mother, she had a thick mane of red hair. Both of whom clearly remember the horror and crushing effect the loss of her husband, and father to the youngster.

"How do they feel about the possibility of a different man coming into their life?" The Pastor asked.

"Brad and I sat down with them and explained our feelings for one another, and when they heard everything, they rushed to us and wrapped themselves around us. Ian told Brad he was the perfect person for me and couldn't be happier. He explained how much he looked up to Brad as the submarine's captain and had looked up what he could find about Brad's career. So, Pastor Dick, Brad has become Ian's hero by helping get our people to safety. And Eddi, Edith's nickname, thinks this man is a naval hero and is her knight in shining armor.

As for me, somehow, from the first time I set eyes on Brad, I knew there was a rare life ahead for us. I can't explain it, but it's here." As she pointed to her heart.

"Brad, how about you?"

Brad Holeman covered the highlights of his life's early history. Then his commission as an officer and early career. His two-year marriage ended with Emily's untimely death from cancer. "After Emily, I devoted myself to the Navy to the exclusion of any hope for a future life with another woman. The recent disaster of our former nation told me to get out of the Navy before I planned. Through my church, I became part of the plans to get Christians out of the country before the Communists seized control and began their agenda of eliminating all religions, especially Christianity. Helen and I met on an evening stroll about the boat, and I, too, knew there was an open door for us. Ian and Eddi have tremendous potential, and I want to make it happen. They are great children.

I talked with both of them, together and separately, and told them I am not their father, nor will I ever try to replace him. I explained that they must keep their dad in their hearts and memories because he is, and always will be, their daddy. I also told them I loved their mother and wanted to marry her. As before, the two of them jumped into my lap, holding tightly. They sealed any doubts I may have about our future."

"You have both been married and know the sometimes-difficult road ahead. Are you certain you are ready to embark on that journey?"

"Yes," the two chorused. Then Helen said, "Pastor, we have taken all of what we have talked about to the Lord in prayer. We laid our lives, the lives of the children, and our future, at Jesus' feet, and He gave us his answer, Timothy."

"Pastor Dick, I carried a message from He who created me; he said, Tell Brad and Helen I approve and bless their union."

Pastor Dick and his wife Linda sat, sharing tears of joy with Helen and Brad at the beautiful gift from on High.

After recovering from the blessed message, Pastor Dick said, "Today is Tuesday; we have time to tell everyone and take care of the legal requirements in time for the ceremony on Saturday if you wish."

Helen held tightly onto Brad's arm in response, who said, "That will be perfect, Pastor Dick. What will we need to take care of?"

"Have you thought of the attire you want to go with?"

"We talked about that, it is too hot for anything formal, and the people don't have those clothes available. So we plan to wear casual clothing, and if anyone needs to, whatever they are wearing is fine by us. And please make sure everyone knows no presents or money, just love, best wishes, and of course, their prayers."

"Well done, Bradley; now, may I take my leave? I am needed elsewhere at the moment."

"Certainly, Timothy, and we trust you will come to the ceremony."

"Without a doubt."

After Timothy's departure, Helen and Brad shared prayers, snacks, and tea with Pastor Dick and Linda.

When alone, Linda stood aside Dick, her head on his shoulder, and he whispered, "Other than our wedding, I have never felt more blessed than today."

Linda responded, "Amen."

THE LORD

CHAPTER EIGHTEEN

With the assistance of the Australian Immigration Ministry, The Salvation Army, and countless members from local churches, it didn't take long for the second load of newcomers to settle in temporary housing while permanent homes still developed. Timothy watched the work and assistance; more importantly, the fellowship and individual friendships blossomed. He smiled at the success of Christians, helping Christians become neighbors, friends, and future families come together as one nation under God once again.

The days slid by quickly, with the townspeople helping and newcomers settling in. By Friday afternoon, everyone in town knew of the submarine Captain Bradly Holeman and Helen Hamilton's Saturday wedding. The wedding would take place in PA Haynes Oval Sports Park to accommodate the expected crowd—the Reverend Richard L. Johnson officiating.

That evening, Pastor Dick and Linda had been invited to dinner at the Hamilton residence with Helen, her children, and Brad. It provided the opportunity for any last questions regarding expectations and releasing anything that may stand in the way of the ceremony and an opportunity for either betrothed to back out.

Following supper, everyone gathered in the small living room for fellowship and prayer. The highlight of worship came from the two children. They stood in the circle of adults, held one another's hands, and bowed heads.

Ian took a deep breath, then began to pray, "Lord God in heaven, we come before You, praising your Holy Name. We thank You for ending our sorrow in missing our Dad and pray for his soul. And we thank You for bringing great happiness to Mom, Eddi, and me; we are happy for her and for bringing us the best father we can have in Mr. Holeman. We already love him. Amen."

Edith stood silent, allowing her mind to reach out for God, "Our Father. Who art in heaven, hear our pleas. We never knew sadness and loneliness until Daddy was taken. It has been a horrible and frightening time. But as You have taught us, we have been able to pray for those misguided men who killed our father and praise You for your mercy for bringing us a wonderful man for Mom and a new and special Daddy for us. The sun shines on us again. Please forgive our sins and guide us until You call for us. Amen."

A pin would have been heard had it dropped. Then a smooth, loving voice filled the room, saying, "Blessed are the children."

No eye was dry as the four adults and two children kneeled and praised God.

That night, a sound-sleeping Pastor was visited by Timothy in a dream, then he slept soundly for the remainder of the night.

Clear skies and bright sunshine brought mild temperatures to the small town of Broome. By 10:00 AM, PA Haynes Park teemed with locals and newcomers for the first newcomer wedding in the town.

At 11:00 AM, Brad, his Best Man, Jonathan Nichols, and two groomsmen, one of which was Ian Hamilton, waited at the makeshift altar. The Maid of Honor was Sarah Sweets, Helen's sister, and two bridesmaids, including Eddi Hamilton.

A piano had been brought in and connected to the sound system. The pianist, a resident of Broome, and the head musician in the Broome High School, who taught classical music, Mrs. Jenny Mefford. Mrs. Mefford opened with Wagner's Bridal Chorus.

Then, with her mane of red hair flowing across her shoulders and a golden tiara on her head, Helen was escorted by her father, Morton Hamilton, who slowly walked the open area between rows of standing friends and neighbors.

At the altar, Bradly stepped forward, facing the advancing lady. Then they met one another and turned toward Pastor Johnson.

The Pastor opened the ceremony with a prayer praising God the Father, the Son, and the Holy Spirit. After that, the ceremony continued, then, unexpectedly, Pastor Johnson stepped back as directed by Timothy the night before.

A cloud of mist began forming above the betrothed, and a full chorus and background harps and horns gently stirred the air. The scarred hands of the Lamb descended from the cloud as it lowered toward the two to be wed. The Lord's arms, draped in a snow-white robe, became visible.

The crowd hardly breathed, mesmerized by the greatest wedding ever seen in all of Australia. People prayed quietly at the sight, and most had tears of joy in their eyes.

The Lord reached out with His left palm up, an invitation for Helen's left hand. She slowly placed her shaking hand in His, and the smooth voice she had heard the previous evening said, "Fear not, for it is I." Her shaken spirit calmed instantly.

Helen and Brad saw a pair of interlocking golden orbs in the Lord's right hand. Then the Lord's hand closed and reopened with two separate rings. "Bradly, take her ring, and place it on her finger." Bradly, also shaken, became instantly calm as his fingers touched Jesus' hand. Then, as she and Pastor Johnson watched, Brad placed the ring on her left finger. The Lord released Helen's hand, then held his left hand up for Bradly. "Helen, take the ring from my right hand, and place it on Bradly's finger."

When Helen finished, Brad's hand was released, and the Lord held his left palm up once again. "Place your left hands in mine." Looking at one another, the two complied, then the Lord placed his right hand on top, and His strong voice rang throughout the crowd and into every person's heart, "Let no man come between this man and woman." And the soft voice returned, "Rejoice, I pronounce you man and wife." The Lord vanished into the cloud, and the cloud began to disappear. The wedding party and crowd recoiled in surprise as two dozen white doves burst through the dwindling mist and into the air to fly around the park.

A gentle breeze rustled nearby trees for several seconds, then Pastor Dick said, "Ladies and gentlemen, I introduce you, Bradly and Helen Holeman."

That was Mrs. Mefford's key to pound out Felix Mendelssohn's 'Wedding March.' At the same time, Pastor

Johnson escorted the newlyweds to the front of the altar and sent them up the aisle.

Linda hurried to Dick's side, always worrying about her husband, and found him soaking wet with sweat, which could only come from being part of a Holy Blessed Wedding.

Tables had been set up with the wedding cake and plenty of tarts, small cakes and snacks, soft drinks, tea, water, and milk for the children. Several townsfolks with musical instruments and experience gathered to one side and began playing dancing music and waltzes for the newlyweds.

The Mayor of Broome stood next to the Johnson's and Holeman's, "If I may, Pastor. If there were any doubts, or weaknesses about God and Christianity among our residents, there aren't any longer. God is indeed alive and well, and we, all of us, will forever be indebted to the Father, Son, and Holy Spirit."

"AMEN," came from everyone in earshot.

Later in the afternoon, Brad and Helen stepped into a black sedan and whisked to their home, where they changed into a casual dress, grabbed prepacked overnight bags, and dashed out to the waiting vehicle. Jon Nichols was the sole person to know where the newlyweds disappeared to. He drove them to the Bali Hai Resort and Spa for their first two days of married life.

Ian and Eddi went to Aunt Sarah's until their parents returned home.

The next two weeks seemed to fly by, and it was time for the *ARK* to head back to Steele Island for another group of refugees. Helen and the children were on the pier to wish their new husband and father a safe voyage and swift return.

At the top of the sail, the OOD took the boat to sea while Brad watched the pier until it disappeared from sight. Glancing down at his ring finger, the ring seemed to glow, and Brad silently gave up a prayer of thanks.

In a pre-voyage briefing, the navigator laid out a different track to follow, curving to the south of the previous path, then turning sharply off New York state to the north while still in deep waters. Brad had the boat dive to eight hundred feet and slow to ten knots. The submarine was a hole in the water, giving off no sound for any vessel to hear it. Before diving, Brad sailed barely under the surface long enough for a burst transmission to Steele Island and received their information download.

With the alternate track in the computers, the submarine followed its orders like a puppy dog. In his first tour of the boat since getting underway, Captain Holeman found the passenger's quarters void of the happy noise of playing children, and friendly faces of the people, thankfully heading for a safe homeland.

The crew in the engineering section couldn't stop praising the precise and simple controls operating the engines. However, one engineer put it in its right perspective; "It's a God thing."

Captain Holeman's last stop didn't surprise the sonar crew. The officer-in-charge reported, "Captain, we have had no passive contacts since getting underway. The change in our track did the trick. If I may, Captain, I would think changing the track at least every other trip will keep us off everyone's radar and sonar screens."

"I agree with you; the Russians want to destroy this boat for unknown reasons. However, I have a theory, they want the secrets of the boat, and if they cannot have them, nobody can have them. And again, in my opinion, the Communists would not hesitate to use the system against those who refuse to bow to them and accept their unrestricted rule. They have already stated that refusal to comply with Communism will result in transferring the holdouts to Siberian retraining camps," Captain Holeman said.

"It sounds like the actions of the pharaohs before God commissioned Moses to lead the Hebrews in the exodus. Every bit as brutal, if not worse," the engineer noted.

"That, and other loss of liberties, makes our job paramount at this time. And why we must all keep a wartime lookout while on watch and remember we are defenseless, except for our speed and stealthiest posture. But our greatest asset is our God; by following His ways, He is our fortress.

One last thing, we have to accept that not all US boats are sympathetic to our cause and may be working for the Communists. But, as the motto of the submarine service has been 'The Silent Service,' we must remain silent and trust none until tried and true." Holeman declared.

"Aye, sir," the sonar Officer agreed.

"I say that because we are most likely to run across US boats on the western part of our designated track."

"Understood, Captain."

****

Special Agent Adrian Gibson arranged to have his operation of finding and stopping the exodus of Christians transferred to a dedicated building on the Air Force base at Bangor, Maine.

Gibson put together another team of dedicated agents for his task force.

SAC Adrian Gibson
S/A   Adam Seltzer
S/A   John Melrose
S/A   Charles Witmer
S/A   James Tanner
Sec   Andrea Monfort
Sec   Sherri Jo Harvey
Sec   Catherine (Cathy) Webb

"Ladies and gentlemen, we will be working outside the regular attachment of Homeland Security. Our sole mission is to stop and apprehend religious zealots' unauthorized departure from the country. After halting the previous weak administration's folly of open borders, another special detachment is assisting the Border Patrol round-up and deporting the illegals. We got a better job.

Our regular hours will be zero-eight hundred to twelve hundred hours. An hour for lunch, then thirteen hundred to seventeen hundred. Saturday and Sunday are off. However, someone will have to remain here in the event something breaks on a weekend. Therefore, everyone is on the weekend watchlist. That way, the weekend duty will have the widest spread possible. I will make up the guidelines and watchlist this week.

Agents will have cubicles, secretaries will have three offices on that wall, and a safe for classified material will be in each office. We have our interrogation room, already wired for video and sound, right behind me.

Every member is assigned an agency vehicle; you will use it on official duty and take it home at night. Likewise, everyone has been issued a communication device while they are off duty. You will be notified to call in if your device activates. Are there any questions?

You are dismissed and use the time to set up your desks and offices. I will be in my office if any issues or questions need addressing."

✳✳✳✳

Sixty miles northeast of Bermuda, the *ARK* turned to course three-four-seven for a straight line to the Pen. The submarine sailed through the five-hundred-foot depth at twenty knots when the sonar watch called the conn.

"Conn, sonar, we have an intermittent transit on a submerged contact; recommend slowing to ten knots for silent analysis."

"Very well, OOD, slow us to ten knots, and set General Quarters, silent running."

"Aye, sir, slow to ten knots and silent running." The orders were given out, and the 688 disappeared while its ultra-sensitive passive elements looked for any submerged vessel within twenty miles.

A minute later, "Conn, sonar, confirmed submerged vessel bearing one-zero-five degrees, course two-eight-five degrees, speed dropping off from twenty knots, twenty, now steady at ten knots, distance nine miles. Our computer identifies the contact as the *USS CARLSON,* an SSN boat out of New London."

"Does he have us?"

"He is still in passive mode, Captain."

"Very well, Helm, maintain course and speed."

"Maintain course and speed, sir."

"Captain, the boat is in our baffles."

"Talker, tell the engine room we may need to increase speed and standby to answer all bells smartly."

"Telling the engine room, we may increase speed and standby to answer all bells smartly, sir."

A slightly garbled voice bounced off the *ARK's* hull. "This is the North American Communist Party submarine Anatoly Vasilyevich Lyapidevsky. You will surface and receive borders for inspection. Failure to comply will result in our sinking you."

The Captain picked up the underwater phone, "This is a private vessel in international waters; you have no jurisdiction here."

"This is your last warning, surface or sink."

"Jack, do you know what the Carlson is armed with?"

"Since it is a former US boat, I would say Mark 48s."

"We will be rising; stand by," Captain Holeman said. "Then he turned to the OOD, take us to four hundred feet and sixty-five knots."

The sound of air forcing seawater from the dive tanks gave off a high pitch sound, masking the rapid increase of its screws. The sub lurched like a race car, surprising the enemy boat. The ARK flew through a thermocline and leveled at four hundred feet. Her speed rapidly increased past forty knots without slowing down.

****

On the Lyapidevsky, the Russian Captain received the transmission of apparent surrender when the interpreter repeated Captain Holeman's words.

"Comrade Captain, the boat has sharply headed upward, then disappeared through a possible thermal layer."

"Helm, bring us up to three hundred feet." In response to the order, the older, renamed Los Angeles class submarine blasted through the thermal layer and settled at three hundred feet.

"Comrade Captain, the boat is rapidly pulling away from us at forty knots on course three-four-seven degrees."

"Torpedo Officer; fire tubes one and four." The order sent two Mark 48 torpedoes after the fleeing submarine.

****

"Conn, sonar, two Mark 48s have been fired by the enemy submarine."

"Very well, Helm, our speed?"

"Captain, we are approaching fifty knots."

"Very well." The Captain's calm voice made the crew in earshot more comfortable.

Three minutes later, "Conn, sonar, torpedoes, and the other boat are falling behind."

"Very well, we can thank God again for keeping us going."

The remaining distance to the Pen continued without incident; however, Captain Holeman had no reservations about the Communist government putting a bounty out for the *ARK* or any boat that did not join their forces.

The submarine moored starboard side to the pier while the big door slid into the closed position beneath the stone overhead of Steele Island. Once closed, lights illuminated the long boat and dock.

Captain Holeman met with church leaders working the sending end of the underground sealift.

After the usual salutations and handshakes, the representative said, "Captain, join us in the briefing room; we have much to discuss."

A hot cup of coffee warded off the chill of a cold late February night as Brad sat at the briefing table. "What is the latest news? We have been out of touch with world events."

"Captain," Evert Ames, the senior guidance counselor of the board, began. "In your absence, the Communists have gained complete control now. Freedom and liberty are now forbidden words, and the users are punishable by twenty-five years in prison. The prisons we used to have were vacation spas compared to what they have become. Everyone imprisoned has barely enough to survive, and heat is a luxury now. So far, no more than a handful of people have been sentenced to incarceration. But unfortunately, there will be more. How are things progressing in Australia?"

"Quite well. The Australian government has been bending over backward to integrate our people into the population, and the folks in Broome are some of the nicest folks I've ever met. In a month or two, I'd wager the people won't be American or newcomers but Australians," Brad answered.

"Under the circumstances, we couldn't get better news," Evert Ames smiled.

"How secure is our operation here?" Brad asked.

"As far as we know, the Communists haven't found out about Steele Island; God knows when we will have to evacuate. We plan on continuing operations until every Christian or person of other religions who wants to leave has made it here. Christians from the Japanese, Chinese, Korean, Filipino, and others have elected to go. Hardcore religious leaders have persuaded the remaining people to stay under the promise of freedom for their religions. We cannot believe that for two reasons. First, their history has been one of totalitarian and anti-religion. Second, the Communist czars have stated they will stamp out all religions; nothing else except absolute fidelity to the party is acceptable."

"Why doesn't that surprise me?" Brad said.

The board counselor continued, "We want you to assume the command of the receiving facility in Broome upon your arrival with this group of people. How is the housing situation coming along?"

"Very well, sir," Brad answered. "Homes are being constructed as fast as people can work. The great weather from the Indian Ocean has been a favorable asset. It will be a wonderful place to live and raise families as it develops. Almost all those there now have adopted Australia as their home country. The government is amazingly efficient in its resettlement assistance. As a result, everyone is learning excellent ways to live and accomplish things they thought impossible.

I have one or two questions for you. First, how many vessels made it free from the Communists, and where are they? Second, we are discussing warships here. We cannot assume to become citizens of Australia and keep warships," Holeman stated.

"To answer your first question. We do not have a total, but of the carrier forces, only three survived massive air attacks, and they have surrendered their vessels—one to Australia, one to New Zealand, and the last to the Japanese. The crews left the ships, planes, and munitions and were given transportation to Australia, with some staying in the nations where the ships stood down.

We have seen dozens of destroyers, some remaining cruisers, and at least two dozen submarines interned in various UK ports. Those nations will integrate the warships into the Australian and UK Navies as manpower becomes available. We have also heard that many of the ship's crewmembers are filtering back to serve for freedom.

At this point, the *ARK* is the lone boat with the special engineering alternations; all the remaining submarines maintain their original engineering departments. Therefore, no subs or surface vessels will be located at Broome, at least for the foreseeable future. The Seawolf apparently was taken by Timothy; that's all we know of it.

One of the worst parts of all this, the families of the servicemen are on their own in getting out, yet a number have been able to get to us. We intend to keep the lights on, so to say, until all God's children are free again."

ANOTHER EXODUS

CHAPTER NINETEEN

During his first administration, the world watched in disbelief as an aged and clearly impaired president invited the people of every nation south of the then United States to 'Come to America' without opposition. They did, with others from over a hundred different countries. No papers or visas, all they had to do was plea for political asylum. Millions poured over the porous national boundaries and into cities nationwide without medical protection, little or no education, without any skills and a little more than the clothes on their backs. Thousands more escaped detection and disappeared into the cities, including drug runners, Russian and Chinese special forces troops, and spies.

As in most countries, the laws allow a certain number of people to enter once they demonstrate they have complied with the entrance requirements and laws. Among those to read and write the national language, understand how the national, and lower governments are established and operate, and they must be sponsored. In addition to those requirements is a regulation requiring the individual not to become dependent on the people or government. The reigning administration ignored the laws and regulations, resulting in dividing and weakening the people and the nation's foundations. Covert Communist agents succeeded in using this division and discord to begin the overthrow of the United States.

Before the Communists closed all borders, thousands of people, the vast majority of religious beliefs, reversed the direction of the flow of humanity. Along the way, local Christians, Hebrews, Moslems, and Buddhist leaders assisted the growing numbers to ports where surface ships of every type took them aboard and transferred them to their home or different nations. Many ships took the refugees to Ireland and UK destinations. Finally, many of those folks made it to Australia and a host of Island nations, which took in the numbers they could manage. Many had the brilliant minds and national dedication the Communists feared the most.

Unknown to the Communist government, the military men and women in the American nuclear forces rendered their missiles and nuclear devices inoperative, spiked, and booby-trapped to explode if they were tampered with or used. Once the hated government took solid control, several atomic weapons were transferred to one of Russia's major nuclear development locations. There, scientists immediately began to disassemble a 20mt nuclear weapon and tripped the detonator. Additional armaments, unprocessed ore, and stocks of radioactive uranium and plutonium increased the weapon's strength in terms of intensified radiation, contamination, and damage, impacting everything within a hundred-mile radius of the site. Air contamination figures would take time before they could be released; but deadly contamination was assured over an additional hundred miles, and long-term illnesses such as cancer would overwhelm hundreds of thousands of people.

The first Russian response was to determine who, in America fired the missile; however, with the world on alert, advanced radar systems proved the detonation did not result from a missile attack but was initiated at the nuclear weapons development site. The investigation continues.

****

The Reverend Michelle Leonard sat at her desk on a Saturday afternoon, reviewing her notes for Sunday's sermon in the Church of the Brethren. Unfortunately, her concentration interfered with her hearing a slight rustle behind her, and when a soft voice called her name, "Pastor Leonard," the woman was so startled that her notes scattered across the desk onto the floor. Being a retired police officer, she almost instantly recovered and turned around and into a combat stance. Pastor Leonard looked at the six-foot individual, taking everything in the area that could be used as a weapon against this intruder.

"Have no fear of me; I am Timothy, a messenger from the Most High."

With her mind still geared toward self-defense, Timothy's words didn't register with her. "Who are you, and what do you want?"

"I need to speak with you, Michelle."

"How do you know my name?"

Timothy repeated his first sentence.

"Timothy, who? And by the way, normal people come to the front door."

"Michelle, I am not a person; I am an angel sent by God."

"Yes, and I'm Mother Teresa."

"No, you aren't you are Michelle Leonard, Pastor Michelle Leonard, are you not?"

"Look, buster…."

"Maybe this will convince you." Timothy slowly unfolded his wings and lifted into the air, until his head bumped into the ceiling.

It was then that Timothy's identity broke through Michelle's resistance.

"What do you want?" she asked in a weaker voice.

"I need to speak to you about moving your small church to a safer land; otherwise, people could lose their lives."

"WHAT?" Pastor Michelle growled.

"Michelle, let's sit and talk, I have much to tell you, and you have much to do."

****

In Ethan's concentration on setting up his desk in the small Sturgis office of Homeland Security, he failed to hear the soft entry and footsteps of Myra Dickenson stop at the door to the office. Instead, she watched the man diligently clean and set the tools of the work in the proper place on the less-than-large desk.

Myra still sensed a major change in the man's demeanor, and what impacted her the most was the tune he was softly humming. One of her favorite hymns, 'Leaning on the Everlasting Arms.'

This hymn was inspired by ***Deuteronomy 33:27, "The eternal God is thy refuge, and underneath are the everlasting arms." (KJV)***

"That's a wonderful hymn, Miles," Myra softly said.

The man turned around and said, "It's Ethan now."

"Ethan, what happened to your hair? It was blond, but now it's soft and pure white. And why did you change your name?" she asked with hope.

"The Lord gave the name after I kneeled before my God and asked Him to forgive my sins and guide my life."

Myra, overcome with joy, pulled Ethan into a hug and whispered, "God has blessed you, Ethan." When she backed away, her eyes glistened with joy.

"Yes, He has, but I'm not yet sure what He wishes me to do, so I will continue to do my job and, more importantly, praise God and thank Him daily for His bounty."

"You know, the Lord has everything planned, and each part will occur in its proper time, including our parts in the plan. And you are right; we will stay quietly here, do our work, and help those we can."

"There is a desk and phone in the next room, with a small bookcase, two straight chairs, and what looks like a comfortable office chair for you. May I assist you in setting anything up?"

"Probably not this minute, but if I need you, can I call on you then?" She asked.

"Well, it's not like I have a lot of open cases right now. But I plan to visit the local Sheriff and Police Chief this afternoon to meet them and offer them any services they could use. I want to find an office store and have new business cards made. Come to think of it, it would be a good idea if we both made the rounds; you will be their first contact point if I'm out or tied up. You're great at making friends, and right now, we could use them."

"I wonder if DHS will ever get a favorable following in Chicago, everything has gone so negative," Myra said out loud.

"I'm not sure they will, not with the mindset of the leadership now in control; I'm afraid was a force for good has become a national Gestapo," Ethan answered.

"For sure, by the way; why did you wind up here?"

Ethan replied, "For the same reason you're here, we're Christians, and Gibson has no love or trust of us. There are two good things about his move to eliminate us. First, we are together; second, this is a quiet town, although when the rally begins, it will change. But our part in it may be light with the Sheriff and police taking the lead. But for some reason, I feel it could be busy for us too."

Myra added, "Let's take it one step at a time until we get our feet on solid ground."

By eleven-thirty, hunger caused Ethan's stomach to growl. He stepped to Myra's door. "Myra, it's heading toward noon, and we're both strangers here; how about joining me in a hunt for a decent café or eatery?"

"Well, it's been years since I've been asked to lunch; I'm flattered."

"Don't be yet; I have no idea where to go."

"Hold on a moment; I'll find somewhere we can go without being rushed."

"Okay, I'll be counting my pencils at my desk." Myra smiled as he turned away.

Five minutes later, the trim woman exited her office, "I found a nice place boasting home-cooked meals not far from here. It's called Uncle Louie's Diner."

"What's the address?"

Myra responded, "1039 Main Street. It has good reviews, and we can always make a fly-through to assess it."

"Sounds like a workable plan to me."

At the diner, they found it clean and well set up. First, the two strangers sat at a table and checked the menu. Then, settling on a hot roast beef sandwich and coffee, they chatted until a young waitress stopped by to take their orders.

Ethan quietly asked Myra, "Before you left, had you heard anything about the movement to get our people out?"

"Gibson didn't know I was keeping his activities under the spotlight and knew he had changed his base of operations to Bangor, Maine. He thought he had located the main transfer point for Christians to escape the country.

"No, he'd raid it in a heartbeat," Ethan said.

Another Christian worker forewarned Martin and Elie, and a pre-set program went into effect, changing the property into a local high school administration center overnight. I understand that a cleaning crew headed up by a minister was present when he did get there. Then after a day or two, they were gone as well."

"PTL," Ethan said.

Following lunch, Myra and Ethan returned to the office to find the mail had been slipped through the brass mail drop in the door. One official plastic envelope bore Ethan's name. Myra took the rest to her office. Sitting at his desk, Ethan opened the envelope to find a file folder and a self-addressed return envelope.

Inside the folder. A letter outlining an interview with a witness, an interview sheet with her name, address, telephone number, and other pertinent information on the woman. Ethan reviewed the material and then stepped over to Myra's office.

"Myra, what is your official designation and duties?"

Looking at Ethan in surprise, she said, "I am a Special Agent with full duties and responsibilities as you; why?"

"I'm glad I asked. Sometimes I need a backup; without another agent, it makes for a dangerous job."

"For sure. You weren't at the Chicago office when my late husband was the Chicago Office Bureau Chief, were you?"

"No, I was in St. Louis."

"I worked cases for quite some time; then we ran short of secretaries, and I was asked to fill in. It appears they forgot I was an agent too."

"I doubt they forgot, particularly after the loss of your husband. Sometimes I think the Neanderthals among us haven't reached maturity or come out of the dark ages, probably both."

"Thank you."

"For what?"

"Not making me say that," Myra laughed.

"The case that came in from Rapid City requested an interview with a woman. I have no problem with the request, but in today's insane world, a male agent would be foolish not to have a lady backup. Sometimes a female agent can do a much better job of speaking with a female subject than with a man trying it."

"You're smarter than I thought. I'm serious; I see a different man than you were. And you better believe I'll back you up; better yet, I'll do the interview, and you can back me."

"Deal," he held out his hand, and Myra took it in a strong grip.

Agents Dickenson and Vickers jumped into the bureau vehicle and headed for the woman's residence.

On the way, the two agents talked about their past lives leading up to the current stress most of the DHS agents were beginning to bend under. Ethan told Myra of his encounters before the interrogation room episode.

"I know Pastor Carvour is connected with his missing congregation; he is probably with them where the people are sane."

"You are correct, Ethan," a voice from the back seat said. Ethan checked his rearview mirror, and Myra turned around to look at a man dressed in white robes with a broad smile. "Good day to you, Myra."

"You're Timothy, aren't you?"

"Yes, I am."

"From what I've heard, Timothy," Myra said, smiling back, "You've been very busy."

"Our Lord has me looking over a large flock, keeping me out of trouble."

Their laughter set a happy tone about Timothy's visit.

"You, in trouble? I've heard so many good things about you. And I'll bet you are one of God's top angels."

Timothy's shyness showed on his face.

"What can we do for you, Timothy?" Ethan asked.

"It's not what you can do for me; it's what I am going to tell you."

Myra and Ethan looked at one another, and then Myra looked back toward their visitor, "Timothy?"

"Exercise caution in your interview; a man is in the woman's closet, and he is armed. Stay at the front door and ask you questions there; the man is going to be apprehended at a later date."

"Thank you, Timothy; we will do as you say."

"Good, you make a nice couple," and the angel was gone in a puff of mist before either could say a word.

Ethan and Myra looked excitedly at one another. They drew up to their destination, and Myra exited the vehicle with a slight smile showing her pleasure at Timothy's visit.

The interview went as planned, then the two agents returned safely to their car, and Ethan drove back to the office to file their reports.

Neither person said a word during their trip as they swelled on Timothy's words. When they arrived, Ethan opened the office door for Myra, who smiled and said, 'Thank you."

"I'll type up your report as soon as you finish it," the shapely agent said.

"You completed the assignment; I watched your six, looking for any overt moves. You can fill in the first-person viewpoints better than I; thus, you deserve the credit."

Toward the end of the workday, the report was completed, signed, and prepared for the mail when they reached the Post Office.

"So, what are your plans for supper?" Ethan asked.

"I haven't made any yet."

"I found a respectable restaurant and would enjoy your company for dinner; otherwise, it will be a can of hash from the microwave for me."

"Ugh!" Myra grunted. "Well, since you watched my six, and you did, I guess it would be agreeable," she played with him.

"I'm glad that guy stayed in the closet." Ethan tried to change the direction of the conversation.

Giving Ethan an unbelieving look, Myra said, "You know what six I was referring to."

"Oh, that; how did you know?"

"I'm a woman, and we know those things." With a sly smile.

"I can't help it; you're an exceptional lady. And I want to thank you for understanding and accepting the new me. I'm just gonna tell you the truth; I admit that I like you."

"You're welcome," her head dropped to her chest in thought. When Myra raised her head, the serious-looking woman looked Ethan in his eyes and said, "I like you too; pick me up at my apartment at six." She walked to the front door; as she pulled the heavy door open, she looked over her shoulder and said, "A lot." The door closed softly on the pneumatic closing dampener, leaving the dumbfounded man in the hallway.

By six-thirty-five, Myra and Ethan walked into the mid-to-upper-class restaurant, where the Maitre-d' seated the couple in a quiet corner booth.

Each declined the offer of alcoholic drinks, opting for water instead. A waiter brought a light house appetizer for the different customers.

Myra and Ethan looked at one another, then their eyes met, and Ethan held out both hands, palms up, inviting Myra to take them, which she did. Finally, Ethan offered an old Grace for supper. "Bless us, oh God, as we partaketh thy gifts, help us in all things, that we may further thy name and cause. Amen."

Myra added, "And we thank you for the safety you gave us on our appointed rounds and for guiding us to ensure we follow only your path. Amen."

Myra wouldn't let go of Ethan's hands but looked deep into his blue eyes again. "Ethan, I have been praying for years that God would guide the right person into my life. True to His promise to grant honest requests, he has brought us together. I heard it in Timothy's words today. I believe this as I believe our time on this earth is growing short, and God is guiding our lives," and tears rolled down the woman's cheeks.

Ethan, could not hold back his joy at what God had done in answering his prayers. "I believe as you, but you say it so perfectly. We will work to be patient and wait upon the Lord; He will lead us where we are to go."

The waiter appeared with menus and fresh water. He then returned to take their orders.

Ethan and Myra talked, cleaning their plates of years of anguish, sometimes fear, and confusion in these perilous times. Ethan said, "I accumulated years of pent-up pain, anger, and embarrassment at following the wiles of Satan for over ten years. He held me tightly in his claws of sin. I felt as if I were falling into a dark pit of hatred and frustration until I found Martin's Bible and was confronted by Timothy. When I confessed my sins to the Lord and asked forgiveness, He washed my sins away with the Lamb's blood, and the miraculous transformation of life with Him was restored." He finished with, "I have no doubt the Lord led us together, here, where we can mature together."

This time Myra laid her palms out, and it was Ethan's turn to take hers. The woman across from him unloaded her past burdens, saying, "After Chad's passing, I felt as if life had ended for me. I wouldn't listen to anyone trying to tell me otherwise, even the Lord.

I started drinking, then dreamed of good things to come, but I was cautioned to be patient. I was brought up in a 'right now' environment so that wasn't easy. I had to learn to be patient all over again. That's when I buried myself in my work, even when assigned secretarial duties. I prayed for relief from my self-induced torture. Then you transferred to the Chicago office. At first, I ignored you and disliked you and your attitude. I was wrong because I didn't consider your tragic sufferings; I was selfish and self-centered and felt sorry for myself. That is not the Christian way of life; I know that again," Myra struggled to keep her composure.

"It is as if we were two ships, lost at sea, then brought together by the breeze of God's breath," Ethan said.

With supper arriving, Myra ended her testimony of having a good life, losing it, and now embarking on a better life with the guidance of the Almighty.

The two Christians sat in quiet conversations, enjoying their meal but enjoying their company much more. When finished two hours later, they held hands and thanked the Lord for the evening and the beginning of a brand-new life.

The months that followed tightened the two people's bond together, and they attended a local church pastored by an elderly Pastor that believed in the importance of the Book of Revelation and its meaning to everyone. The promise of life everlasting by men and women who devote themselves to the Lord, and how it will shelter those called by His name from the dark times of the coming tribulation.

It was a clear and warm day in the early spring when Myra entered the office to find Ethan sitting at his desk reading reports.

"You're in early, Mr. Vickers," she said in a soft voice.

"Yes, I wanted to catch you before you dived into the mountain of work you have."

Myra laughed; "This time of the year, Sturgis is pretty quiet, and I don't have anything on my desk, my dear."

Ethan rose and walked to the lovely red-haired woman; "I'm glad to hear that. I hope you don't mind, but I wrangled the day off for us. So, we can go and do anything we wish, and there are many sights I have always wanted to see."

"Well, now, what brought this on?"

"If all goes as planned, we can have a great day to relax and see things."

"What are you planning?"

Ethan knelt before the lady he fell in love with, then held up an open two-inch square felt box.

"Myra, I love you dearly and want to spend the rest of our days together. Will you marry me?"

Myra dropped her purse and gasped; her hands flew to cover her mouth, and tears of joy welled into her eyes as she almost screamed, "Oh yes, darling, I've waited so long to hear you ask that." Myra held out her left hand, and Ethan slipped the gold engagement ring on her finger.

Ethan stood, and the excited and happy woman threw herself at him, wrapping her arms around his neck, and their lips met, sealing their promise to one another.

The two jumped at the sound of clapping from behind them, and they whirled around to face a white-robed personage.

"Timothy!" the two chorused.

"Let me be the first to congratulate you on your engagement."

"Oh, thank you, Timothy; coming from you is the best ever," Myra cried.

"I have something for you both," and he handed over a special envelope.

"What's this?"

"Open it."

Myra and Ethan read the eloquent papers, directing them to drive to the coast of Maine to meet Captain Brad Holeman, who would provide you with a peaceful cruise on his boat.

"What is this all about? We have responsibilities here."

"I know, and you will again, in the proper time. Take your time driving and see your sights, but the letter has an arrival date, do not miss it.

You may want to take at least a week's worth of clothing and pack three changes of warm-weather clothing," Timothy said.

Ethan shook his head, saying, "Timothy, you don't understand; we have so much to do, especially now with our engagement."

"Am I to understand I'm to tell our Creator you are declining the vacation He planned for you?"

"Ahhh, no, forget everything I said; I must have bumped my head."

"Oh, are you going to be all right?" the now concerned angel asked.

"No…no, everything is fine; we will leave and begin packing right away and thank you for your wonderful gift."

"You are to stop at the Church of the Brethren in Panora, Iowa. There you will meet the Reverend Michelle Leonard, and she will explain everything to you." Then the angel disappeared into the mist.

Ethan looked at his love, "Well, my dear, we have our marching orders."

"Ethan, we take our belongings from here, and when we leave, we drop the keys in the mail drop; we won't be coming back."

Ethan smiled, "No, we won't."

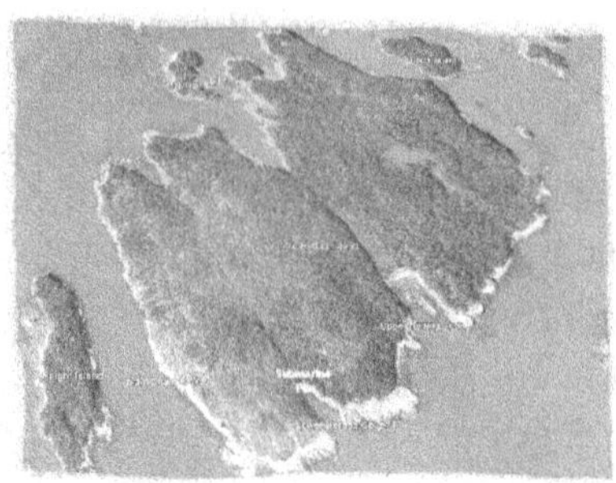

STEELE ISLAND SUB-PEN

CHAPTER TWENTY

Ethan threw the keys to the bureau vehicle in with the building keys; then, he and Myra jumped into her truck and drove to Ethan's apartment. He quickly packed the clothing Timothy directed him to and a second bag with expendable travel clothing. In addition, he brought along a small bag containing shaving gear and personal hygiene items.

Myra drove to her apartment, where she repeated Ethan's packing and, as he had, closed her apartment and returned the keys to the manager.

Before leaving Sturgis, they parked in the parking lot of a large box store, where they mapped their route to sights they wanted to visit, knowing they would never see them again. One, Mount Rushmore, was closed but viewable from numerous locations. Both checked their cameras for fresh batteries and spares. Myra also marked the better overnight locations for rest.

Their first night came at Keystone, South Dakota. They rented two rooms at a Comfort Inn, and Myra secured two rooms at each location in the corporate chain along their route. At each site, she registered the two rooms under the false identities Ethan had created to thwart any trace of their movements.

The couple finished their farewell sightseeing, during which over a hundred photos had been taken. They knew before too long that photos would be the best way to see these historic sites. Their final stop was the sleepy summer town of Panora, Iowa, and the Church of the Brethren. The reddish-brown brick church has sat on the northeast corner of Lake Panorama since its construction in 1862.

Myra and Ethan walked in the front door at the time noted in Timothy's papers directed. The time was one PM on Saturday, and to their surprise, Timothy met them at the door.

"Come in, Meet Pastor Michelle Leonard. We have everything taken care of; your wedding license needs nothing else than your signatures, as well as the Pastor's, at the completion of the ceremony."

Looking around, the two saw a dozen church members of the small congregation sitting in the front pews.

"Timothy, we aren't dressed for our wedding, and I still need a shower and my hair done," Myra complained.

"Myra, our Lord will help; Michelle will take you to a room for preparation. And Ethan, follow me."

Sensing celestial help, the two followed their caretakers to separate rooms. When Myra entered the room, Michelle indicated, she saw four women her age dressed in maid's clothing.

Myra, feeling out of place and insecure, was startled when one of the helpers said, "Myra, don't be concerned; we are from our Lord and will tend to your needs. Step into the bathroom and shower. Ten minutes later, Myra Dickenson stood looking in a full-length mirror at a beautiful woman staring back at her. Her hair was done in a professional manner, and she wore a white bridal dress with small sequins and blue trim; a chin-length lace veil covered her face, held in place with a diamond tiara. Another of the helpers handed Myra a bridal flower bouquet of white roses and Baby's breath. Her face was void of makeup, and her natural beauty with rose-highlighted blush brought her beauty superior to makeup.

Myra was escorted by two men dressed in light-blue tuxes into the church foyer with flower and leave arrangements covering the windows to the church sanctuary. When Myra reached the entrance to the sanctuary, the organist began the Bridal Chorus.

Myra, accompanied by a handsome fatherly figure, slowly walked down the aisle, flanked by rows of well-wishers tossing rose petals in front of the stunned woman.

Ethan met the lady of his life at the altar. Pastor Michelle, Wearing her white ceremonial attire, began the ceremony of Holy Matrimony. At the exchange of the rings, the Pastor stepped back, and the celestial mist formed, announcing the presence of the Lamb.

Background music preceded the appearance of the blessed hands, and He opened his right hand to reveal the twin golden rings locked together. Closing and reopening His hand exposed two rings; the Lamb's soft voice commanded, "Ethan, place her ring on her left finger. Then, holding Ethan's left hand, the Lord repeated the ceremony for Myra to place the other ring on Ethan's left ring finger, and the Lord clasped their hands together, charging the world not to come between the newlyweds.

Myra and Ethan glanced upward to see the serene and loving face of their Savior. His smile was instantly sealed in their hearts and into their minds for the rest of their days.

Pastor Michelle completed the ceremony and announced the presence of Mr. and Mrs. Ethan Vickers to the congregation. The Wedding March sounded as the married couple walked to the back of the sanctuary.

That's when a loud gasp and echoed exclamations attracted the newlywed's attention, and they turned around to see Timothy, the Bride's Maids and groomsman, and Myra's helpers, now draped in white robes and hovering at the ceiling, casting rose petals on the couple.

Such a wedding had never before taken place in the church and stood in everyone's memory. Myra and Ethan stopped briefly to sign the marriage documents, then; finally, they made it to their car and drove to the nearby highway.

Timothy stopped to visit with Pastor Michelle. The Servant of God picked up the marriage documents for the newlyweds, and Timothy told the Pastor to gather her flock and travel to Maine with all haste.

In town, Ethan turned east on state highway 44 until they arrived at state highway 141, which took them to Interstate 80. The newlyweds drove east on I-80 to the Amanas' Colony, where they toured and ate at the famed Ox Yoke Inn and stayed at a hotel. Following breakfast at the OX Yoke, they headed east to Maine.

****

Once Myra and Ethan arrived at the Christian Homestead, near Jonesport, Maine, still known as the local school administration building, their vehicle was sold off, the plates removed, and the car shipped to Las Vegas as a used vehicle for sale under a salvage title. Meanwhile, Miles "Ethan" Vickers and Myra Dickenson disappeared from the Communist nation's web.

Myra and Ethan were assigned married accommodations in the underground facility inside Steele Island to wait for the arrival of the *ARK*. On their first evening in the facility, they were in the deserted dining area, relieved to be free from the closing doors of isolation finally. Holding hands, they gave thanks for the safe journey and the last opportunity to see the heritage of their former homeland.

"Myra, I feel as if a yoke weighing a ton has been lifted from my shoulders; as it turned out, other than our coming together, looking back, I can see it was a horrible life to lead."

"You're right; even as a Christian, I feel dirty from my work and efforts on behalf of DHS."

"No more; we are free and live under Jesus' form of true liberty. Not that the future isn't going to have its challenges, but God won't allow us more than we can handle," Ethan said.

****

The next week saw the influx of the next group of Christians arriving at Steele Island. Unfortunately, the flow showed signs of waning due to those who refused to leave their homes, the excessively aged, and defectors from what many began calling Christianity a myth based on ancient and irrelevant writings. Much of the terminology came from anti-religious advertisements on the now state-owned television, radio, and social media.

Men began running to specific stations as a bell sounded, signaling the arrival of the *ARK*. The working party waited at the mooring bollards for lines from the submarine to secure it to the pier. Then, finally, the lights in the huge bay went out to be replaced by red night lights.

It wasn't long, and the blunt-round nose of the *ARK* materialized from the black, foggy waters. Soon the sail of the boat appeared with dark figures on top, occasionally moving around. The boat floated in at less than creeping speed. At the proper time, the mooring lines were thrown from the submarine and quickly wrapped around the bollards to secure the boat to the pier. Two gangways floated through the darkness of the bay toward the after end of the sail—each set of walkways close to a hatch. The crew placed stanchions along the deck to keep anyone from slipping off and into the water.

"XO, I'll be ashore submitting my report; please continue preparing the boat for our next group of people."

"Aye, sir."

Ethan and Myra watched from the back of the pen as the submarine inched its way to its berth. Then they heard the big motors start the hydraulic pumps, and the great door began shutting behind the boat. Once closed, the pale lights came on, bathing the scene like a hundred-year-old night scene from a black-and-white movie.

The forming of the mist alongside the two signaled the arrival of Timothy. "Good evening, Timothy," the couple said.

"Good evening; I see you arrived here safely. Were you able to see the sights you were looking for?"

"We did," answered Ethan, "and we took many photographs, suspecting it is the last time we will get to see them."

"I understand. You may want duplicates and storage-grade copies made as a historical aid. There may come a time they will be a treasure of the past. Here is a packet for you, with your marriage documents and two copies of wedding photographs."

"Timothy, that is so precious of you. You are a special angel to us; thank you again. But, I sense you have need of us. Is there something we can do for you, Timothy?"

"Yes, there are three Christian ladies in your old Chicago office; they must be rescued, so to speak."

"What about their families?" Ethan asked.

"They are the single believers in the family, who are Muslim, and their lives have been threatened. So we are going to rescue them and bring them here."

"Are you expecting trouble?" Myra asked.

"With the dragon and his minions, it is almost always assured. If you would rather not help, there is no problem."

"Timothy, you have been around humans for how long?"

"Since our Creator created me," the angel said.

"And you believe we wouldn't help you?"

"I was offering you a choice."

"Thank you, but we're in for the duration."

"I will enjoy your companionship and help."

"Do you want us to bring our weapons along?" Ethan asked.

"No, I believe we can handle anything that happens."

Timothy moved to stand next to the former DHS couple, then a mist formed about them, and the three found themselves floating in a partly cloudy sky. Myra tightly held onto Ethan's arm, not wanting to look down.

"Do not fear, Myra; you are safe," Timothy said with a smile.

The night faded into the day with the rise of the warm sun. Then the mist surrounded the three again, and when it dissipated, the three stood in Myra's old office, now showing the lack of an occupant.

"You must bring the three women to this room and offer them the opportunity to join the Christians in a safe environment. You should not divulge the method of travel."

"Why?" Ethan asked.

"Should one or both decline, that is of no consequence to those who have gone forth. However, if they deliberately or inadvertently informed the agency for an unknown purpose, lives might be in jeopardy or lost."

"Yes, you're quite right, Timothy. We will be back shortly."

"Ethan, I will know what is transpiring, but I will not be visible to them unless they choose to join us."

"Another precaution?"

"If there is no belief, how could they believe an angel?"

"Certainly, why not? By the way, we know the ladies we're here to see; each has suffered beatings and threats to their lives but did not want charges brought against their father and brother. So we will return shortly."

Ethan and Myra stepped into the first women's office, startling her. "Miles, Myra, what are you doing here? Gibson told everyone you were transferred to no man's land, somewhere out west."

Then her eyes caught sight of the golden wedding bands. "Are congratulations in order?"

Myra smiled softly, "I would say yes, but we are no longer with DHS."

"Are you working for someone else?"

Ethan tried to come up with an answer other than no. Finally, Myra said, "We now work for the WFJ."

"WFJ? What's that? I've never heard of it," Saba said.

"Working for Jesus."

Smiling, the dark-clothed woman said, "Take me away from here; I am ready."

"What about your family?" Ethan pressed.

"My father is a fundamental Muslim. He has declared that I have dishonored him and embarrassed the family because I want to see an American. He told me he would enforce an honor killing of me at his first opportunity."

"Do you think he would carry that out, knowing it violated the law?"

"Absolutely. He has already told the family to pack the belongings they wore when coming here. He plans to kill me before they leave the house to catch their flight to Bagdad."

"What about Fareen and Urwa?" Myra asked.

"Fareen and the boy she was seeing, Kevin, shared a light kiss as they parted at the front door later in the afternoon. One of the family saw them and told her father, and he beat Fareen last night. After her family fell asleep, she slipped out of the house and stayed with me; now she fears he will shoot her for kissing her boyfriend."

"Is she here today?"

"Yes, she is in her office as we speak and is terrified of leaving it."

"Can you get her to follow you here?"

"I think she will come; she trusts me."

"Bring her here, now."

Saba ushered Fareen into the empty office a minute later, where the young woman cowered behind Saba.

Myra asked Saba, "What about Urwa? Do you know anything about her?"

A scowl crossed Saba's pretty face, "She, as it turned out, is a devout Muslim who now chastises us for seeing someone outside the Muslim community. She is, how you say…a hardcore Muslim and would never consider leaving their violent world."

Ethan asked, "Are you proclaiming yourselves to be followers of the Son of God?"

Still trembling, both women acknowledged they had accepted the Son of God into their hearts and souls.

Timothy took this opportunity to make his presence known.

Seeing the mist beginning to form, Myra quickly closed the door, barring any exit. Ethan stood aside, allowing the two women to see but a small sample of God's power.

Timothy stepped from the cloud; the two women were terrified at the sight they beheld.

"Have no fear; I am Timothy, an angel sent from God."

The women clutched tightly to one another for support in the face of a celestial being speaking to them.

"If you reveal your beliefs of Jesus as your Savior to your families, what will happen?" Timothy asked.

With no hesitation, both young women said, "My father would kill me, and if he did not, a Sharia official will."

At that moment, a DSH agent walked by and saw the wanted people in Myra's office, yelled for assistance, and pulled his weapon. As he aimed it at those in the room, he screamed, "Don't move."

Timothy, not intimidated by the overt move of the agent, said calmly, "Quickly, come to me." The four mortals clustered around the angel, and the agent opened fire. In rapid succession, he fired four rounds. The first going over the heads of those in the room. Timothy's wings swung out to protect his four charges, but not before a bullet drilled its way into Myra's back as she shoved one of the girls between Timothy and her.

"Oh, Lord," the seriously wounded woman moaned before collapsing into the angel's arms.

Timothy's impregnable wings whipped about the women and Ethan, then, in a snap, they disappeared.

The Creator's four beings rematerialized in the medical infirmary on Steele Island, where Timothy released his charges to the staff and picked Myra up to lay her on a table.

The woman was growing cold and grey with the loss of blood and barely breathing. Ethan watched, seemingly frozen in grief at the sight of his new wife dying before him. The two rescued women knelt where they were and prayed for Myra's life.

Timothy placed a hand over Myra's midsection, his face contorting into a gravely concerned picture. His eyes closed as he praised his Creator, then begged for her life, telling Him how Myra had protected a young woman with her body.

The all-knowing Lord blessed Timothy for his efforts, then reached through a forming mist to lay hands on His child, saying, ***"Greater love hath no man than this, that a man lay down his life for his friends." (Including women—John 15:13)***

Upon the touching of the Lord, Myra breathed again, and as the oxygenated blood coursed through her body, the gray waned for her natural peaches and cream color.

The woman's eyes fluttered open and centered on the smiling face of Jesus. She instinctively reached for her midsection, then seeing the Lord's hands still on her; she stopped, her hands shaking.

"Have no fear, child; hold my hands," the voice said above her.

Myra laid her hands on top of His as He commanded. She stopped shaking as the spread of pure love overcame her. But, the woman could not stop the tears from running from the corners of her eyes. It was the same magnificent, loving face that wed her and Ethan.

The Lord wiped her tears away, saying, "Your tears of love have been accepted, now rise and follow your husband."

Jesus and Timothy were gone, and the infirmary was quiet; the medical personnel, although strong Christians, had never seen the physical presence of the Lord and were speechless.

Myra tightly clutched Ethan, and as he felt for the wound, there was none; not even her clothing had been damaged. So it could not be found if there was any trace of Ethan doubting God's love and power.

Myra looked into Ethan's eyes; she sobbed in happiness as she murmured, "Oh, Ethan, the Lord healed me and rescued me from death again. He touched me with His scarred hands as he did when He married us. Then wiped the tears from my face. He has given us our lives back, Ethan. There is no god before Him; blessed be the Lord."

"Myra, my dear, we are forever in the service of God, and I pray He uses us to His glory."

"Amen," came the muffled voice from his chest.

AUSTRALIA

CHAPTER TWENTY-ONE

Captain Holeman looked at the last keeper of the Steele Island Complex, Terry Wilcox, and saw the sadness of the loss in his eyes. But, unfortunately, Holeman had seen it too many times in the eyes of ship and submarine captains as they left their stations for the last time.

"Terry, it's time to let it go. As a true professional, you manned your station with honor and excellence, as you have all your work. And I wouldn't be surprised to see you assigned to another important post."

"You're right, Brad. I know you have been through this feeling more than once."

"True, But something may change, and we could bring our people back to our homeland. But, for now, we have a safer homeland, and we owe the people of Australia the same allegiance we had to America."

"I have no problems with that; after all, they are our cousins. The Steele Island complex was placed in the best deep state of preservation for extended periods available. If we need it again, it will be ready to serve us," Wilcox said.

"You can never tell. Mr. Ackerman single up all lines and inform the engine room to standby for all bells. Have the work party remove the forward gangway."

"Aye, Captain."

Two minutes later, Captain Holeman said, "Release all lines and get the men aboard."

The five men at the shore bollards threw off the remaining lines and ran for the one gangway left. Once aboard, the men pushed off the gangway, leaving it to hang over the side of the pier. At the same time, Mr. Ackerman took the boat to sea. When the stern of the submarine cleared the bay doors, a remote signal started the closing cycle, sealing the Pen from prying eyes and the sea.

A heavy fog layer moved in on the Atlantic Ocean along Maine's coastline south of the New Hampshire state line. The *LOS ANGELES* class boat's radar watched for any surface vessels as the boat made for the Continental Shelf. Once the GPS and depth sonar confirmed they were over deep water, Captain Holeman ordered the boat to five hundred feet, speed forty knots.

A modification to the engine nacelles placed the exterior motor and screws within a tunnel, helping to dampen what little noise they made; thus, the submarine rivaled diesel-electric boats for silent running.

"Mr. Ackerman, you have the conn; I'm going to take a walkabout."

"Aye, Captain."

Brad Holeman stopped by his cabin to check on Helen. She said her stomach was a little upset, but she was fine. Helen didn't want to be away from her husband after being alone for so long. His cabin was comfortably large enough for the two of them, and this was her third trip in the boat. She helped wherever needed and developed the respect of the engineers as an accomplished mechanic. By noon, the red-haired wife of the captain felt back to normal.

Brad stopped by the sick bay and visited the boat's Doctor. "Hi, Tom, how's business?"

"Pretty quiet on this run, and fewer kids running into objects. How about you, enjoying your run?"

"The serenity is great; I enjoy the quiet, especially with Helen along."

"I'm glad to hear that, yet I feel a 'but' coming up."

"Yeah, Helen said she was feeling queasy for a while; I was wondering if you could stop by the stateroom and check her out. We don't need any illness down here, especially one which could be contagious."

"Sure, I'll let you know if Helen is catching or caught a bug."

"Thanks, Doc."

An hour and a half later, Doctor Tom Ingleside caught up with Brad as he entered the control room.

"Do you have a minute, Brad?"

"Sure, is everything all right?"

"Yes, Helen is feeling well. Everyone has felt the stress of the times; it's nothing to worry about."

"That's a relief, Doc; I guess I would rather error on the positive side than the reverse."

"Most certainly, nothing to worry about," and the Doctor left the conn with a slight smile.

The faithful ship's clock chimed zero-seven-thirty, and the conn watch was ready to change the watch. Brad stopped by the stateroom to check on Helen. He found her listening to soft pop music and reading a novel.

"Hi, hun; how about breakfast? Are you up to it?"

"You bet; any suggestions?" Helen asked.

"You need to get out of here; what do you think about eating in the wardroom?"

"Well, fancy you are inviting me on a date to have breakfast with you in a submarine. How deep are we?"

"Five hundred feet," Brad replied.

"That will be a smooth ride."

"You bet."

"Brad, before we go, I want to talk," Helen said with a serious look.

"Are you all right? Doctor Ingleside said you were fine."

"Oh, I am it's something else."

"Helen, what is going on; you have me worried."

"I'm pregnant."

Brad took a step back; his eyebrows arched in surprise. Then he grabbed his wife and held her as tightly as he dared. "Helen, there is no better news you could give me; I love you."

Helen returned the tight grasp, then whispered in his ear, "I was so afraid you would be upset this early in our marriage; I didn't think it was possible."

"Oh, no, Helen, I would never feel that way; I always wanted a family. I'm delighted with Ian and Eddi, and now it's even better."

"Thank you, darling," she looked him in the eyes, her own rimmed with tears of happiness; "I want to give you a son; I just wasn't thinking it would happen so soon."

"I am happy as it is," he said. Then he giggled; "I wonder what the kids will say?"

"I bet Ian will hope it's a brother; he says too many girls are around now. And Eddi, she will be as giddy as I am, whether it is a boy or girl, and I think she will try to mother our baby."

"All of that is great. All I want is for you to come through the pregnancy and safely deliver our first child, and second, I pray for a strong, healthy baby."

"That's the prayer," she agreed.

"Now, how about we have some breakfast?"

"Lead the way, sailor boy."

Helen and Brad had finished breakfast and enjoyed coffee and one of their increasing chats when the 1MC blared, "Captain to the bridge, on the double."

Helen urged him, "Go; your boat needs you; I'll get to the stateroom."

On the way out, the Captain met one of the Stewarts, "John, would you get the wife to our stateroom? I need to find out what's going on."

"Right away, Captain."

As Brad Holeman burst into the conn, the OOD called out, "Captain in the conn."

"OOD, what happened?" Holeman asked.

The OOD gave him a quick update on the boat's orders, "Sixty-five knots, maintaining course and depth. Captain, a Russian Akula jumped us from behind, and I upped the speed to fifty knots; then the Russian fired a type 53 torpedo at us. That's when I called you. So now we're at sixty knots and climbing to sixty-five."

"Good work."

The boat responded as a racecar, lunging ahead and rapidly increasing speed.

Then the Captain heard, "Conn, sonar, torpedo has locked onto us at five hundred yards."

"Sonar, do you have a thermal layer above or below us?"

"None, yet, Sir, but we're searching."

"Very well, if you find one, sing it out, don't waste time with phone protocol."

"Aye, sir."

Three minutes later, "Thermal layer a hundred feet above us."

"OOD bring us up quickly, maintain speed and course." The deck tilted up at the bow as the helmsman watched the depth gauge unwind. Then the bow dropped to a level plane and charged on at flank speed ahead.

"Conn, sonar, the Russian boat is off the screen, probably still below the thermal layer and behind us. No indication of the whereabouts of the 53, but the torpedo was falling behind when we went through the layer."

"Very well, Mr. Ackerman, check with engineering for operating conditions; if everything is normal, reduce speed to forty knots in fifteen minutes and remain above the thermal layer."

"Aye, Captain." Two minutes later, "Captain, engineering reports everything is at normal temperatures and operating normally, and we have capabilities of sixty-five knots at our call."

"Very well, you can't beat that."

All seemed to be quiet, and that is what bothered Captain Holeman. He sat in his chair, praying for no further encounters with hostile boats. Brad informed the passengers and crew of the reasons for the maneuvers and assured them they had cleared the danger zone; however, the chance of another encounter was always with them but considered slim.

Two hours and ninety-two miles later, the boat felt like it wasn't moving, and the lonely sound heard came from the whisper of the blowers. Captain Holeman called the engine room, "This is the Captain; how is the plant?"

"Running smoothly, sir." The watchman pulled the last hour's readings, "All our readings are normal, and everything is whisper quiet, and for an old sailor, it's eerie."

"Check the pit log."

"Forty knots, Captain. The motor RPMs match the pit log and ordered speed, and the external bearing temperatures are right where they are supposed to be."

"Thank you, I think everyone on the boat is ready to fall asleep because it's so quiet."

"Yes, sir, we're running hot laps back here to stay awake."

"Have any of our passengers taken an interest in engineering work or studies?"

"As a matter of fact, we have almost a dozen ladies learning how to run the plant, distiller, and other machinery in engineering. And I must say, they are smart as a whip; they will make great engineers."

"We are all indebted to the efforts everyone is doing there; keep up the great work."

"Thank you, sir; I'll pass it on to the crew."

"Well, now OOD, it would appear that we are now a training vessel as much as a passenger boat."

"Okay, Captain, would you care to clarify that?"

"The snipes in engineering have about a dozen ladies in training for jobs in engineering. If they keep that up, we'll have to revamp our terminology."

The OOD quietly murmured, "Oh, how I long for the old submarine days," bringing out stifled snickers.

"You gotta get current, me lad; one of these days, you'll have a lady for a skipper," the Captain teased.

Fortunately, the remainder of the voyage was contact free. And as the boat approached the Australian coastal shelf, Captain Holeman brought the *ARK* up to hundred-fifty feet until they were a hundred miles from Broome.

The Captain cautiously approached the surface with sonar passively scanning around the sub. He intended to avoid the possibility of a collision with a surface craft with their final load of Christians aboard. After being assured that there was no surface traffic on the black sea, he surfaced the boat for the remaining hundred miles to home.

Following the docking maneuvers, the boat was moored under a newly constructed overhead cover, and the parade of busses awaited the newcomers for their ride to the temporary facility.

After the final passenger disembarked, the submarine became almost as quiet as a tomb were it not for the ventilation fans.

Brad made his report to the church leaders, then, he and Helen, who left their vehicle at home, were given a lift by one of the councilmen. No matter how comfortable the restricted stateroom had been, it couldn't match the feeling of home.

On the first day home, Helen called to make an appointment to see a physician at the community clinic. An hour later, the smiling redhead walked out with the confirmation of her pregnancy. Her physician had laid out a diet and exercise regimen to put her in the best condition for delivery in about eight months.

That evening, she and Brad sat down with Ian and Eddi to explain the forthcoming changes in the Holeman household.

As predicted, Ian wanted a brother. On the other hand, Eddi said she thought she would want a sister when the time came but sided with Ian for now. Helen and Brad simply wanted a healthy baby.

Although Helen had educated her two children on the basics of reproduction, She and Brad shared the responsibilities of educating the two on the details, not particularly on act causing procreation but the role played by God in creating the life in her womb, how it is a blessing as well as a responsibility to the new one's parents. They wrapped it up with the future roles they would have in their families and how, with the Lord's guidance, they would have full lives. Brad and Helen emphasized how and why God set the guidelines for sexual behavior and how to avoid the pitfalls of secular behavior. And they did not leave out the possible results of failing to remain virtuous.

Eddi asked, "Mom, what if one of us makes a mistake and crosses the line? Will we go to hell or that other place the Pastor once said was worse?"

"Where was that?"

"I don't remember for sure, but it was some lake."

"That, my dear, is the Lake of Fire, from which there is no return."

"That's the one."

"First, if you know you have sinned, that is, disobeyed God's law, go to your room and pray. You remember How we taught you to pray; humble yourself before the Lord by praising Him. Then thank Him for all the wonderful things He has provided, which is everything, not just physical material things. I'm talking about His love for you. You are very precious to God; never forget that. Then you must admit your sin and tell Him what you think you did or actually did. Ask Him to clean your soul with the blood of Jesus and ask Him to guide you through life. Then thank Him again for His mercy. You must listen every day, all day long, for that voice whispering in your ear telling you not to do something, especially if you know it is wrong. God will hear your prayer and pleas for mercy and forgive your sin. Last, you must make a serious effort not to commit that sin or other sinful acts in the future."

"Wow, that's serious, isn't it, Mom?" Eddi asked.

"Yes, dear, but it is part of life as an adult, and you cannot dodge it," Helen said.

The young girl got up and rushed into her mother's arms like a five-year-old.

"Mom, I don't know if I will be able to keep from making mistakes."

"Oh, sweetheart, you won't live a perfect life; all you have to do is make an honest attempt to live by God's law. He knows you will slip and fall; we all do. That's why he gives us a chance to talk to Him and admit the problem, and He will forgive us. As you continue to grow, you will gain more knowledge and remember how to conduct your life. And the best place to learn it all is by studying the Bible. You will get nothing by just reading it; you must attend Bible studies and Sunday School and read the Bible daily. All of us must do this."

"How did you get so smart, Mom? What school did you go to?"

"First, I went to the school of life. I had wonderful teachers in our Pastor, and especially in my Grandmother, and she learned from her mother and grandmother. One of our most important responsibilities is to teach our children about God, who He is, and His plan for Salvation. One of those ways is to pray for understanding before we study the Bible, then follow every reference attached to words, as I shown you."

Ian asked, "What if I don't want to read the Bible every day, or even at all?"

Brad answered, "Ian, do you listen to the Sunday school teachers?"

"Sometimes."

"Do you listen to your Mom? You know, like what we have been talking about?"

"Yes," he said a little sheepishly.

"Ian, you are still young, but as you grow, you will realize how important it is to learn everything you can about the subject before you. Because as an adult, you will be held accountable for your actions, what you say, even what you think."

"But who will hold me accountable?"

Smiling, Brad said, "Now, as long as you are young, it is Mom's and my responsibility to hold you responsible, and your teachers in school hold you accountable for your schoolwork.

Once you become an adult, teachers, your Mom and me, and the police, then the judge in court will hold you accountable if you go wrong.

But, if you fail God, and do not go to him for mercy, He will hold you accountable, and sometime after you pass away as an old man, you, just like everyone in the world, will have to answer for what they did during their life. And remember, Jesus keeps a scorecard on each of us, and He knows what we are doing and thinking every day of our lives. We will talk more about these things as time marches on, but you have a lot to think about right now."

With the family meeting over, Eddi went to her room, and Ian went out to find other kids to play with. Helen and Brad sipped coffee at the open kitchen table and discussed their meeting.

Brad went to the Submarine the next day to check on the usual minor inport work. In the back of his mind, Brad wondered what would become of the submarine. *'God has said he didn't want the secular world to have the engine or concept because of their propensity to turn everything into a weapon. I'll have to ask Timothy about that if I see him again.'*

The on-duty crew worked on several non-critical repairs and maintenance at the submarine pen. Captain Holeman spoke with the officer's present who wondered about the sub's future. They expressed how they were in the dark as much as he was.

"Has anyone seen Timothy?"

Del Ackerman said, "I don't believe our angel has been seen since we hit port."

"Okay, if anyone does, would you ask him to contact me? I have a question."

"Yes, sir. Is there any information on other sorties coming up?"

"I haven't heard anything, but I'll let you know when I do."

SEAWOLF

CHAPTER TWENTY-TWO

Brad met with Martin and Elie two days later.

"How are ya doin, Brad? And how is the boat fairing?"

"That boat is the fastest underwater craft in history. Tom Latham brought his boat into Steele Island, and I think he will be headed this way. I haven't heard from him since we passed outside the Lower Cove."

"While you were making the run you just finished, The *SEAWOLF* docked with a full load."

"Where is she now? Steele Island is in mothballs."

"It's with the Master Designer and Timothy."

Laughing, Brad said, "I'll bet the NACP is in a fit over the loss; I wonder if they declared the boat missing?"

"I haven't heard anything about a missing sub, but as paranoid as the commies are, they probably won't make a 'SUBMISS' announcement," Martin said.

"The socialists and Communists lied through their teeth to hook those people who are driven by greed and laziness to get something for nothing. Khrushchev was right; the people did it to themselves. Now it's time to pay the piper because they have lost every protection against a tyrannical and predatory government," Brad added.

"Martin, may I have a word with you?" A familiar voice said.

The two men turned around to see Timothy standing behind them. "How do you do that, Timothy?" Martin asked.

"It's a God thing I use. We have need of you and Elie's skills."

"We are ready to serve our Lord, Timothy."

"Thank you, under the second security dock is another addition that will need engines installed. The engines are in the engine room, along with all the tools needed. You have proven you turn out superior work, and the Master Designer is pleased with your efforts. And yes, Brad, your newly trained engineers are welcome to help and learn under Martin and Elie."

Martin smiled at his friend, "He grows on you, doesn't he?"

"He sure does; thank you, Timothy."

"You're welcome."

Martin quietly asked Brad, "Where did that structure and boat come from? There wasn't anything but shoreline there a minute ago."

"I noticed that; I would say it behooves every man, woman, and child to mind their thought and words, as we are living under the highest authority," Brad added. "I know two pastors who could make excellent use of this information, and spread it to the other ministers, thus the people. And come to think about it, maybe that's exactly what the Lord intended."

"You are very astute, my son."

The two men looked around for Timothy, then Martin said, "That wasn't Timothy."

Both men heard the angel's familiar voice, "You are correct."

"Good idea," Martin agreed. "I better round up Elie and get started on our next job."

"If it's all right with you, the women who have qualified as watchstanders on the 688 have been trained by the Snipes in mechanical design and repairs; I think you could benefit from their assistance."

"Certainly, good help is difficult to come by these days, send them over."

"I'll get right on it."

Brad stopped by the house, finding Helen cleaning a clean kitchen. "Bored?" he asked.

"Yes, I've cleaned the house twice in two days."

"How would you like to join the other trained women in installing the engines and motors on a boat we just acquired?"

"Lead the way, my darling."

"Not so fast, remember you are a new mommy-in-progress again. All I ask is that you call the Doctor's office and get an okay to work, including the limitations and the weight you are allowed to lift. I know I'm being a bit bossy, but I'm justifiably concerned with your health and our baby's safety."

"I understand and appreciate your concern. I will do that straight away."

Brad laughed, "You're starting to sound Australian already."

"I suppose that is true, but when in Australia…."

Helen hung up the phone, "Doctor Thompson cleared me for light work with a twenty-pound lift restriction, and since I would be working, he wanted me to begin monthly checkups. And, of course, if I tire, I'm to sit for fifteen to thirty minutes."

"Well, dear, can you live with that?"

"Oh yes, I need to get out and move."

"All right, I can take you to the boat, and if it's like ours, it will have an elevator in the sail. Have someone call me when you are ready to come home; you have my number."

Helen stepped up to her husband, "How did I get so lucky to get a wonderful man?"

Brad smiled and said, "God."

After he got in their small van, Brad called four of the women from the engine room watch list he carried and arranged to pick them up on the first load.

Before leaving the dock, he watched Helen maneuver to the sail elevator in the *SEAWOLF's* sail. From the distance that separated them, he couldn't even tell his wife was pregnant, so his worry meter settled down.

Three of the remaining eight engineers were working in Broome, and Brad picked up the remaining five and took them to the boat.

Holeman called Pastors Johnson and Carvour and offered to treat them to coffee and a roll as an enticement to meet with him. At a local café, the two men lightly chided him for thinking he had to bribe them. Then Mickey said, "Of course, it helps."

Brad mentioned an issue brought to his attention by three church members. They had noticed how a few Americans have a bad habit of forgetting manners and the narrow path Christians choose to follow. He asked, "Am I off base, or is there a bit of drifting by some of our people, especially the youth? We owe these members an answer and solution."

Mickey said, "No, you aren't off base; Dick and I have noticed the same concern, and we have bantered the subject around a bit. Maybe it's time to bring all the ministers in on it. For my two cents worth, Every Christian needs to think of Jesus, speak with Jesus' thoughts coming from his mouth, and behave as if Jesus sees our every move, which He does. The short answer is; to keep their eyes on Jesus."

"Great advice, Pastor Mickey, Pastor Dick."

"Brad," Mickey spoke up, "There is another matter to discuss."

"You have the floor, sir."

"As you see, the *SEAWOLF* is in our custody now," Mickey stated.

"For now, yes."

"You must know the naval forces in our former land will want it back if they know it's here."

"Yes, they will. Do you know if the boat has been altered?" Mickey asked.

"Altered? I have no idea; it just appeared this morning; the *SEAWOLF* cannot be returned to NACP hands," Brad flatly said.

"What's the problem?" Mickey asked.

Thinking for a moment, Brad recalled the information he wanted. "The I AM contractors took possession of it when Tom Lathem moored her to the pier at Steele Island. They made considerable alterations to the boat's engineering section, probably the bow structure, and certainly the interior accommodations. The engineering alterations with the special engines will be completed by Martin and Elie, and I believe they have already started on that today. That alone will prevent it from going back to the Satanists. It's no longer a warship; it's one of two underground transports in God's service."

"I was unaware of that. Will you have command of the added submarine?"

"I do not want that. First, I am an experienced 688 driver, and second, Tim Latham is the Captain of the *WOLF*. Third, I'm not checked out nor qualified for that class boat."

"I understand; I was unaware of the requirements. But, speaking of requirements, I think it would be prudent to have a person in training to fill in if either of you is injured or otherwise unable to fulfill the job," Mickey suggested.

"I agree it's an excellent point; in that event, the Executive Officer should be a trained Officer for such an emergency or the Captain's advancement to other duties," Brad explained.

"It's clear I am out of your league in these matters. Could you take on the responsibility of setting up an organization to cover this issue?" Mickey asked.

"Although these boats have non-nuclear plants, I recommend that the crews who were with them when we acquired these complex machines remain with them. Although they are all volunteers, to begin with, I believe they will probably want to remain aboard. At the same time, each man could supervise the training of a backup replacement. It will be much simpler than with a nuke boat."

"I seem to recall there is a retired Admiral in the church family; what do you think of him taking the administrative reins of our fledgling navy?"

"It will be a good start, and he may know of other former senior officers who could greatly benefit the organization," Brad said.

Pastor Dick interjected a different line of thought, "We're entering an unknown territory here in that we accomplished our mission to the best of our knowledge in North America. Now, we find ourselves a second and most advanced submarine and crew in our possession. A question for thought; Why? Why do we need a second vessel? I would suggest our Lord may be gathering His people from across the globe and bring them into one place. For what remains an enigma for now? A possible purpose for the second…what do you call your ships, Brad?"

"Boats."

"Two boats could be used for gathering people from two parts of the world simultaneously, saving more of the church. Just a thought," Dick added.

After digesting what his friend said, Mickey replied, "This endeavor is not unlike when the Lord removed His people from bondage under Pharoah and moved them to His mountain to receive His law."

"Sounds like a good analogy to me," Brad put in. "Maybe we can call Timothy, and he can give us a little insight."

"Let's do it," agreed Mickey. "Dick, you brought us to this field of questions and unknown. Would you lead us in asking for Timothy?"

The three men stood under the warm sun and asked the Lord for His guidance and if He would direct their efforts as He wanted. Then, before the prayer was complete, Timothy stood quietly behind them, his head bowed, joining Christ's followers in worship.

When finished, the men began to talk among themselves, and Timothy coughed to let them know he had joined their meeting.

"The instant answer to prayer is somewhat unnerving," Dick said. "We're accustomed to answers coming on God's timetable."

"I understand," the mild-voiced angel said. "I understand your questions regarding our actions; is that correct?"

"Yes. We are ready to serve the Lord in every manner He wishes; we need nothing else except His directions."

"Let's walk," and the angel led the trio toward a strip of beach. "Our Creator has not mentioned His return to me and is unlikely to do so. However, at this time, our Lord does appear to be gathering His people, possibly in the line of thinking offered by Pastor Mickey. Many square miles of land here could hold the Christians in safety. The King, the United Kingdom, and the Australian Prime Minister are quite open to having the Lord's followers settle here. The Australian government is transporting materials for building homes, stores, and manufacturing facilities. This will provide work for the people to build, grow and manufacture a good living in a safe land. The growth will help the local and national economy and living standards.

To accomplish these events, you will sail to different ports where the refugees will still wait for you; that is why the two submarines exist. And they are not to fall into Satan's or his minion's hands. You have good men to sail the vessels and deal with pirates and hostile forces. You will have the Lord's protection and the speed of your boats and capable minds to avoid problems. Most of all, you have prayer and faith, the two best assets for your work.

You are wise to develop a second crew for each submarine; you do not want to…as you say, burn out your men. And you are to create an organization for operations."

Brad said, "When we began this work, we felt it might end in the rapture of the church, but for some reason, I'm beginning to think that event is still in the future, and we will graduate from strangers in a strange land, to citizens of Australia, and our colony will disappear as we become Australians. There is no doubt that our yet-to-be-born children will be Australians. And I'm sure that will be a good thing."

Timothy replied, "Brad, your children will be Australians, as all the newcomers will become citizens of this vast nation. In addition, the Christian newcomers will become Australian Christians.

As I have said, I do not know when the Lord will return. As you noted, God has His schedule concerning the future, which will occur as He decides. Until that time, everyone must remain true and strong as the lion. And Christians must put on the armor of God, as the dragon will not repent nor cease his efforts to steal, destroy and kill. Beware of the attempts of the dragon to use any Christian's weakness to destroy him and his loved ones. Are there any other questions? If not, I must see to the work on the *SEAWOLF*." Then the angel disappeared.

"Well, gentlemen," Brad said, "you were right; it looks like we have plenty of work to accomplish. I'll arrange a meeting with the XOs and Tom Latham, and we can begin developing training programs for the second crew. I congratulate you both on correctly assessing the purpose of two boats, and I wouldn't be surprised to see more join our little fleet."

Mickey asked, "Is there a reason for concern in notifying the authorities that we have the submarines?"

He got a pair of chorused "No." from Dick and Brad. Then, Brad added, "This is the Silent Service, which means we remain silent. Besides, I have it on good advice that the Prime Minister and Australian Navy are aware we have the boats and that they are no longer nuclear powered and are unarmed transports now."

****

Three days later, the church leadership sat before a group of former officers and men who served in the Navy. The group learned that the newcomers now had two submarines at their disposal and, following a lengthy meeting, proposed a program for using the boats.

Former Rear Admiral Michael Adberry suggested, "Offering potential positions for those who were qualified. Then establish a program to train those persons willing to learn and operate the vessels.

The applicants, both men and women, must read and sign non-disclosure documents before beginning their service."

Three men raised questions regarding the submarines and were told the secrecy documents must be signed for that information due to security requirements. "Under no circumstances must the NACP know we have the missing submarines."

The church leadership expressed surprise and appreciation for all of the attendees standing up to join the crews of the submarines; the established Officers and men expected nothing less.

Admiral Michael Adberry, a former submariner, took the reins of the force and asked for a meeting with all the members from both boats and the new inductees.

Two days after announcements were made in secret after church services, two-hundred-fifty crewmen of the two boats and thirty-one volunteers met with the Admiral and staff of the force.

"Ladies and gentlemen," the Admiral addressed the volunteers, "We have been handed the formidable task of creating a manning force of two crews for each submarine in our possession. However, with the conversion by the I AM corporation, we will be able to concentrate on the manning issue.

Our mission is no longer combat; it is search and rescue. Our job will be to travel to foreign locations to recover escaping and refugee Christians and return them here. It may sound like a milk run, but it isn't. We will be hunted and shot at by Russians, Chinese, and several other countries where Christians are under surveillance, even under guard. That makes our job no less dangerous than it has been. We have had an adversarial encounter with a boat out of New London. Our only friends on the sea appear to be from the UK. Therefore, you must consider all submarines an enemy until proven otherwise.

I had a reputation for supporting women's efforts to advance in the Navy, which will not diminish. However, to those ladies who have bravely stood up to be counted, I must ask that any mothers with young children or who need to assist elderly relatives consider weighing the need to join and those other responsibilities and the fact you will be at sea for weeks at a time. There is always the possibility of not coming home due to attacks or unforeseen accidents.

There is no compulsory duty in this force; everyone is a volunteer. We have two weeks before we begin training; you can help by reading the material we have accumulated and conducting daily physical activity as directed by Chief Jared Neimeyer. Please ensure your decision is final. We plan on conducting interviews and will have a list posted addressing ships and duty assignments before training begins. Unless there are any questions, you are dismissed."

The Admiral requested the boat Captains and XOs stay behind for further discussions with him.

"Gentlemen, as well as being a Captain, you will begin to carry additional responsibilities. I will not burden you with our former Navy protocol requiring inspections, evaluations, and the seemingly thousand time-consuming busy jobs we used to have. First, we do not have time for it, and second, everyone will have to double their workload until we reestablish the best manpower requirements and fill the billets. However, I have been put on notice this will not become a career endeavor; when the need for the boats is exhausted, they will be removed.

Regarding communications with our boats. As some of you know, there is a VLF antenna array about five or six hundred miles south of us. I will be visiting the Defense Ministry regarding our boat's communications and the possibility of establishing us as a private organization under their control to avoid the possibility of collisions or misidentifications. I will keep you updated as information comes in.

With your engine and accommodation alterations, you must determine the crew billets necessary for your boats. We have decided to develop two crews for each boat, as was done with the boomers. To make the system work, we will build a chain of command along the lines of what you have worked under when in the USN. It will be streamlined to your needs, and I will need input from you for the implementation of the billets. If there are any other concerns, I will be available 24/7 at these numbers and locations; later, we will have a command post for contacts." Then, assistants handed out a sheet of paper to each person.

We will meet again on Friday, a week from today, at ten hundred, in this room. Thank you, dismissed."

THE ARK

CHAPTER TWENTY-THREE

Six months later, Admiral Adberry picked up the desk phone, "Adberry speaking."

"Admiral, this is control; we received a notification from our Fort Myers center. The director, the Reverend Michelle Leonard, reports they are nearing their capacity, and the heathens are closing in."

After checking his reports, he said, "*SEAWOLF* is too far away and out of position to be of help; we'll dispatch *ARK* by tomorrow."

"Thank you, sir."

****

Brad Holeman picked up his home phone, "Holeman speaking."

"Brad, we have capacity run with the heathens closing in at the Fort Myers center; you are the best help available."

"Aye, sir, the boat is ready to set sail as soon as the crew is aboard."

"Good, that's better than I expected; we will alert the crew and get them started for the boat. As soon as they are aboard, get underway, and this will be a fast run around the horn; we can't use the canals."

"Understood. Sir. We have the maps we need aboard. Our food and supplies were topped off yesterday; we are ready to go."

"Good job, watch your six, and full speed ahead."

"Aye, sir." Turning to his wife, "Helen, we have an emergency run. Will you be all right?"

"You know I will, and I'll keep you in my prayers, come on, I'll drive you to the boat."

"I love you." Then the Captain gained control, grabbed his ready bag, and headed for the car, where Helen slipped behind the wheel. With Helen's expert driving, the usually seven-minute drive ended four minutes later at the pier. The feisty redhead parked near the gangway entrance, and as she and Brad exited their vehicle, others began arriving. As soon as the crewman left the car, their wives drove out the far exit to allow the growing line behind them to do the same. Then four vehicles parked outside the overhead, and the man and wife sailors grabbed their gear from the trunk, called the boot in Australia, and headed for the gangway.

Half an hour later, Captain Holeman appeared at the open bridge of the sail. Looking around, he spotted his fiery redhead waving to him. She signed, telling him she loved him, and he saluted her in return. Then the lines of the submarine were cast off, and the boat began backing from its shelter. Helen watched her husband's sub turn around and head into the blue-green Indian Ocean.

Helen Holeman had fallen deeply in love with her husband almost overnight. He not only filled a terrible void in her life but became the peaceful completion of her life. Then their wedding flashed before her eyes, reminding her of the strength of their union.

Helen watched the black vessel skip across the placid Indian Ocean, throwing up a rooster tail that melted into the spray from the bow charging through the water at thirty knots.

****

Captain Holeman ordered a course that would put them east of Florida's southern coastline. His plan called for working past Cuba; and swinging north off the peninsula's western coast to a preset location near Fort Myers, where the *ARK* would meet a ferry carrying two-hundred-forty-eight Christian refugees.

****

Meanwhile, Captain Holeman submerged the boat to a hundred fifty feet while still in relatively shallow water. Four hours later, the sub reached deep water, and the order to dive to seven hundred feet was given, along with the order to turn to the southwest.

****

When the *ARK* reached three hundred miles south of the apex of Africa and Cape Agulhas, they exited the Indian Ocean and into the South Atlantic Ocean. There, the Captain ordered the boat to the northwest toward the peninsula of Florida. With time running out for the Christians, Captain Holeman boosted his speed to fifty knots. At fifty knots, the submarine covered hundred-fifteen miles every two hours.

Ten days and sixteen hours later, the *ARK* arrived fifty miles off Fort Myers, Florida, where they would wait for the ferry. Captain Holeman's speed put their boat in position eight hours early, so the Captain ordered her to the bottom, where the sonar suite listened for the loud sounds of the ferry.

Several surface vessels motored overhead, each classified as a fishing trawler or a smaller fishing boat. The *ARK* put out the sound level of a tomb and was not detected by a reserve destroyer that steamed above the sub on a training mission. However, its presence was noted and plotted because they posed a threat if the ship remained in the vicinity during the transfer of the refugees.

The hours slowly passed until a sonarman called out, "Conn, sonar, a vessel is approaching our location from the Fort Myres direction and sounds like the ferry. No sounds in the area of any other vessels."

"Very well, Diving Officer, bring us slowly up to seventy-five feet, sonar listen for the location of the ferry and coordinate with the Diving Officer."

The orders were repeated, and the *ARK* began to lift off the bottom. At a hundred feet, the boat stopped to give sonar time to generate a clear picture in all directions.

"Conn, sonar, all clear, and we just received an all clear from the ferry."

"Very well. Bring her up to periscope depth." After a careful three-hundred-sixty-degree sweep, the Captain looked at the ferry, noting everything looked as it should. Next, Captain Holeman pointed the lens toward the stars in the sky and the glow of Fort Myers and the coastline. "Prepare to surface the boat." Then a minute passed, and "Surface, surface, surface," the OOD said.

With the compressed air forcing water from the dive tanks, the submarine broke the surface, and the lookouts scrambled to their stations, followed by the OOD and Captain. Every eye in the sail scanned the waters for any signs of shipping or boats, but all they saw was the ferry.

Captain Holeman maneuvered to the stopped civilian vessel, and once moored together, men on the ferry slid a wide gangplank onto the sub's deck. Crewmen set up stanchions and lifelines to prevent anyone from slipping into the water.

Several sub sailors assisted the passengers aboard and to either the after hatch or elevator. The passengers had been coached to maintain silence for safety, and the transfer was completed within an hour. Then the ferry crew withdrew the gangplank and cast off the submarine. Captain Holeman immediately pulled away while the elevator was restored, and the crew disappeared down the hatches and secured the covers.

"Green board," called the Diving Officer after the sail was secured and the pressure hull sealed.

"Diving Officer, prepare to submerge the boat."

"Prepare to submerge the boat, sir."

"Sir, the boat is ready to submerge."

"Dive the boat to one hundred feet, Diving Officer; make your course two-one-seven, speed 20 knots. Sonar keep a tight watch; we will be in restricted waters for almost seven hours."

The crew repeated the orders and settled in for the long haul.

"XO, would you give our passengers the welcome aboard talk and have the crew speak with everyone about the head operation?"

"Aye, sir."

"Navigator, plot our course for home."

"I have it ready for your approval, sir."

"Well done, Mr. Ingleside."

Several hours later, "Conn, sonar, surface contact, a destroyer in passive mode, bearing three-two-one, course one-four-one, at eighteen hundred yards to starboard, speed fourteen knots."

"How much water beneath us?"

"Seventeen hundred feet and slowly sloping to over eight thousand, according to our charts," the Navigator said.

" Sonar, any indications he has us?"

"He is still in passive mode; we may be too quiet for him."

"Very well, we will continue on our course and speed. Sonar, keep a sharp eye on him and sing out if he shows an interest in us."

"Aye, sir."

"Diving Officer, prepare to crash dive to eight hundred feet on my command; maintain current course," the Captain ordered.

"Aye, sir, on your command, crash dive to eight hundred feet, maintain current course."

The waiting began. The Captain said, "OOD, have the XO ensure everyone straps themselves in or takes a braced position, then have the talker call for silent General Quarters."

Things began to happen slowly as the boat prepared for harsh maneuvers and the call to arms for sailors with experience.

The Captain began to think they had slipped by the destroyer; then, a loud ping bounced off the hull. "Crash dive."

The Diving Officer called out, "Down bubble, crash dive to eight hundred feet, all ahead thirty knots."

The boat leaped ahead, leaving a knuckle in the water behind them. Then, at five hundred feet, they went through a thermal layer that temporarily hid them from the pursuing destroyer.

"XO," the Captain got Kevin Bach's attention. "If you were a can driver, where do you think we would go?"

"If their CO is from our old navy, he would expect a sub to go deep, maybe a thousand feet, and try to hide. So what are you thinking of doing?"

"We're dealing with a whole different animal here. We have played with the Russki cans and subs over the years and pretty well have their playbook figured out—the same with the boys from Beijing. But now, we have a hybrid, a Communist-controlled former American CO. Probably with a trigger-happy Political Officer behind him.

What do you think of a burst of speed and heading for the shallower banks east of Miami, where we can either sit down for a few hours or make a run for it, using the normal boat traffic for cover? He may think we will run for the depths of the Caribbean; instead, we turn and follow the deep water around the peninsula of Florida up to, say, Melbourne. There we do a hard right to zero-nine-zero and run up to sixty knots. We would be backtracking, but the water is deeper in the channel. If we push on, we'll be over the shelf and gone in a few hours, leaving a frustrated tin can well behind us."

The XO digested the scenarios for a moment, "I like the latter of the two, around the tip of the peninsula and up the east coast of southern Florida."

"So do I. Navigator, plot us at five-hundred-seventy-five feet to zero-eight-eight degrees where we can turn north and run as far as Melbourne, at thirty knots, then a hard right on zero-nine-zero and increase our speed to sixty knots," the Captain ordered.

"Aye, sir. OOD come to zero-eight-eight degrees for two-hundred-eighty-eight miles at five-hundred- seventy-five feet, thirty knots."

The OOD repeated the sequence, the ship quickly rose to the ordered depth, and the helm rang up thirty knots. The Navigator double and triple-checked his figures, depth, and course. He had to avoid hitting bottom, which, at their speed, would destroy the submarine and kill everyone aboard.

"Conn, sonar, a Mark 48 torpedo just popped through the thermo layer and is seeking a target. It has acquired us, sir."

The Captain said, "Maintain last orders, but increase speed to sixty-five knots."

"Conn sonar, the Mark 48 is falling behind."

"Very well," Holeman said with a slight smile.

****

On the Burke-class destroyer, Russian Captain Third Class Nikita Sokolov stood looking out the forward windscreen as the destroyer pursued the unknown submarine at thirty-one knots and helplessly heard it had run from him at over fifty knots. Having nothing to lose, he ordered a torpedo fired at the fleeing submarine. Minutes later their sonar reported the target eluded their torpedo, and it ran dry, then sunk to the sea floor.

****

"Thank you, Lord, thank you for taking care of us." Bradly Holeman was startled when a soft voice whispered in his ear, "You are welcome, My son." The man froze for a few seconds to gather his wits. Then he heard a slight commotion behind him. Turning around, he saw the crew looking at Timothy, standing by the rear bulkhead.

Captain Holeman motioned for the angel to join him. "Timothy, I have a question."

"Most certainly; what is it?"

"I just heard a whisper in my ear, and it wasn't your voice."

"No, it was not I. However, our Creator has taken an interest in you and wanted to let you know it by speaking directly to you."

Not knowing what to say in response, Brad murmured, "Thank you."

Timothy gave him a knowing smile, then a light squeeze to his arm before returning to the after-bulkhead.

The Captain looked at the angel and asked, "Timothy, would you like to do me a favor?"

"Anything, Captain."

"Would you visit each cabin of passengers and speak with them about our restrictions for the safety of the boat and use your great bedside manner to calm any fears? And if you come across anyone suffering from claustrophobia, let the boat's doctor know?"

"I would be glad to help, Captain."

****

An hour after the attack by the destroyer, the Captain reduced the submarine's speed to forty knots. The following days were filled with tours for young people and interested adults, none of whom had ever been on an operating submarine. Several teenage youths expressed an interest in sailing with the *ARK* and were told to learn everything the teachers had to teach, especially mathematics and science. And those having serious inclinations about making the submarine service a career should attend college with mechanical engineering and nucleonics majors.

****

"Captain," the OOD called, "We're about fifty miles from Broome, sir."

"Have the Bo'sun pass the word for the passengers to clean their staterooms and pack their belongings. We will dock in two and a half hours. The Australian Ministry of Immigration and Christian assistants will assist them to quickly settle in the temporary accommodations until permanent housing becomes available."

Captain Holeman docked the *ARK* with his usual precision in two and a half hours, and soon the first newcomers stepped on Australian soil for the first time.

****

Martin, Elie, Brad, and Helen sat talking at a table in one of the town's homelike restaurants.

Elie said, "The number of Christians has grown to well over a thousand souls in and around town, and the original population of Broome found that we have many of the same values and beliefs as themselves. I've seen many friendships and integrated groups develop since we arrived. Now our people are referring to themselves as residents of Broome."

"That's good news, Elie. I know there has been concern among the elders that the local people may not care for our presence."

Helen said, "The local schools are first-rate; they seem to be years ahead of most urban schools we left behind. And the people here are serious about parents being active in their children's education; I think that is one of the best programs for youngsters. The schools work with the parents to ensure students have the best education, emphasizing English, humanities, mathematics, and science. Higher (tertiary) education is excellent and well-adapted to international levels. Our people have a new respect for Australia and their values."

Martin added, "The additional mandatory educational classes for all adults and drivers cover the laws of Australia, civics, and Australian history. Some complained until one veteran told them that they could ask for transportation back to wherever they came from."

"What did they say?" asked Brad.

"Every one of them backed down, and two received the evil eye from their wives."

On the third day after arriving home, Brad visited David Forman, the newly elected head of the Christian counsel.

"Good morning, Brad; how nice to see you."

"Thank you, sir, and congratulations on your new position."

"It's temporary; the council has voted to dissolve their control and move the people under the general council of Broome. It is fitting with everyone now a citizen; it's time to take their place alongside the town's other citizens."

"I agree; it was a wise decision. How did the city council take it?"

"One member voiced an objection, and his concerns were laid to rest. The final vote was unanimous."

Brad thought for a moment, then said, "All-in-all, I couldn't be happier with the effort everyone has put forth. How things have been developing must be due to God's efforts to care for us."

"Here-here," the others cheered and held up their iced tea.

Then Elie whispered something into Helen's ear. The redhead's face brightened, and her radiant smile brought the attention of the two men. "Why, that's wonderful, Elie."

"What's that, Helen?" Brad asked.

"Martin and I are going to become parents," Elie bubbled.

Everyone began congratulating the couple, and Helen said, "It appears we may become two of the earliest people to have natural-born citizens of Australia in our families."

"Maybe not the first," Brad corrected; "I've seen at least two other passengers who were probably six months along on the last run."

"I didn't know that," Martin said.

Elie asked, "Helen, have you heard of advanced education here in Broome?"

"Yes, first, there is a Notre Dame Campus not far from the airport. There is also the Broome Residential College, St. Mary's College, the North Regional TAFE Campus, and the Primary grade school, all in the same area. Oh, and Broome High School is in the same area, about five blocks from the hospital."

"What is the TAFE Campus?" asked Martin.

Helen answered, "TAFE institutes are state-administered Technical and Further Education. They offer courses leading to certificates and diplomas in a wide range of vocational topics and sometimes higher education."

"I have good feelings about the people in this town and the planning they put into building Broome," Elie chirped.

The party enjoyed the food and company, but the next day was still a workday, and each couple left for home. When Brad and Helen arrived home, the light on the house phone blinked, and a message waited in the voicemail.

Brad returned the call to the Admiral. "Brad, this is a movement warning; Timothy had to leave for the Chicago DHS office when we learned four Christians are in confinement. And there is the question of who sent the information. Timothy said he knew who it was and would handle it."

"All our collection centers are closed and overrun by the government. And to make it worse, even though there is a way to enter the Great Lakes through the Saint Lawrence Seaway, that is no place for a submarine operation."

"I agree; the situation is too volatile to risk sending either of our boats in there. This is but a warning. However, I don't expect any sorties; this one will be all Timothy. Look at it this way, that angel has the best backup in history."

"There is no doubt about that, Admiral. Good evening, sir."

Brad respected Timothy and his zeal. He had helped him and the *ARK* more than once.

TIMOTHY

CHAPTER TWENTY-FOUR

There is no calculation for the speed of an angel. However, it is above man's comprehension. Timothy is known to the Christians as one of God's messengers, sent to help those called by Jesus' name. God's angels are also known to be capable of powerful and devastating rebukes in the name of the Lord, lest unbelievers test him.

Ethan and Myra's detention cell locations could not be hidden from God's creation. Myra prayed in her isolation room, praising the Lord and honoring Him. Timothy was no stranger to Ethan's wife. Myra prayed for her and Ethan's imprisonment to end and the safety of Nora Richards, the eyes of the Australian Christian board in Communist North America.

The woman sensed an arrival and turned toward the mist from which Timothy emerged. "Welcome to my little world, Timothy. I wish I had a refreshment for you."

"Myra, the wife of Ethan, let the words of our Creator refresh you and bless you, for you have found favor in His heart. Take my hand," he commanded. When Myra's hand touched the angels, she found herself standing behind Ethan, kneeling before his cot, deep in prayer.

"Husband, stand and be refreshed in God's love as I have."

Ethan stood and turned, "Hello, Timothy. Thank you for bringing Myra."

"Are you ready to continue your journey for the Lord?"

"Yes, we are," the couple replied.

"Take my hand," Timothy commanded a second time.

Instantly the three appeared in yet another cell. A young woman kneeled on the hard concrete floor, her raw elbows supporting her beaten head, as she prayed for relief from the pain inflicted by her captors. When Nora looked up at the sound behind her, Myra gasped as Ethan's jaw tightened in anger at what evil men do. Nora's eyes were badly bruised, and bleeding, and a rivulet of blood came from the corner of her mouth at the hands of her tormentors. Two teeth had been knocked out of her mouth, and she held her stomach to protect herself from further pain. But the pain of shame from the sexual torture and rapes would never disappear.

Timothy released the hands of Myra and Ethan, and he approached the wounded woman. "Nora, what have they done to you?" He whispered. Nora's mental and psychological shock kept her in a daze.

"Do not be afraid, Nora; the Lord will help you." The angel reached out and gently placed his hand on Nora's head, closed his eyes, and began to praise the Lord. Myra and Ethan bowed their heads, joining in with Timothy's prayer for healing and forgetting the pain she received from others.

As Timothy and the Vickers prayed earnestly, Nora's injuries healed instantly. Her body renewed in the Lord as if she had never been violated, and her memory of the shame she felt left with any sin as far as the East is from the West. The beautiful woman was whole again. Nora's hands flew to her face now without pain. Tears of gratitude and happiness rolled down her cheeks.

"Praise the Lord, Nora; He has made you whole again," the angel proclaimed.

Nora bowed her head with the angel and the Victors and thanked God for His mercy.

Timothy explained, "The Lamb of God, sitting on the White Throne, will judge these people who prey on their captives and the innocent."

"What will become of them? Nora asked.

"All who are called by His name will witness the Lord's law in action as saints at the time of Judgment."

The detention guards watched as Timothy did the bidding of God. Then, several armed guards ran to Nora Richards' cell and burst in on the four occupants in the cramped space.

Having heard dozens of stories of this being and his jailbreaks, the guards pulled their handguns, aiming them at the angel. Timothy menacingly lowered his head. His eyes became red beacons of justice, staring at the guards.

The smooth voice of the heavens said, "Timothy, I know they deserve what you could give them, but let's leave them trying to explain what they saw before you left with our people."

The angel smiled, his impenetrable wings shielding his three charges, then said. "Gaze upon the face of the woman you defiled and beat. See the glory of the Lord in her being made whole again. You can also be made whole in the Lord for all eternity; all you have to do is ask for Him." Then, holding the three Christians securely, they vanished before the guards.

The lead uniformed man said, "That man and woman, they were in other cells; how did they get here with that weirdo? And who cleaned up that broad?"

"I dunno, sergeant, but I'm glad you have to write the report," the second man snickered.

"I wouldn't laugh too loud; you have to write up a report backing up the facts. I suggest you look mine over before you write your report to ensure you get your facts straight." Those men lined up in the hallway behind their leaders and were released without requiring a report.

Special Agent Adrian Gibson became livid upon learning the angel struck again, and he was getting the information a day after the action. He immediately filed dereliction of duty reports against the sergeant and the second man present for allowing the four people to escape.

Gibson's anger and embarrassment over the strange being's jailbreaks were beginning to cost him power and standing in the power structure. He became paranoid about the probability of demotion, if not outright dismissal, for incompetence. The only people in the immediate office were lower-level laborers and secretaries, and they shied away from his vile anger and feared undue punishment.

The SAC called his contact in Bangor, Maine. "Laughton, is there any activity at that place we raided a couple of months ago?"

"No, Chief, it's only a school administration building now, and at most, three or four vehicles appear for short periods, then the same people drive away. I developed an inside agent, but whatever went on before the school district acquired the property is a mysterious past. Nothing interesting is happening there."

"All right, give it thirty more days, and if nothing breaks, shut down the surveillance and return to your regular duties."

"Yes, sir."

****

To the Vickers and Nora, their travel time felt nonexistent, and they found themselves in a warm, sunny tropical town with red-colored soil.

"Where are we?" asked Nora.

Myra and Ethan looked around, eyes wide in wonder at the instant change in the weather. The air in Chicago was cold and damp, with old, dirty snow and ice on the streets.

"Western Australia," said Timothy. "This is the town of Broome. You will find the relocated Christians here, and the Australian people are also friendly Christians. Come with me; this building is the location of the Christian resettlement organization."

Upon entering, Mavis Johanssen looked up from her work. "Oh, hi Timothy. It's been a while. Who have you brought in for us?"

"Mavis, meet Myra and Ethan Vickers, and this young lady is Nora Richards, all from Chicago. I'm afraid we left in such a hurry; they have nothing with them."

"Oh, my. Well, don't worry, we have clothes here you can have. I'm afraid you will be starting from scratch; we all did. But don't let that worry you; we have a bank of clothing, food, and toiletries for newcomers. For now, we will get you an apartment; it will be small since it is temporary, and you will have the opportunity to share a larger room with another young lady if you wish. We work with the Australian Ministry of Immigration, and they will interview you and try to match your skills to employers. Homes are being built daily; we have a list of families, couples, and single adults to which your names will be added. You can select one or pass it by for another as soon as homes are available. The houses are reasonably priced, with your income and number of occupants setting the home size. There is no welfare as the states had; everyone over the age of seventeen works; it is the law."

Myra and Ethan looked at one another and nodded in agreement, and Nora said, "That's very reasonable."

Mavis called an associate in, and she took the three new people to the back room for fitting and the proper clothing.

"They are nice people, Timothy; where did you find them?"

"DHS in Chicago detained them; it saddens me to find they were the only Christians there. They were in serious trouble, and faced certain death if we hadn't been notified. But our Creator brought them home, as He always does."

"Yes, Timothy, we are blessed to have such a merciful Lord."

"I agree. I must take my leave; I'm being summoned. Have a good day." Mavis looked up, and Timothy had vanished. The woman smiled and shook her head, wishing she had his energy.

****

A European television and radio broadcast ran a documentary of the exodus, "Time continued to move forward, days ran into weeks, and weeks into months. The rush of the second exodus was over, bringing just over six-hundred-thousand Christians into the free world, which have been assimilated into the new lands. New Zealand, Fiji, the Solomon, Gilbert, Microncsian, and other island groups. All of these locals gained military aid in ships, planes and boats, and weapons.

The fanatic NACP first demanded the return of the hardware, then threatened to destroy all the nations that held more than half the weapons the former United States had produced. Notification by the free people that nuclear weapons were included in their new arsenal convinced the NACP leaders to back off, bringing about an unofficial agreement to let the exodus people keep the property but never attempt to return to North America.

Many more immigrated to Canada, the rest of the UK, Ireland, Israel, and other free nations.

News of communist terrorism in the form of torture, killings, and imprisonment for many captured Christians was leaked to the world, revealing the true face of communication. Additional clandestine releases disclosed people were summarily put to death for being active drug dealers and users, and all those of sexual perversion beyond the natural man and woman relationships. Trumped-up treason charges were used to get rid of potential political rivals, who were quickly shot to death.

Mexico suffered a massive attack from its northern neighbor, the primary targets being the drug cartels and corrupt officials who worked for them. Russian and Chinese troops occupied their country and threatened the surrounding smaller nations with annihilation if they failed to comply with Communist ideology.

Information had filtered that the Russian and Chinese lines of support were thin and subject to attack by rebels who still fought against the Communist invasion. As a result, the movement to enslave the world stalled and ground to a halt. Further information escaped claiming that the Communist forces were not the type to listen to the large numbers of college-educated socialists, and thousands of would-be socialist leaders suffered the same fate as the drug lords. Every college professor run down was summarily executed when caught, along with the city mayors, council members, and county supervisors and police. Former US congressmen and women, senators, and the few-living former presidents were all put in graves. They all suffered the long-standing policy of Communism; kill all former opponents and every family member, and there will be no trouble from them.

****

In compliance with the will of God, the *ARK,* and *SPIRIT,* disappeared, and all systems powered by the celestial turbine were mysteriously converted to electric motors.

Timothy said, "The Lord has fulfilled His promise that the power device would not fall into Satan's hands."

It was several months before Timothy again appeared before the Christian leaders.

"I see you have successfully transitioned to the Australian culture and life. It is a good life, and you will thrive here with the people. Keep the faith, my friends; I will miss all of you, but you will not see me again until we meet in heaven. Our association has enriched me, and I thank our Creator for the opportunity to help you.

I know you have questions about rapture. It will come, and it will come in the time God determines. However, as it tells you in your Bibles, Be watchful; no man knows the time but the Father. And it will happen in the twinkling of an eye. Do not read the Bible; study the Bible. Keep the Lord's Commandments and love one another as He loves you.

Now I must leave you, and I leave you with these words; *Let the words of my mouth, and the meditations of my heart, be acceptable in thy sight, O Lord, my strength, and my redeemer. Amen." Psalms 19:14."*

H. Nelson Freeman is a Vietnam Veteran. He enlisted in the US Navy in 1958 and served on five ships. The USS Norton Sound (AVM-1), USS Midway (CVA-41), USS Kitty Hawk (CVA-63), USS Nicholas (DD-449), a Fletcher class destroyer, and the USS Goldsborough (DDG-20). He attained the rank of Machinist Mate Chief Petty Officer. Later he enlisted in the Iowa National Guard, serving another 15 years, retiring as a Master Sergeant.

Sgt. Freeman graduated from Upper Iowa University with a BSPA. After over 30 years in law enforcement, Mr. Freeman retired as a Sergeant from the Urbandale Iowa Police Department and law enforcement. He was a Criminal Investigator, CSI, court qualified Polygraph examiner, fingerprint and handwriting expert. He now enjoys writing in Iowa.